Igniting Social Action in the ELA Classroom

Igniting Social Action in the ELA Classroom

Inquiry as Disruption

Robyn Seglem and Sarah Bonner

Foreword by Antero Garcia

TEACHERS COLLEGE PRESS

TEACHERS COLLEGE | COLUMBIA UNIVERSITY
NEW YORK AND LONDON

Published by Teachers College Press,® 1234 Amsterdam Avenue, New York, NY 10027

Front cover art by amtitus/iStock by Getty Images.

Library of Congress Cataloging-in-Publication Data

Names: Seglem, Robyn L., author. | Bonner, Sarah M., author.
Title: Igniting social action in the ELA classroom : inquiry as disruption / Robyn Seglem and
   Sarah Bonner ; foreword by Antero Garcia.
Other titles: Igniting social action in the English Language Arts classroom
Description: New York : Teachers College Press, [2022] | Includes bibliographical references
   and index.
Identifiers: LCCN 2022031432 (print) | LCCN 2022031433 (ebook) | ISBN 9780807767542
   (Paperback : acid-free paper) | ISBN 9780807767559 (Hardcover : acid-free paper) |
   ISBN 9780807781326 (epub)
Subjects: LCSH: Language arts (Secondary)—Social aspects. | Literature—Study and teaching
   (Secondary)—Social aspects. | Empathy—Study and teaching (Secondary) | Civics—Study and
   teaching (Secondary)
Classification: LCC LB1631 .S4545 2022 (print) | LCC LB1631 (ebook) | DDC 370.11/5—dc23/
   eng/20220718
LC record available at https://lccn.loc.gov/2022031432
LC ebook record available at https://lccn.loc.gov/2022031433

ISBN 978-0-8077-6754-2 (paper)
ISBN 978-0-8077-6755-9 (hardcover)
ISBN 978-0-8077-8132-6 (ebook)

Printed on acid-free paper
Manufactured in the United States of America

Contents

PART III. SEEING IT ALL

Foreword

From Dewey's vision of a progressive education to a Silicon Valley–informed endorsement of a student-led "Genius Hour," inquiry has been of interest to teachers for generations. In the form of the past repackaged as the new, inquiry often comes down to the salient aspects of ensnaring student interests in adult visions of learning and assessment. It's the same trap that school leaders have been trying to set out year after year. It's not enough. The sentiment of inquiry is an important one, but if we're being honest with ourselves, the needle of academic progress has not changed substantially in more than a century. Our schools remain inequitable at best and inhospitable for many on a daily basis.

Whither inquiry amid this educational crisis?

Enter the powerful work of this book. Robyn Seglem and Sarah Bonner remind us that inquiry—when done with the intention of justice-driven transformation—isn't just old pedagogical wine decanted into shiny new bottles. Instead, throughout *Igniting Social Action in the ELA Classroom: Inquiry as Disruption*, Seglem and Bonner demonstrate how inquiry breaks away from traditional forms of education that are historically rooted in capitalist, settler colonial legacies. This is a disruption that does not necessarily come easily or readily in classrooms from the get-go. It seeps slowly from the tapped trunks of hard-won trust in our classrooms, like a stubborn and slowly yielded molasses.

Let's talk about the sticky, invaluable role of disruption at the heart of this book. Think about the portrayal of disruption in the cultural world of NPR and mass media. Speaking of billion-dollar valuations and unicorn apps that will fix everything with the tap or swipe of a screen, we love disruption. At least as long as it resides outside our classrooms. Apps that disrupt familiar industries have realigned much of our daily lives. The taxi industry has been reimagined entirely through app-based ride request platforms like Uber, grocery shopping has been transformed by Amazon and Instacart, and entertainment now no longer requires venturing to theaters for the most recent Hollywood blockbusters, thanks to Netflix and other online streaming platforms. What a world.

Of course, the convenience of all this disruption comes with the cost of individual labor exploitation and a reliance on tools that routinely surveil upon and limit the choices of their user base. Disruption comes with a moral cost that most of us try to look beyond. We like disruption when we can benefit comfortably from it and avoid reminders of the ills it might impose on others.

In schools, though, disruption is discouraged entirely. This is not because of some moral compass attempting to push students away from the machinations of capitalism. On the contrary, disruption in school impedes the alignment of young people to the goals of consumption and passivity that go for instruction these days, and it is viewed through the lens of inconvenience and dissonance. Literally, disruption announces itself loudly; typically, it is the outbursts of students we presume are off task. Let's be honest: School community members might claim that these are students impeding the learning of other students, but it is often the case that adults feel annoyed and irked at students' gall at breaching an authoritarian din in schools. It is the fragility of adults that winds its way to criminalizing exhalations of joy and playfulness in our classrooms and labeling them as "disruptions." As an overgeneralization, we don't like young people's vocalized testaments of agency; they clash with prudish sensibilities of school orderliness.

Who gets to disrupt and who gets to label something a disruption? These are acts maintained by adults and often funneled through white privilege.

But we could disrupt this narrative of disruption, and we could do so alongside our students.

As I read Seglem and Bonner's book, I was reminded that our efforts to disrupt normative, school-based stifling of disruption is a courageous act. It is also one that we are not alone in working toward. Your race, your gender, your various markers of cultural identity do not impair your ability to be a disruptor. Frankly, if you match the general demographics of the teaching profession—if you are a white woman reading this—you have an advantage and an obligation to disrupt boldly, loudly, and in solidarity with your students and with the BIPOC members of our school communities. It is exactly what the authors are doing in the pages that follow.

Returning to the often-hackneyed nature of inquiry that began this foreword, becoming a critical disruptor requires stepping into and beyond inquiry. It means asking hard questions, gathering data to inform your answers, and seeking others to join you in prodding the membranes of schooling policies that hold in student potential every day.

Book after book speaks of the voice and courage that are required in innovative inquiry projects. Such pep talk–driven texts overlook the very hard work and planning that come alongside a modicum of interest in resisting the status quo. Disruptive inquiry is hard to pull off. That's where this book's chapters and detailed examples

come in. There is a blueprint for progress offered here. What might we build collectively?

The world that students are inheriting from us is a bleak one. From ongoing mass violence to climate devastation to the erosion of individuals' rights at the state and federal level, these are times when it is perilously difficult to maintain the spark of inquisitive dreaming. And yet we must dream intentionally and encourage our students to do so as well.

Dreaming big with your students is not only a possibility but—in these times—a necessity. As Robyn Seglem and Sarah Bonner make clear, it is something we can do with our students as we inquire about disruption and break past the assumed limits of schools today.

—Antero Garcia

Preface

What's the point of having a voice if you're gonna be silent in those moments you shouldn't be?

—Angie Thomas

WHO ARE WE?

We need to state this upfront. We are white and able-bodied. And, as such, we don't look that different from 79% (National Center for Education Statistics, 2020) of the teaching field. We are also straight, cisgender women. And this, too, is the norm in classrooms.

Robyn grew up in a small town in Kansas. Her educational and lived experiences in her early years were very monocultural. It wasn't until she went away to college that she gained a deeper understanding of the diversity within our world and began to recognize the systemic inequities that form the foundation of our society. Before moving to university, Robyn taught middle and high school English Language Arts (ELA) across contexts—mostly suburban white spaces. But even in the 3 years she worked in a middle school that was shifting toward urban, she witnessed teaching colleagues engaging in micro- and macro-aggressions toward students of color.

Sarah grew up on the Illinois side of St. Louis—where rural life was met with city living only minutes apart from each other. Heading to a university in Central Illinois, she knew that teaching was both her calling and her passion. Over time, Sarah taught middle school students in urban, suburban, and rural classrooms. However, it wasn't until her 10th year of teaching when she met Robyn and realized that teaching had the potential to do more than just participate in study guides, book reports, and short stories.

So, why are we here? Why do we do the work, and why did we write this book? The answer is simple: If we, as teachers, don't do the work, who will? If we, who have the voice, stay silent in this moment in time, in these moments of social injustices, what is the point, to borrow from Angie Thomas (2017), of doing what we do? We do the work because we must, because we have the voice, because we have the opportunity to assist our students in learning how to ask the critical questions needed to change the world. We don't want our students to have to wait until college or adulthood to recognize the need to ask important questions and to disrupt the systems that oppress so many in the world. And this is especially important in the predominantly white spaces we work within.

We started this journey together 8 years ago, and we've learned so much about our students, our teaching, ourselves along the way. The work began as a simple desire to empower students through inquiry. We wanted our students who lived fairly insulated lives to have opportunities to be curious about the wider world. We began with Walter Dean Myers's *Monster*, hoping to demonstrate to students how media and other systems can shape narratives around groups of people. We wanted students to recognize that this story—so many stories—exists because it reflects a reality many in our world face. And we hoped that this recognition would prompt questions that students would want to explore in order to have a broader and deeper understanding of our world. It worked. They did. And we continued studying issues such as homelessness in Jennifer Richard Jacobson's *Paper Things* and PTSD in Laurie Halse Anderson's *The Impossible Knife of Memory*. These were important realities to explore. And upon reading about them in fiction, students wanted to know more about how these issues existed and were dealt with in the world.

We could have stopped there. Students were excited about learning. They were asking questions and willingly seeking out answers. They were no longer wondering why they had to read books. They began to see novels as representations of the world, and they were engaging with issues that impact humanity. Then, other factors converged, prompting us to consider ways to push the work in new directions. Small groups of students started asking for more—they wanted to move beyond educating themselves and work toward making change. Society was becoming more divided as politicians ramped up the rhetoric around immigration and America's place in the global economy. Our students and their families were being inundated by media that created echo chambers, reinforcing their thinking rather than causing them to ask important questions. So, we began to evolve our work to disrupt the forces we—and many of our students—were seeing as harmful to our world. We became even more selective in the books we chose. Current titles were privileged because they reflected the events society was grappling with in the here and now. We sought out books written by and about people of color. Titles such as *Internment* by Samira Ahmed and *Dear Martin* by Nic Stone introduced students to characters oppressed by societal systems. We encouraged them to ask questions around why this might be so. We spent more time helping students examine echo chambers, introducing more media texts for students to examine through a critical lens. Students began questioning spin, bias, and outright fabrication as they worked to better understand the world. And we began to look for opportunities to build action into the units that followed, urging students to identify causes and injustices that mattered to them to begin the process of changing our world.

Once again, we could have stopped there. Students were identifying real problems represented in literature and examining how those problems impacted their communities. They were starting to recognize that they had the ability to make a difference in the world and starting to take small steps toward answers. Yet, in many ways, they were still working as individuals. In 2020, we recognized that wasn't enough. In a world upended by a pandemic where people found themselves isolated, it became even more evident that we needed each other. The protests that followed the murders of Breonna Taylor, Ahmaud Arbery, and George Floyd reminded us of the power of collectively working toward a goal. So, we're evolving once again. While we realize that inquiry around social issues initially started our work, it continues to grow with an emphasis on collaborative action and a focus on community. As national issues continue to inspire our work, we also know that inspiring students to take actions in their own communities brings forth a positive change that stays with them beyond the classroom. Focusing on the importance of community empowers students to speak up and speak out about the issues that matter the most to them as a means to create tangible change.

HOW CAN YOU DO THE WORK?

You are reading this book because the work matters to you too. You recognize that your voice cannot be silent and that you must help students find their voices. If you've been doing work such as this for a while, we hope this book offers you new approaches to consider in your own space. If you're new to this work, don't think you have to do everything at once. Regardless of where you are in this process, the work you do matters. You may be thinking as you consider many of the ideas presented in this book: "I like these ideas, but I could never do this with my kids," or, "These ideas are great if I didn't have required texts mandated by my district," or, even, "I don't think my school administration or the community I serve will approve of this work." We acknowledge that there is both fear and vulnerability to changing your practice with students. But even making changes on atomic levels can expand your thinking and invite you to try new things.

While this work directly impacts learners, it must start with teachers. This work requires a mindset that supports change, flexibility, and a willingness to learn and grow. As we position our mindsets as learners, we invite the possibility of generating new ideas, taking risks, embracing failure, and listening to others. If we, as teachers, are willing to embody these traits for ourselves, then it becomes natural to embody these traits in the classroom culture we build with students. When thinking about the value of meaningful and important work with students, there are considerations teachers can make when taking steps to transform their own practice.

1. **Overcome fear.** Take time to think about the barriers you might face. Unpack your fears and think forward with solutions.
2. **Know your *why*.** Rather than making change for change's sake, explore your *why* behind these changes to your practice. This justification enables you to weave your *why* into your curriculum design, affords you conversations with others connected to this work, and, provides context to others who might be interested in learning more from you.
3. **Find your people.** Whether you're continuing to do the work or you're just starting, find people who will keep you moving forward. There will be successes and failures. Knowing that you have people to inspire you to think differently will prompt you to continue changing for the better.

Finding your own entry point into this work becomes fundamental to its success. While you may be committed to district-mandated texts, how might you think about the implementation of these texts differently? How can the work centered on mandated texts invite students to think critically about the world they currently live in? We owe it to our students to engage in meaningful conversations and learning experiences.

HOW IS THIS BOOK STRUCTURED?

We begin this book with an invitation to join us on the journey we began more than 8 years ago. We provide you with a bird's eye view of how to structure a unit, as well as a year, of how to get started, and of how to think about assessment as you read through the book. We then divide the book into three parts: "Seeing Big," "Seeing Small," and "Seeing It All." In many ways, this book is linear, following the scope and sequence we outline in our invitation. But in other ways, it's malleable, allowing you to start small as you begin the work and to adjust your approaches to your own contexts. Each chapter shares vignettes, quotes, and student work that highlight the ideas in the chapter and are used with permission from our students and their guardians. Most of their names are their own— again, used with permission. Our students are proud of the work they've done and are eager to share their expertise. Others have been changed to protect their identities, and we've noted those when they are introduced. Each chapter (except for our concluding chapter) also shares examples of learning experiences that move students toward using inquiry as disruption and social action. We provide specific steps to take to enact these experiences, as well as additional resources and points to consider. You will also notice that we thread a multitude of voices throughout each chapter, tapping into authors of young adult literature, as well as researchers and theorists, who have inspired our

work along the way. This work is grounded in theory, and we want to provide you with the resources to demonstrate its connections to sound educational practice to those who may question your efforts. And we want to share with you the voices who have inspired our students, as well. We conclude each chapter with a series of questions for you to consider as you set about designing your own disruptive inquiry approaches, because this book is just a sampling of how you can get started.

Part I: Seeing Big

In Part I, we introduce you to cultural anthropologist Michael Wesch's notion of seeing and begin this book by providing approaches to helping our students see the bigger picture. By getting a sense of the bigger picture they exist within, students are better prepared to identify problems that merit further study.

Part II: Seeing Small

In Part II, we shift students' focus to the details that make up the bigger picture. We ask students to consider how language choices and individuals' experiences impact that larger whole. Through identifying these details, students begin to find entry points into doing the work of igniting social change.

Part III: Seeing It All

The final section of the book helps bring everything together. We explore shifts in thinking that will assist students in designing and persisting through work toward social change. We suggest approaches for how students can do this meaningful work. And we conclude by helping you see how to bring it all together in your own contexts, as well as how to approach assessment and grading complex work.

Acknowledgments

We would like to thank our Teacher Church colleagues for their support as we developed this work. Special thanks go to Winnie Nuding Slater, Kristina Falbe, Lynne Olmos, Kyle Rich, and Greg Kocourek for reading and providing feedback on our chapters. Additionally, we want to thank Wanda Turk who kept us organized as we prepared this book for publication. We also could not have taken this to the finish line without the love and support of our families. Lastly, to all the students who help us do this important work, this book is for you! We appreciate you all!

Igniting Social Action in the ELA Classroom

An Invitation: Seeing Differently

The funny thing is that I never see the world any differently through new glasses. I only ever see things differently when I look in the mirror.

—Jeff Zentner

WHO ARE WE TEACHING?

As you begin reading this book, we invite you on our journey of seeing differently. Like most experienced educators, we look back on our early days as teachers and cringe slightly, wanting to send apologies to every student who attended our early classes. But the truth is, we always did our best, and our students walked away knowing more about the language arts than they did when they entered our classrooms. We still get the occasional note from a student who wants to share the impact we had on them—even from those students we had in our early years of teaching. That's because we recognized what cultural anthropologist Michael Wesch (2018) has since stated: "People are different. These differences represent the vast range of human potential and possibility" (p. 9).

It was because we could see our students that we were able to provide just the right book to the student who was wrestling with her sexuality or to say the right words to the student who was cutting and just needed someone to affirm her self-worth. Seeing these students and students like them demonstrated to us that the language arts could do more, *be* more, than reading about the human condition and writing essays that explored our responses to those books. We started to see the language arts differently. If one book, one word, one project could affect one student, how could we amplify the power of the language arts to have a larger impact on the world?

So, we begin this journey by exploring who we are teaching, because it is the students we teach who will drive each decision we make along the way. Think about the communities you serve. What beliefs, values, ideas, and assumptions do your students bring with them to class every day? How do those communities shape their thinking, their responses to both the experiences within your class and the

larger world? In our work, most of our students are white, many are conservative, and few have traveled far or often outside of their communities. Recognizing these factors shape how we approach this work. They have impacted our sense of urgency as we seek to broaden students' perspectives and understandings of other humans who live in the world, as well. But we also remind ourselves that we cannot see our students as one homogenous group. Instead, we must get to know each student as an individual because when we start seeing individuals rather than groups, we can identify the strengths the individuals bring to the learning experience and leverage those strengths toward making change happen.

In addition to considering the roots of students' ideas, assumptions, and values, we must also examine their prior educational experiences. For students who have only had traditional ELA, and even social studies, experiences, jumping right into inquiry is jarring—and unlikely to succeed. Recognizing this shift in educational experiences does not mean we are passing judgment on their previous teachers. It simply means that we know we must provide more scaffolding for students as they learn how to ask their own questions rather than answering a teacher's and as they learn that failure is expected and celebrated rather than simply a negative mark on their report cards. Conversely, when students come to our classes having experience in an inquiry or social justice–based classroom, less time can be spent scaffolding, and we can lead with students' questions.

Evaluating student needs is also an important part of getting to know our students. While looking at data around reading and writing scores is important, we cannot limit ourselves to quantitative data. Quantitative data by nature groups people, situating them next to each other to make comparisons in relationship to a construct that someone decided was important. This is not to suggest that there is no value in it, particularly in a system that rewards high numbers, but test scores provide a very narrow view of a student. If we want to get at what our students need, we must talk to them and listen to what they are saying to us and to others. Through these conversations, we can often identify our next steps in the classroom. If the students seem susceptible to what they are reading or hearing on media platforms, then we design with an eye toward media literacy. If there is a culture of bullying, then students may need to read literature that explores the root of bullying. If students seem to accept, and even reinforce, stereotypes that flatten or damage other racial, social, or cultural groups, then we bring in as many different texts as we can to disrupt those stereotypes and provide students with positive counterexamples.

Seeing our students as individuals, as well as a part of a collective whole, allows us to design learning experiences that meet the needs of our students and our communities. When students know they are seen and that we recognize all the parts that make them who they are, they are willing to trust us when they feel uncomfortable taking risks or considering a new perspective.

SITUATING THE WORK

When designing meaningful and purposeful learning experiences for students, it is essential to think about your practice through a variety of lenses. The approaches in this book aren't singular, stand-alone lessons that students engage in once or twice a year. They take time, planning, and scaffolding throughout the year as students continue to build on their experiences.

Scope and sequence. Starting with a scope and sequence—or a sketch of teaching and learning over the course of one school year—allows you to view your practice from a bigger lens. Simon Sinek (2009) talks at great length about "The Golden Circle" or the notion of how great leaders inspire action. Throughout this conversation, he points to key questions that drive these leaders to

promote action among others. Sinek's questions include What, Why, How, and What. Highlighted in Figure I.1, these driving questions identify the vision of what we want to do with students throughout the school year. Traditionally, planning may be centered on a required text or a type of writing format, but if we think about planning differently—leading with the interests and issues important to our students—then curriculum design has the potential to transform requirements into learning experiences for everyone.

Once those questions have been answered, developing a scope and sequence for an entire school year becomes a natural next step. Thinking through and justifying these ideas provides insight into the design and planning that goes into teaching and learning. If one of our main goals throughout the school year is to promote social action among our students, our year-long scope and sequence must unpack what this means. Figure I.2 illustrates a sample scope and sequence that supports the scaffolding students need to understand what it means to take action on issues.

Unit design. Devoting time to unit design allows teachers to design with the end in mind and provides an opportunity to think about the support students will need. Unit design shifts the teaching focus from day-to-day planning to ongoing facilitation and student responsiveness. Using Sinek's "Golden Circle" framework, those driving questions can help situate and plan the details of the unit itself. Figure I.3 uses Unit 3 from the scope and sequence in Figure I.2. As these driving questions continue to layer within the unit itself, these questions highlight the details needed to develop this work.

Traditionally, it's easy to place the literature in the very front of unit design for reasons like "it's mandated by my district" or "in 7th grade we always read . . ." However, if we commit to viewing practice differently, we must also rethink the questions we use when engaged in design. When we place our students and the social issues that interest them in the center of unit design, we have the potential to transform the ways in which we implement learning. If we're willing to transform how we design teaching, then we're also transforming the dispositions our students hold

Figure I.1. Using Simon Sinek's framework, these questions are ones to consider when designing an instructional year.

WHAT	WHY	HOW	WHAT
What do you want students to learn this year?	*Why is this learning significant? Why does this matter? To you? To students? To others outside of the classroom?*	*How do you plan to connect students with this learning?* *How can you think about the role of teaching and learning differently in your classroom to support learning?*	*What supports do you need when connecting students with this learning?* *What skills, support, and experiences will students need in order to achieve this learning?*

Figure I.2. A sample year-long scope and sequence that scaffolds students through the inquiry as disruption approach.

Unit 1: Personal Identity & Understanding Perspectives	Unit 2: Critical Media Studies & Social Issues	Unit 3: Using Literature to Help Unpack Social Issues	Unit 4: How Others Take Action	Unit 5: How I Can Take Action
This unit affords students time to think about their identities, beliefs, and core values. It builds community by introducing other perspectives through others' stories.	This unit speaks to how issues that students care about are portrayed in the media. Building this critical lens affords students practice with developing and asking questions connected to the world around them.	This unit uses literature to drive inquiry around topics that students may not understand or have been exposed to. The literature drives the questions and students research answers based upon their curiosities.	This unit seeks to provide insights around and to prompt students to critically examine how others have engaged in social action around social issues.	This unit invites students to take action around issues that matter to them.

Figure I.3. Sinek's Golden Circle can help teachers develop instructional units in ways that push them toward their end goal.

UNIT 3: Using Literature to Help Unpack Social Issues			
WHAT	**WHY**	**HOW**	**WHAT**
What issue or issues do my students not know a lot about? What literature can help my students talk about this issue or these issues?	Why should we study this issue or these issues? Why does this work matter to my students?	How will we study this issue or these issues? How can I provide multiple perspectives throughout this unit? How can I design learning experiences that matter to my students? How do I want my students to engage in this learning?	What support will my students need in order to examine these issues? What practices or skills will my students need to develop throughout this unit? What support will I need to better facilitate this content?

toward learning to become more personal and meaningful to their everyday world.

In our work, we broke down the unit illustrated in Figure I.3 into weeks. Figure I.4 demonstrates how to take these unit-driving questions, and apply them to unit design. In addressing the question "how will we study these issues?," we wanted students to develop an awareness campaign. A campaign highlighted the research around their questions and integrated literacy and technology in meaningful ways. In many traditionally designed units, the literature is the unit. However, with our work, the literature inspires limitless curiosities, questions, and ideas for students to pursue.

The tasks. For units like the one featured in Figure I.4, we must devote time to identifying texts that will help support students' understanding of the social issue. Then, knowing the culminating goals of the unit will help develop the tasks around the texts. We know that one of the first tasks that we need in our unit revolves around building schema for our students to connect to the learning experience. Acknowledging students' interests and needs provide an easier path in cultivating resources that will help students develop their connections to the unit study. Figure I.5 illustrates how to design for this task.

SELECTING YOUR TEXTS

Text selections—specifically book considerations—can be seen as one of the cornerstones to situating inquiry as disruption with the classroom. From police brutality to toxic masculinity to drug addiction, our students have questioned, investigated, and acted on a variety of social issues that are inspired by the books we read and experience together. When it comes to considering texts for your students, there are a few questions that can be helpful in the decision-making process:

- *What questions are your students asking? What questions are you asking?*
- *What topics or issues do your students know very little about or have little exposure to at this point in their education?*
- *What books can help students process those questions?*
- *What books can help expose students to current topics or issues that can inspire a deeper line of inquiry and action?*

In our experience, once we've determined the text selection for our students, we then make a point to think

Figure I.4. A sample timeline for a unit.

		UNIT 3: Using Literature to Help Unpack Social Issues
TIME FRAME	**FOCUS**	**TASKS**
Week 1	Build schema and begin reading	Engage with texts that can help students make connections to the content, introduce the literature, begin new reading routines, and introduce anchor activities
Week 2	Continue reading	Continue with reading routines and new anchor activities
Week 3	Finish reading	Finish reading routines and complete all anchor activities
Week 4	Socratic seminar discussion	Prepare and answer questions for a Socratic seminar, host Socratic seminar discussion, and invite students to ask questions that ignite research
Week 5	Research	Collaborative groups research and discover answers to their questions developed in Week 4, curate credible sources, and annotate for meaning and connections to student questions
Weeks 6 and 7	Campaign development	Collaborative groups determine what information has relevance to the issue they want to convey awareness around, identify target audiences, participate in design thinking, provide feedback to each other's prototyped designs, and produce a final product
Week 8	Campaign launch	Share campaign work with audiences outside the classroom, participate in feedback and reflections related to the unit

Figure I.5. Breaking down the tasks using Sinek's framework.

		UNIT 3: Using Literature to Help Unpack Social Issues	
WEEK 1 TASK	**WHY** Why does this task matter?	**HOW** How can I complete this task with students?	**WHAT** What can I use with my students to complete this task?
Building schema	*Our students may have limited experience or a surface level understanding of many of the social issues found in the literature we choose to use. Taking time to build schema affords every learner an entry point to make connections with the reading experience.*	*Our students have interest in multimodal texts. Additionally, they can connect their own personal identities to some of the core conflicts within the issue.*	• *Podcast episodes* • *Documentaries* • *TED Talks* • *Journaling* • *Reflection* • *Discussion*

not only about the learning experiences we can design from this text but also think deeply about who can support our students throughout this reading. Think about the variety of roles and perspectives that come with stories and pair that with the realities of these perspectives within your communities. In many ways, this book experience serves as a launchpad into inquiry and practice with criticality. When working with these books and your students, it's important to remember that you should not only consider ways in which your students can begin to think differently and critically about the text, but you should also nurture skills they can practice and apply. A way to think about this design can be seen in Figure I.6.

Thinking through the questions in Figure I.6 can lead to reimagining reading experiences for students. For our work, we know we want students to take action on the issues that matter the most to them, but we

also recognize that they need practice in developing this mindset. We structure learning experiences into anchor activities as a way to bridge the book with deeper thinking (see Chapter 5). To see the questions in Figure I.6 in action, see Figure I.7.

Selecting meaningful texts can open students to a new world of thinking and questioning. The experiences we pair with these selected texts afford students the opportunity to connect with a variety of social topics as well as an agency to act.

WHERE DO I START?

Implementing this transformation to practice doesn't happen all at once. Examining the scope and sequence work along with the unit design proves that this work takes time. Attempting to change everything at one time not only can

Figure I.6. Questions to consider when selecting books for inquiry as disruption.

	QUESTIONS TO CONSIDER
Perspectives	• *What roles are represented in this text?* • *Who can speak to these roles?* • *How can I connect with these experts and connect them with my students?* • *What questions do students need to consider when speaking to experts in efforts to learn more about existing perspectives in the reading? In our communities? Beyond the classroom?*
Skills	• *What skills do I want students to practice?* • *What writing, technologies, speaking, listening, thinking do I want my students to practice during this experience?* • *How can elements of the book help students practice their skills?* • *What learning experiences can I construct that support the practice and development of these skills?*

Figure I.7. A model for how to use the questions around text using Jeff Zentner's book *In the Wild Light*.

	BOOK SELECTION: *In the Wild Light* by Jeff Zentner	
	EXAMPLES	POSSIBLE LEARNING EXPERIENCES
Perspectives found in or related to the book	*Roles in this book include, but not limited to:* • *A poet* • *A scientist* • *A person experiencing addiction* • *A professor* • *A person with emphysema*	• *Connect and conduct interviews with people from the community who identify with these roles or perspectives* • *Watch and connect to documentaries, TED talks, pre-recorded speeches/lectures related to people with these experiences.*
Skills	*Because we'll be designing an awareness campaign (Chapter 8) after our reading experience, I'd like students to practice visual literacy skills.*	• *Construct a photo essay related to issues, characters, or events within and around the book.* • *Construct a détournement (Chapter 2) that challenges students to take an issue from the text and create commentary around it through hijacking original art*

be overwhelming as a professional, but it could also deflect from the core reasons you committed to when starting this transformation journey.

For New Teachers

For new teachers, getting a handle on the everyday routines of the classroom can be a large task itself. At a novice level, channel your energy in the design of your units. As you focus your attention to the questions, skills, experiences, texts, and tasks you want your students to engage in throughout the course of a unit, daily planning becomes easier.

For Experienced Teachers

We know you've experienced your fair share of professional development seminars, district initiatives, and new design frameworks. We ask that you allow yourself to see these experiences and the work that you do differently. To start, we recommend designing one unit that encompasses the questioning and thinking we've outlined throughout

this book. Think about your mindset toward learning, how your mindset can change based on the needs of your learners, and how this experience can ignite other learning opportunities as the year progresses.

ASSESSING THE WORK

Seeing differently in your instruction will more than likely lead you to start questioning your assessment practices. On the surface, some of the experiences and approaches we describe in this book are not that different from what you might find in a typical ELA classroom. It's the lens of student-centered inquiry and social action that shift the way we use them. Rather than analyzing characters to better understand the book, we encourage students to explore what the characters can teach them about the world. Rather than developing projects that create artificial inquiries, we prompt students to identify questions that matter to them, so they can begin to take real action in their schools and communities. And rather than handing out points and letter grades, we work collaboratively with students to provide ongoing meaningful feedback.

Yet, our work didn't always embrace nontraditional grading practices. Like most teachers, we weighted assignments, calculated points, and designed elaborate rubrics. As we began to make the small changes that led to the bigger changes described in this book, we began to recognize that traditional grading, like traditional teaching, just didn't make sense. It didn't meet the needs of our students, nor did it accurately reflect the work they were doing. But it took making changes to our instructional approaches for us to recognize the disconnect with our assessment and grading practices.

We state this upfront because we have no doubt that as you read this book questions about assessment and grading will arise. We encourage you to think about how you would approach assessment as you read. What changes would you make? Where do you see disconnects between traditional grading practices and the approaches described in these pages? Why might you want to rethink how you grade? We'll share some of our own approaches to assessing and grading in the final chapter of this book, but in the meantime, think about your own contexts, your own students, and your own goals. What would grading and assessment look like in your classroom as you do this work?

Part I

SEEING BIG

Cultural anthropologist Michael Wesch (2018) talks about the essence of learning as mastering the art of seeing. Truly seeing means that we must look at the world in different ways. Helping our students practice these different ways of seeing is key to using inquiry to disrupt the social problems we face in the world today. To initiate the process of seeing, we must begin to examine how we see the world and *why* we see the world in the ways we do. This allows us to set aside the assumptions we bring to the experiences we had in the past, the experiences we are living, and the experiences we will encounter in the future. Wesch begins the outward journey of seeing by encouraging us to "see big." When we *see big*, we look at the systems that shape our and others' lives. We explore culture. We delve into social forces. We consider the impact of economics. We listen to the reverberations of history. And we recognize how politics influence the decisions we make.

Part I of this book introduces ways we can help our students *see big*. Chapter 1 begins with the importance of students getting to know themselves before shifting to what Kalina Silverman (2014) calls Big Talk. Through Big Talk, students connect with others, often strangers, to better understand the complexities of others' stories. And by engaging in Big Talk students start to identify the cultural, societal, economic, historical, and political forces that mold who they and others are. Chapter 2 introduces approaches that help students grapple with the systems they have begun to explore through the experiences described in Chapter 1 and throughout the book. Students learn the importance of *wobble* (Garcia & O'Donnell-Allen, 2015) in personal growth, and they learn how to leverage their own moments of wobble to create messages designed to prompt others to wobble too. Finally, Chapter 3 prompts students to begin asking their own questions rather than waiting for questions to be posed to them. It introduces questioning that is playful, as well as questioning that extends Big Talk. By normalizing student questioning, students take control of their learning. Questioning provides students with a skill that will help them *see big*. And once they can see big, once they can question the systems that shape our world, students can begin the journey to disrupt our world.

ONE

The Dangers of a Single Story

Just because you can't experience everything doesn't mean you shouldn't experience anything.

—Nicola Yoon

Our early experiences with reading were vastly different. Robyn's elementary texts were color-coded and taken from a box labeled SRA. She worked quickly through each color, reading each story and answering each question on the corresponding quiz, until she wrapped up those blue cards, proclaiming to all that she was a great reader. Nearly 10 years later, Sarah found herself sorted in a different way. In Sarah's classroom, readers were categorized as birds—the coveted cardinal, the fierce blue jay, and the simple robin. She was a robin—a part of a group that announced to the rest of the class that she, along with her small circle of peers, wasn't as good at reading as most of the class. Fortunately, those days are long past . . . or are they? Although they may not be labeled as *blue* readers or a part of the *robin* circle, children all over the country are being shaped as readers through leveling systems like Lexiles and programs such as Accelerated Reader. Once our young readers have a solid understanding of where they fall on the reading totem pole, many of these readers enter middle and high school where they are handed books from the canon or books their parents fondly (or not so fondly) remember reading back in the day.

If they are students like Robyn, they approach each book confident they know the answers. If they are students like Sarah, they approach each book confident that they don't. And unfortunately for both kinds of readers, they more than likely are presented with books that share with them a single story. That story may be the interpretation of the test maker or teacher. It may be focused on the story of the protagonist rather than on the other characters who help make that story whole—and given publishing statistics, it is highly likely that this character is white. Or, if the protagonist does represent a historically marginalized population and this is the only story our students hear from this perspective, we risk doing the very harm we seek to undo: perpetuating the misunderstanding of others who are different from ourselves. Chimamanda

Ngozi Adichie (2009) warns us: "The single story creates stereotypes, and the problem with stereotypes is not that they are untrue, but that they are incomplete. They make one story become the only story" (12:50).

It is the dangers of perpetuating those single stories that demand we shift our focus away from leveling and labeling readers and toward an exploration and attempt to empathize with multiple stories. It is vital that teachers displace misunderstandings and limited perspectives, so that when our students meet others with different experiences, they do not approach them with, as Adichie (2009) describes, "patronizing, well-meaning, pity" (4:42). Students need to understand the complexity of stories everyone brings with them, so that they look for the connections that make them human equals.

As ELA teachers, we have long been believers in Rudine Sims Bishop's (1990) conception of literature as "mirrors, windows, and sliding glass doors." It has been through holding up mirrors to our own practices that has helped us shift from reading books and doing projects that made us comfortable to engaging with books and doing work with students that, at times, has made us uncomfortable. While we do this work to help our students who have been historically marginalized find stories that serve as mirrors, we also do this work so that our white children find those windows and doors into realities that Bishop called for 30 years ago.

But if teachers truly want to help students see past single stories, it goes beyond mirrors, windows, and sliding glass doors. Rather, as Uma Krishnaswami (2019) wrote in a blog post, teachers must also consider literature as a prism that refracts light in multiple directions. In selecting the stories we present to our students, we want to seek out books that "disrupt and challenge ideas about diversity through multifaceted and intersecting identities, settings, cultural contexts, and histories" (para. 6). These books give their characters the "power to reframe their stories" (para. 6), providing students with the power to reframe their own understandings of the world.

While we believe that inquiry is a positive step in learning, we—and others—make the case that inquiry for inquiry's sake is not enough to tap into this form of change (Beach et al., 2022; Juliani, 2014; Mirra et al., 2015). Teachers and other stakeholders may find comfort in the inquiry process using safe and distant materials— the *books we've always taught in that assigned grade level.* But, if we want to cultivate long-lasting change, then we must be willing to disrupt our own lenses, break down our established comforts, and participate in experiences that allow us to become uncomfortable in order to experience the world differently.

Throughout this chapter, we demonstrate that the need for disruption is not only necessary for students as they continue to make meaning of the world, but also because students deserve engaging learning experiences that matter to them. As we speak to the beginning stages of this framework, the power of *why* connects to our actions. Along with disrupting traditional practices, we know this framework also invites students to ask questions that take them out of their comfort zones. As Yoon (2015) reminds us, it is important that we, as humans, experience *something*. This chapter, as well as the rest of the book, outlines pedagogical approaches that seek to provide meaningful experiences that help our students see the world differently—and, hopefully, move them to act even after they leave our classroom spaces.

OUR STUDENTS' LIVED EXPERIENCES

It was our first year embarking on the work described in this book. Students had finished Walter Dean Myers's *Monster* and had decided that they wanted to learn more about gangs, an idea loosely associated with the book, which features a young Black man on trial for participating in a burglary that led to murder. It was evident that the students, in their insulated world, equated juvenile crime and violence with gangs, pointing to the dangers of a single story. Yet, it was important they follow their curiosities because it allowed them to examine the complexity of why teens join gangs and to consider experiences of youth different from themselves. It allowed them to begin to add dimension to what began as a single story.

On this day, students were trying to capture their research in images and slogans as they worked to create an awareness campaign to present to other classes. As they worked on their ideas, it soon became apparent that students who had already come so far in their thinking still

had a long way to go. The ideas overheard from group to group continued to perpetuate the very stereotypes the unit was intent on disrupting. Given their lack of experience with youth of color, students, when asked to create, were falling back on their own experiences and their own perceptions, and these experiences and perceptions were largely divorced from the ideas they had been researching. It was time to intervene and prompt students to consider why their current ideas were problematic.

At this moment, Ashley, the only young lady of mixed race in the room and one of very few in the school, raised her hand. And then she began to talk. She voiced how troubling the Ferguson conflict was for her and made connections between herself, Michael Brown, and Steve Harmon (*Monster*'s fictional protagonist). She asked her peers to think about their experiences at the local mall. She wondered if they had ever been followed or asked specific questions about the purpose of being in that store or even had their bags searched. As all around her the rest of the class sat quietly, uncomfortably, Ashley spoke about the voices of the Black Lives Matter movement and the response of law enforcement. She helped the class to see that while most of them did not correlate these real-time events that were occurring less than 3 hours away from them with the events happening in the novel, the story of Steve Harmon was not that much different from the story of Michael Brown. The story of Steve Harmon alarmed the class, and so should, Ashley argued, the story of Michael Brown. At this moment, Ashley was inviting her peers to empathize with the experiences people of color encounter. This moment was a turning point for Ashley because it became more than reading an engaging YA text, asking questions and cultivating readings. It became a path in which she found a means to find and use her voice. It was also a time of pivot for the rest of the class.

We want to pause here and acknowledge that while Ashley chose to speak up in the moment, it was not her responsibility to do so. While she found it an empowering moment, other students may not and should not be expected to speak up. It is up to us, as teachers, to identify instances such as this and create a space for these conversations to transpire. We must approach these conversations with strategies that prompt students to empathize with others and to identify their own biases, and to dismantle stereotypes. One way to do this is by modeling the if/then statement approach Jason Reynolds and Ibram Kendi (2020) take in their book *Stamped: Racism, Antiracism, and You.* We offer example sentence starters such as, "If a policy makes someone feel unsafe" and invite students to explore the rest of the statement, leading to responses such as "then we need to revise the policy."

This offers students entry points into conversations that can begin to dismantle biases and stereotypes.

In our experience with Ashley, when the conversations finally resumed, their tenor had changed. As ideas emerged, they paused to reflect upon whether these ideas were rooted in stereotypes. They began to think about ways to symbolize the information uncovered in their research that more accurately represented their messages.

IN DIALOGUE

Throughout the school year, students kept a blog where they reflected upon their questions and insights across units. For many students, the blog was simply a part of the classroom process, but for others like Samantha, it became a place to reflect upon the lessons in the class without prompting. Samantha wrote this post in the summer following her time in Sarah's class. It demonstrates how she was able to recognize that there is no single story, even within an individual, and how she pushed back at being defined in a singular way. Once students can see this about themselves, they are better prepared to recognize the complexity of others.

"S" by S

A wise and generous teacher once asked me, "What does it mean to be you?" Sure, it might have been a project that I accomplished with other papers and assignments, but I felt like it was a shallow and generic teenage answer. I wanted to explore more, so here I am, writing this for the world to see, so Mrs. Bonner, "what does it mean to be you?" for me, it means so many things.

It means so much more than that project that you had us do all the way at the beginning of 8th grade. It means that I am shy around people I don't know or trust. It means that I have friends, best friends, and family who love and support me. It means that I am shy, happy, scared, stressed, mean, rude, sad, disappointed, excited, grateful, and so much more all at the same time. It means that I am loved, even when I make mistakes. It means that I get into drama and fights with fake friends over and over. It means that I have real friends who know me

> In recognizing the multiple facets of herself, Samantha is prepared to see the multiple facets of others, which is necessary to disrupting a single story.

and who will try and protect me from many things. It means that I am the only one of me, and that only I know what it means to be me.

Most of you have probably stopped reading by now or got bored and skimmed until you got here. Well, I have exciting news for you, you have made it to the end of part one. Yes, I will continue to write about who I am and what it means to be me. Why? Because this is MY anthem and this is who I want to be. I want to share myself with the world. So, please, if you made it this far, spread the word. I want people to know who I am. I want people to read this and be inspired. And most importantly, I want people to read this, and I want them—I want you—to know that no matter what, just keep being you in a world full of non-yous. You make a difference. You matter. You are loved. You are strong. And you are the only one of you.

Sincerely,
S.

> Samantha writes for herself, but also to make a difference in the world. In celebrating herself, she is also reminding everyone to celebrate and love who they are.

TRANSFORMING THROUGH PRACTICE: HELPING STUDENTS UNDERSTAND THEIR STORIES IN ORDER TO PREPARE THEM FOR OTHERS' STORIES

As Adichie (2009) explained, a single story creates stereotypes that share only a fragment of the larger narrative, leading to those who only possess that fragment to misinterpret others' stories. Ashley shared experiences with the rest of the class that demonstrate how deeply those fragments can go. Left alone, these single stories will continue to cut away at our students and society. Teachers must create spaces for students to learn the untold stories so that they may piece together the larger narrative. Samantha demonstrates how this can begin by helping students examine the multiple stories that make up their own identities. Understanding the complexity that resides within themselves better prepares students to complicate the single story about others that often dominates the media they consume and the conversations they overhear.

The work of Russian philosopher and literary critic Mikhail Bakhtin (2010) provides a lens to understand how to approach stories. Bakhtin reminds us that the telling and hearing of stories is greatly influenced by social and cultural influences. To fully understand stories, it is important to consider the perspective of the storyteller and the listener, the ways participants evaluate the experience, and the ideology the story is positioned within. Teachers must recognize that language is not neutral and teach students to examine how culture

and experience shape what we say and what we hear. The lessons that follow are two that embody the dialogic nature of learning described by Bakhtin. Used early in the year, these lessons prepare students to look beyond the single story.

THEORY TO PRACTICE

Mikhail Bakhtin: Bakhtin's work in *The Dialogic Imagination* (2010) examines the relationship between novels and language. Bakhtin saw the novel as the text most closely able to represent the world, and as such it provided opportunities for dialogue to help shape social understandings. The approach to inquiry through novel study builds upon Bakhtin's work as it asks students to consider the voices present within the texts they read and to engage in dialogue with these voices as students pose the questions that will shape their inquiries. The following highlight how Bakhtin's theories influence the learning experiences presented in this book. They can serve as models for how to think about putting his work into practice.

- **The Words We Use (see Chapter 4):** "There is no such thing as a 'general language,' a language that is spoken by a general voice, that may be divorced from a specific saying, which is charged with particular overtones. Language, when it means, is somebody talking to somebody else, even when that someone else is one's own inner addressee."
- **Surviving the System (see Chapter 5):** "What is realized in the novel is the process of coming to know one's own language as it is perceived in someone else's language, coming to know one's own belief system in someone else's system."
- **The Investigation Mixtape (see Chapter 3):** "Truth is not born nor is it to be found inside the head of an individual person; it is born between people collectively searching for truth, in the process of their dialogic interaction" (Bakhtin, 2013).

For more about Mikhail Bakhtin's work around dialogic meaning-making, check out the following resources:

- "In Theory Bakhtin: Dialogism, Polyphony and Heteroglossia" by Andrew Robinson at https://ceasefiremagazine.co.uk/in-theory-bakhtin-1/
- "Three Minute Thought: Mikhail Bakhtin on Polyphony" at https://www.youtube.com/watch?v=InLfLXWQkzY

THE MULTIGENRE ABOUT ME PROJECT

What is a Multigenre About Me Project?

Developed more than 20 years ago by Tom Romano (2000), the multigenre research project blends research with creative writing, allowing students to identify topics of passion, research these topics, and craft their new understandings through multiple genres to capture the essence of the topic's story. Romano describes multigenre writing as "an immersion in a big topic of personal importance. I want students to taste such passionate immersion. I want them to experience how that immersion, combined with the possibility of multiple genres, can waken a boldness of expression in them" (Romano, 2013, p. 193).

The Multigenre About Me Project takes up the concept of the multigenre research project, but rather than asking students to research a topic of their choice, students research themselves. Within the Multigenre About Me Project, students develop a minimum of five genres of writing, each sharing a different aspect about themselves. In addition to these five genres, students also create a "Dear Reader" letter that previews their project and unique packaging that symbolizes an important element of their selves.

How Can a Multigenre About Me Project Help Students Understand Multiple Stories?

Multigenre About Me Projects require students to examine multiple aspects of their identities. It requires them to interrogate who they are through an exploration of their values, their experiences, their passions, and their interests. This interrogation leads to an understanding that answering the question, "Who are you?" requires careful consideration and complex answers. And once students realize that they are not made up of a single story, they are more likely to recognize that the single stories they often hear about others are incomplete and often inaccurate.

Multigenre About Me Projects also prepare students for an inquiry-centered learning environment. By asking students to explore the question, "What does it mean to be you," they begin to understand that deep learning begins with an important question that demands them to slow down and look for answers in multiple spaces. The multigenre format demonstrates that there are multiple ways to demonstrate their understanding, and it prepares them for developing the authentic texts needed to engage in work outside of the classroom.

Before You Begin

Prior to starting the multigenre writing project, engage students with the driving question, "What does it mean to be you?," but also ask them to dig deeper beyond the surface understandings of how they might generically describe themselves to others. To accomplish this, students participate in a series of schema building exercises that speak to core values and personal beliefs, add the concept of *writer* to their identity, and create a childhood map that outlines memories.

This schema building time also affords different activities like understanding personal enneagrams (The Enneagram Institute, 2021) or explorations of learning preferences. The data collected throughout this week of experiences serves as a platform for prewriting. While students may not use all their collected data from this schema building week in their final product, it ultimately allows students to generate choices and topics to think about when moving forward in constructing their writings. Designing a space for students to have access to resources and mentor texts becomes key prior to diving into this project. Students can engage and play with a variety of nontraditional writing genres and styles.

In the Moment

Step 1: Develop a writing proposal. Allowing students to develop a writing proposal offers an opportunity for students to not only personally take ownership of their writing, but it also invites students to answer the essential question using their chosen content and chosen format. Additionally, as students venture through the writing process, they have the option to design their own writing order, allowing for personal ownership of learning.

Writing a proposal consists of identifying four author-based decisions: (1) the writing genre for the piece of writing; (2) a mentor text or a text that demonstrates the same writing genre for a student writer to use as a guide when constructing their own authentic pieces; (3) the topic of the writing; and (4) the author's purpose or what readers should know because of reading the writing. Once students identify the parameters of their writing projects, teachers set project milestones so that students can use these set times to manage their time, receive meaningful feedback, and maximize their workshop experience. While students are required to propose five pieces of writing that support five different writing genres, students also have the option to write more than five pieces, which they identify within their proposals. This planner allows students to not only map out what they want to write about but also how they want to write it: https://tinyurl.com/2p8csx9k.

Step 2. Allow for writing time. Participating in the multigenre project not only unearths unique personal explorations for students, but it also offers an opportunity to demonstrate and participate in workshop models. Throughout this writing, a writer's workshop supports a culture of continuous writing, sharing, and feedback.

Step 3: Turn rough drafts into final drafts with the help of a playground. At this point, students have chosen their topics that attempt to answer the essential question, "What does it mean to be you?," their proposals outline how they will write about their topics, and the workshops invite draft writing around these topics. Before entering the final draft stage of this project, students participate in a publishing playground (see Chapter 3). In that playground, students can play with different publishing tools—such as digital tools, quill and ink for calligraphy, typewriters, book binding, sketchnoting, and so on. Students use their playground experiences to make further decisions on their final drafts.

Step 4: Create a "Dear Reader" letter and the final packaging. As students finalize their projects, they construct a "Dear Reader" letter that outlines what readers should know when reading the project in its entirety. This letter serves as a capstone to the experience as it highlights the various genres, topics, and the reasons decisions were made by the individual writer. For example, in his letter, Nate explains why he focused on his love of laughter, "The third writing I did was a Manifesto about laughter. There wasn't a super specific reason I did this; It's just that I laugh a lot. I always try and make people laugh, and it's weird, but when other people laugh, I laugh even if I don't know what they are laughing about or what the joke is." In addition to this letter, students construct some form of packaging to house their writings. Their individual packaging should correlate with the driving question and be relative to their identities (See Figure 1.1).

Step 5: Celebrate what it means to be you! As a closing to this writing experience, students celebrate their writings in the form of another playground. Prior to this, students had the opportunity to understand the nature of a playground with the help of publishing tools. This time, students serve as part of the play as the classroom is divided up into players and presenters. The presenters display their packaging and their writings in an assigned space within the classroom. The players walk around the classroom and play with projects by questioning and interacting with the presenters. Additionally, the players provide peer-supported feedback to the final products. In the next class, the players and presenters switch roles to allow everyone an opportunity to interact with and celebrate the work of all students in the class.

Making Learning Visible

By celebrating student writing, students display pride in their work and demonstrate the elements of their identities that make them unique, which cultivates a sense of agency in a classroom of writers. After experiencing the proposal writing process, workshops to construct individual writings, and the whole-class sharing of writing, teachers can examine the connections this project makes with students by inviting them to engage in a structured reflection activity using Well-Remembered Events (Carter, 1994). While originally created to help pre-service teachers process their teaching experiences, Well-Remembered Events have also been effective for helping students process their learning, as well. Figure 1.2 demonstrates how these reflections are structured.

Well-Remembered Events help surface for teachers the moments in learning that stand out to students. For some students, these reflections consist of the pride they feel as an author, such as adding author as a name within their personal identities. For other students, the reflection provides space to consider other writing experiences they would like to engage in if given another chance to write. Adria (see Figure 1.3) discovered through the Multigenre About Me project that the freedom it offered allowed her to express herself in a way that matters to her:

Publishing my drafts allowed me to be creative. I liked having the freedom to publish them in a way that reflected my

Figure 1.1. Examples of students' Multigenre About Me Projects that include genres such as letters, poem, infographic, and word art.

Figure 1.2. Well-Remembered Events provide a structure for students to identify learning events that stand out to them and reflect upon their importance to their learning.

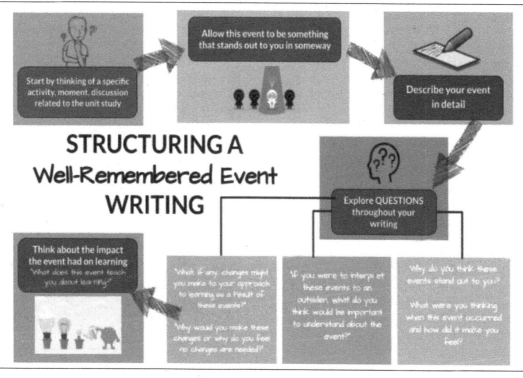

personality. It was one of the first projects that I've gotten to do the way I wanted. I actually had fun with drafting and especially publishing this project.

These moments of visible learning invite new conversations into practice as students begin to transform their

Figure 1.3. Adria chose to package her Multigenre About Me Project in a guitar case to reflect her love of music.

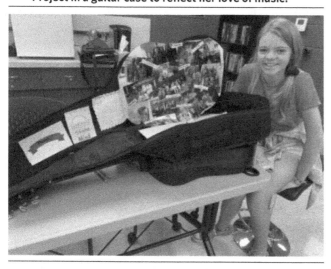

identities from students to writers. When these openings occur, teachers must carefully consider the next steps that will keep the momentum going so that students continue to think critically about their personal identities and what it means to be them in today's world.

WHAT WE KEEP

What Is What We Keep?

Adapted from the journalistic minds of Bill Shapiro and Naomi Wax (2018), *What We Keep* invites students to think deeply about the objects that matter the most to them and to share the stories connected to those objects. In addition to exploring their own objects, students are also challenged to connect with strangers in their community, cultivate stories related to other people's objects, and curate these stories in unique ways.

Students, who only know their own experiences, frequently hold an ethnocentric view of the world. Through this lens, students believe their values, ideas, and assumptions are the correct ones (Wesch, 2018). The act of talking to strangers about their valued objects asks students to engage in cultural relativism because through

MULTIGENRE WRITING IN ACTION

- Romano (2000) introduced the concept of multigenre writing to think differently about research and move beyond the traditional layout of a research paper. Using a multigenre approach to a topic invites learners to think about the topic from different perspectives and constructing writing pieces that demonstrate a variety of writing genres (letters, infographics, charts, graphs, poems, etc.).
- When presented with driving questions like, "What does it mean to be you?," multigenre writing can serve as a platform for students to explore their values, beliefs, and identities that go beyond a surface understanding of each student.
- Meg (see Figure 1.4) constructed a writing within her project that explored her values and beliefs. From her writing entitled "The Meaning of Life in My Eyes," she stated, "What should we do to make a difference while we're here? Some find life as something you just try to get by in, but that's not what it's about. I find that the meaning of life is to learn and grow, meet new people, and experience new things, and never give up. I often think about what we were put on this earth to do, and what I can do to make a difference."
- Reflecting on her overall multigenre writing experience, Meg wrote, "The Multigenre writing

project taught me that there are different ways of writing, and that you can do more than just writing essays about yourself. They teach me that my classroom is more than just writing essays. We try to incorporate our ideas and what is important to us in our projects and learning. It taught me that I can do new things and have fun doing them."

Figure 1.4. Meg sits with her Multigenre About Me Project during the class playground (see Chapter 3).

the learning of others' stories, students begin to better understand a broader spectrum of values, ideas, and assumptions and how this spectrum of ideas relates to their own culture. What We Keep requires students to find someone they have never met and engage in Big Talk around meaningful storytelling. Through these conversations, teachers prompt students to identify an important idea and reflect upon what this idea teaches them about being human.

How Can What We Keep Help Students Understand Multiple Stories?

Through What We Keep, students not only evaluate and justify the objects connected to their own identities but they also collect stories associated with others. And while these conversations may only reveal a single aspect of their strangers' lives, when combined with the kaleidoscope of stories compiled by the class, a larger understanding of the

multiple stories that make up their community emerges. At times, the stories students uncover mirror their own experiences, but at other times, talking with strangers about the objects they keep provides them with windows into worlds they had never previously conceived.

Like the Multigenre About Me Project, What We Keep primes students for inquiry-centered learning because it requires them to frame meaningful questions and explore their answers with people outside their everyday circles. It pushes students outside of their comfort zones, requiring them to try something they might not have on their own. And it teaches students that the world is more complex than schools sometimes present it to be.

Before You Begin

As you can well imagine, storytelling, deeply thinking about the memories centered on objects we own, or even talking to strangers may not come naturally to all our students. To promote healthy, positive experiences with this activity, it's important to think about the resources your students will need for such an experience. One way to begin this experience is by watching the TED Ed talk "Why You Should Talk to Strangers" by Kio Stark (2016). Stark speaks to the notion of engaging in the human experience by finding what we have in common by talking to one another rather than living in a space of fear and ignorance. She invites her viewers to think about the unwritten rules of talking to strangers and makes the overall case that these interactions disrupt our own narratives in hopes to construct unexpected connections.

In addition to this video, collect a series of resources for students in anticipation of their specific needs. Using Shapiro and Wax's (2018) book of stories to both analyze and model as mentor texts provides students the context to which they can start their own thought process. Other example resources for this learning experience may include strategies for eye contact, developing questions, and engaging in meaningful conversations.

It is also important to make time for parent communication and teacher transparency. Inform parents and stakeholders of your intentions with this experience and allow for flexibility within individual comfort levels. For example, some families may be comfortable with going to a grocery store and encouraging their child to approach a completely unknown stranger. However, other families may not be comfortable with that idea and may choose to have students talk to a neighbor or school personnel. The definition of "stranger" can be flexible with your students. While we ultimately want students to engage in new experiences that push them into new and exciting spaces, we also want to engage students (and parents) in safe ways.

In the Moment

> Step 1: *Afford students conversations and exposure to resources centered on the idea of storytelling and eliciting stories from strangers.* When posed, talking to strangers seems like a foreign (and maybe to some students, scary) concept. As young people, echoes of "stranger danger" have rippled into their understanding; this means that the idea of doing the opposite of what they've been taught needs processing time.
>
> Step 2: *Help students understand the why.* Because this can be seen as an intimidating experience, ensure that students understand *why* they are being asked to engage in this type of work. Don't be afraid to highlight work from

experts who do this well—such as storytellers, anthropologists, or archivists. Additionally, seek out examples of how others do this on social media (like https://www.humansofnewyork .com/), or invite students to brainstorm reasons why this act can be seen as a positive step in understanding the world.

> Step 3: *Prepare students for engaging in dialogue.* Provide students with resources that show what meaningful conversation looks like in real life. Take note of the elements that make that conversation meaningful. Students can study videos, brainstorm, construct questions, and even develop a plan before venturing out into the "field."
>
> Step 4: *Discuss how researchers collect data in the field.* When we frame our learning experiences using real-world terms, it can invite a heightened agency toward the work we're doing as both students and teachers. Facilitate discussions around capturing moments as students venture out to talk with a stranger. How will students document the experience? Encourage students to focus on active listening skills when collecting their interview data. Video and/or audio recordings of interviews can help students capture these data points while also processing the information that is being collected.
>
> Step 5: *Create and execute a plan to accomplish this challenge.* Once students experience the lesson (the TED Ed talk, Humans of New York mentor text, etc.), encourage students to think about how they will execute their own plan to curate object stories from strangers. You might discuss possible options for students to participate in this challenge as well as invite students to brainstorm possible ways to interact with this task.

In addition to brainstorming with students, communicate with parents in an effort to help students execute a plan that also supports their comforts. Many students may choose to do this independently within their community; however, many students may choose to do this with parental support or with the safety parameters of their school community (for example, talking with school personnel that students may not have directly spoken to in the building). Allowing students and parents to find their own comfort parameters around this challenge welcomes the success of this learning experience for all students.

For more about how to break this work apart for students, check out the guidelines Sarah provides her students at https://tinyurl.com/9ssw3p6n.

Making Learning Visible

Because this learning experience lends itself to individual interpretations and experiences, finding a way to make learning visible for each student becomes essential. One way to do this is to develop a classroom blog and invite students to construct their own blog pages that are linked to the classroom blog page (to serve as a collaborative space). From there, students can post their documentation of their experience and reflect on the lessons this experience gave them in the moment. Creating a space for students to share their individual experiences allows the opportunity to be shared and celebrated among all students as well as other classroom stakeholders.

Olivia—a student who initially expressed hesitation toward this learning experience—found comfort from talking to a distant neighbor and reflected on her learning experience by saying:

> To start with, I'd say that one of the biggest discoveries I made with this experience is that not all strangers are bad and that even sometimes talking to strangers you can find out some of the craziest things. I just think that maybe you shouldn't always think the worst of strangers and maybe sometimes you might even make a friend talking to them or find out new things that maybe you had no idea about. This experience impacted my thinking in moving forward because it will really help with asking good questions and trying new things but also to make me think about different things in a different way from others.

WHAT WE KEEP IN ACTION

- Shapiro and Wax (2018) started a conversation with people to uncover the single object that carries the most emotional significance. This work seeks to explore the human experience and how value, sentiment, and storytelling make us who we are as people.
- What if we were to challenge students to engage in a talking experience with strangers? As part of a What We Keep constructed by Natalie (seen in Figure 1.5), she stated,

> The big discoveries I made as a result of this experience are to value what you do in life and recognize all the meaning your life has. Not only does your life have a lot of meaning, but a lot of simple objects in your life have a lot of meaning. Sometimes we take for granted how lucky we are to be able to experience things, but it is important to understand the story behind items you may hold. . . . Though our objects were much different, I used mine as an example, and we connected in that way. I also hadn't ever thought about all the items I hold and how much meaning there is to them. I had to ask myself so many questions, I don't think I've ever known myself as well as I do now.
>
> After this experience, I think about strangers a bit differently. You don't have to be afraid when you come across a stranger; try to connect with them. There may be more people out in the world like you that have very similar interests and experiences as you.

Figure 1.5. Natalie reflects upon what she learned from a stranger who cherishes her late grandmother's mug.

When we invite students to rethink the notion of strangers and partner it with exploring the human experience, we give them an opportunity to practice interacting in learning that goes beyond the classroom. As Olivia concludes, trying new things can be the ultimate reward, and, as students continue to see these rewards, it welcomes the courage to keep trying new things as learning experiences unfold within the classroom.

READING YOUR WORLD

The two activities described in this chapter are just two examples of how teachers can help students understand the importance of multiple stories. Through an examination of their own multilayered stories and a sampling of stories from their communities, we have found that our students begin to make a mindset shift that helps them better understand Adichie's (2009) warning of the dangers of a single story. When teachers afford time and space for students to explore their own personal beliefs, ethics, and identities, we begin inviting our students to ask questions and get curious about the issues that connect to what it means to be them. Students who have a grasp of their own personal identities can better understand, listen to, and empathize with others around them. This shift is a vital first step in our larger work of helping students develop inquiry mindsets and engaging in thinking and experiences that lead to developing social awareness and action.

But these activities are not the only ways to do this work. Your world may (and probably does!) look very different from our world, so we ask you to consider how you can help your students recognize the dangers of a single story. The questions that follow are designed to help you develop your own approaches.

REFLECT, MOTIVATE, AND ACT

Reflect Our Own Stories

- *Why are you here?*
- *What are your students' stories?*
- *Do student stories of learning match your stories of teaching?*

Motivate to Discover Our Own Stories

- *How might you think about your own story?*
- *How might you think about your students' stories?*

Take Action to Understand Your Students' Stories

- *Tell a story about a class/teacher/subject area that represents a positive learning experience. What happened?*
- *How can you create an experience that allows students to learn their stories in more depth, as well as others?*

TWO

Seeing Is Not Neutral

> A compass doesn't tell you where you are. And it doesn't tell you where you have to go. It can only point you in a direction. It's up to you to always find your true north.
>
> —Samira Ahmed

Divisiveness and mistrust in our society has multiplied exponentially in recent years. Looking back upon events of the past several years, we find that our eyes, as well as the eyes of many of our white colleagues, have been further opened to the reality that our colleagues of color knew all too well: Our system is broken. Snapshots of teaching in recent years provide evidence of this over and over. Sarah walked into her junior high school on November 9, 2016, and was met with students chanting, "build the wall!" Twenty miles away, Robyn was working with preservice teachers, and one burst into tears. She had spent the morning staring into the frightened eyes of her Latinx students, students who were terrified by the promises made by the man who was just elected president. Almost 4 years later, we, along with the rest of the world, were stunned to have our time with students come to a sudden halt as a deadly virus ravaged the world's population. Questions of access became more pressing than ever before as we worried about students who completely disappeared from our worlds. Did they have internet access to stay abreast of our work? But more importantly, were they healthy? Were their families still able to work and feed them? Next, we were grappling with our close teaching colleagues around how to acknowledge and address the racial unrest that erupted due to the deaths of George Floyd, Ahmaud Arbery, and Breonna Taylor. We were hurting. Students were hurting. What could we as white teachers do?

We, like the majority of Americans, have found ourselves regularly working through the stages of grief. Climate change. Immigration. Vaccinations. Police reform. *Roe v. Wade.* Voter rights and suppression. The list goes on, and the cycle of numbness, replaced by pain and anger, that stems from the fighting around these issues continues to disrupt our lives, as well as the lives of our students. We struggled with how to continue to teach

in predominantly white communities where a significant portion of our population refuses to see the damage systems are enacting on so many humans. Yet, we recognized that while our whiteness afforded us the luxury of sitting back and bemoaning the state of the world while teaching the status quo, doing so would only perpetuate the problem. David Kirkland (2019) talks about the unseen students, the students who are vulnerable because of "their families, their genders, their socioeconomic circumstances, or anything else about vulnerable youth that deviates from the ideal" (p. 10). If we chose to teach as if these students do not exist, we would continue to perpetuate the injustices these students experience daily in and out of school. It is our duty as teachers to see these students and to recognize that much of the problem stems from what Kirkland reminds us about *how* we see. Seeing, he states, is not neutral.

We must recognize that if we claim to be neutral, we are choosing to believe in equality over equity. If our practice supports what we do for one student, we must do for all students, we are assuming that our students are all the same. To teach toward equity means that we must *see* what is happening to our vulnerable students and make the changes needed to sustain them, not just the students the system already sustains (Ellison & Solomon, 2019; Groenke et al., 2015; Kirkland, 2019; Muhammad & Haddix, 2016; Paris & Alim, 2017). It takes, Kirkland (2019) reminds us, "more than what happens in our classroom. It must be about what happens in our heads and hearts" (p. 11).

The educational system, like other social systems, is not an easy system to change. We know that. But our heads and hearts know that we need to do the work that leads to change. We understand that while we as teachers need to recognize that seeing is not neutral, we also need to help our students and other community stakeholders understand this as well. The more people who recognize that seeing is not neutral, the more opportunities we have to create fissures in the systems. And our understanding of science tells us that a system can only handle so many fissures before it collapses.

When we came to this realization, we had already begun to set the stage for using inquiry to meet all learners' needs. We had begun to teach books in ways to help students see that not everyone's lives mirror their own. And we asked them to look at issues in very real ways, connecting topics to the community so that students could see that social problems exist beyond the pages of a novel. As recent years have unfolded, we began to understand that it is not enough to help our students see the social issues that create tension in our communities. Rather, they need to understand that they cannot see these issues and remain neutral. How can we help students take a well-considered stance that might help move our world forward? One way we can do this is to embrace literature that reflects the world we currently live in. So rather than playing it safe, we started choosing novels such as *Dear Justyce* by Nic Stone to examine the justice system, *Internment* by Samira Ahmed to explore Islamophobia, and *In the Wild Light* by Jeff Zentner to confront living with grief.

While we were asking ourselves this question and making these choices, we were also very conscious of the context we were working in. While we have always held strong equity-oriented beliefs, it was important that our community did not perceive that we were coming in with an agenda. Rather, we needed to keep in mind, as Kirkland stated in a (now-deleted) tweet, that our work was not to change people's minds. "The very act feels oppressive and manipulative. I'm interested in presenting evidence-based perspectives that render to people facts upon which they can make up their own minds."

To help our students grapple with such perspectives, we turned to Garcia and O'Donnell-Allen's (2015) *Pose, Wobble, Flow* framework. Although written for educators to examine their own practices, we found value in using this framework to enable students to examine their own views and explore alternative perspectives. We use this framework throughout the school year by first identifying a pose that we want our students to address. Students have considered their positions on race, gender, and immigration, as well as other important social topics. Exploring these topics is vital if we want our students to truly understand that seeing is not neutral.

Once we ask students to identify their poses, we present them with texts that provide perspectives they may not have initially considered. We do this to help them

wobble, a necessary state that prompts them to critically examine their initial poses and wrestle with how this new information supports or contradicts these poses. Through wobble, change can occur, leading to growth in understanding, to flow, and, hopefully prompting students to move past neutrality and toward the action needed to make positive change happen.

In this chapter, we offer glimpses into how we promote moments of wobble in our classrooms. Some of these moments are small, simply nudging students to be open to new perspectives. But some of these moments linger in our students' minds long past the ending of the unit. In these moments, we see that our students understand Ahmed's (2019) words. They recognize that while we have not told them where they stand in the world or where they need to go, we have given them the tools, the compass, to help them find *their* true norths—not their parents', not ours, not the media's. And once they are equipped to find their way, many are unstoppable.

OUR STUDENTS' LIVED EXPERIENCES

One afternoon in the fall of 2018, rather than gathering with his friends in the lunchroom, Corey, along with a small group of Sarah's students, bounced into the classroom, ready for discussion. Deep into Dashka Slater's (2017) book *The 57 Bus: A True Story of Two Teenagers and the Crime That Changed Their Lives*, students had questions that Sarah, as a cisgender woman, couldn't answer. But Queer EdBirds, an association at nearby Illinois State University, could. The group was made up of future educators who identify as LGBTQ+ or as allies of members in the community. They understood the importance of uncomfortable conversations.

Students shared events from the book with the Queer EdBirds and asked questions that helped them better understand Sasha's experiences as a teen who identified as agender. Together, the group explored issues around gender-neutral restrooms. Members from Queer Edbirds opened up about their own experiences in the LGBTQ+ community. Connections were forged across groups through rich discussion as they worked through their prepared questions, as well as those that occurred while they were visiting.

Grabbing slices of pizza, middle school students blended with college students and sounds of laughter echoed throughout the classroom. Conversations that started formally continued informally, as the middle school students became more comfortable with this group of strangers—a group that represented people who lived differently from them, but who were not, they discovered, that much different inside. They were all human. They all laughed and cried and succeeded and failed.

As the time came for the Queer EdBirds to leave, Corey approached Sarah and whispered, "Hey, Mrs. Bonner . . . this was cool. I always knew I was an ally, but I never understood why until now, so thanks." Then he smiled and left the room for his next class.

IN DIALOGUE

Wobble Journals are one way we ask our students to see the world in a different light. In this response over *The 57 Bus*, Ava considers the impact tragedy has on families.

> *Pose:* Think about your "pose"—what is *your* opinion about a topic found in our text for this week's reading? Explain your opinion: Do you think families are ever the "same" after a tragic family event?

I don't think families stay the "same" after a tragic family event. There will always be some sort of difference, whether in attitude, personality, or state of well-being. There might also be an actual change such as a change in location, schools, people, etc. No matter what, each member will process this traumatic event differently, and it will change them. People may pretend to not be altered, but deep down I believe that everyone has to adjust somehow, whether good or bad. I know when I lost my grandmother we all were affected. It made us truly realize how much we need to appreciate people while they are still here and how we just need to always cherish and love others.

> *Ava demonstrates how poses are initially drawn from personal experiences. Here, she first acknowledges that families do not stay the same after experiencing tragedy. As she explores this thought further, she makes personal connections to her own family to justify her thinking. Recognizing where poses originate helps to develop experiences that will lead to wobble.*

> *Wobble:* What made you think differently (from your original "pose") about this topic? Cite evidence from the text supporting your wobble.

After the fire, Sasha had to deal with the emotional and physical trauma of their injuries. A lot of people would find it hard to stay the same after going through such a traumatic ordeal. Sasha on the other hand, was okay and continued living after their pain went away. In part three of *The 57 Bus*, they said, "Once the physical pain went away the emotional pain faded too." They ended up going off to college and living a normal life.

> *Using a quote from the text, Ava begins to empathize with Sasha and the trauma they suffered because of the bus burning. And, while she acknowledges that Sasha is ultimately "okay," Ava is starting to see the many complex layers to the impact of trauma.*

> *Flow:* How do you think differently about this topic given what you know about the different perspectives? How has this impacted your initial "pose"?

I now can see both sides to the argument "do families stay the 'same' after a tragic family event." Sasha was able to overcome the pain and not let it change them. Their parents were much the same, but it affected them slightly more. Richard and his family, on the contrary, were forever changed. Richard will be locked up for 5 years! This is not just putting a toll on him but on his family and friends as well. This experience changed Richard and will continue to affect him for the rest of his life. So, yes, tragic events can affect families, but, sometimes, they don't.

> *Here, Ava confesses that the notion of staying the "same" isn't simply dichotomous. As Ava empathizes with Sasha, she equally begins empathizing with Richard—the teenager who is blamed for the bus burning. If Ava has the ability to think through the impact of trauma on families through story, imagine how these thoughts can then be applied in real-world context.*

TRANSFORMING THROUGH PRACTICE: HELPING STUDENTS RECOGNIZE THAT SEEING IS NOT NEUTRAL

To assist students (particularly students from privileged backgrounds) in understanding that seeing is not neutral, educators must help them see the vulnerabilities that exist for others because of the larger system. As Corey indicated, providing students with opportunities to talk with people who are victimized by the system allows students to better understand why they think and feel a

---

THEORY TO PRACTICE

Henry Giroux: Giroux is known for his work in critical pedagogy, focusing on the intersections between school and the larger world and working toward citizens who are critical contributors to democracy. As such, engaging students within a culture of disruptive inquiry supports his work by providing students with opportunities to critique and participate in solutions to issues with which society is grappling. In a 2011 interview with C. Cryn Johannsen, Giroux provided his advice on how to fight back when higher education is under attack. Many hold true for pk–12 schools. The following are ways work in this book connects to Giroux's (Johannsen, 2011) recommendations. They can serve as models for how to think about putting his work into practice.

- **Wobble Journals:** "[W]e need to educate students to be critical agents, to learn how to take risks, engage in thoughtful dialogue, and taking on the crucial issue of what it means to be socially responsible. Pedagogy is not about training; it is about critically educating people to be self-reflective, capable of critically address[ing] their relationship with others and with the larger world."

- **Media Campaign (see Chapter 8):** "We need to educate young people to deal with new modes of education that are emerging with the new electronic technologies, and we need to educate them to not only learn how to critically read this ubiquitous screen culture but also how to be cultural producers."
- **YPAR (see Chapter 8):** "I also believe that a discourse of critique demands more than criticism, it also needs to employ a discourse of possibility, one rooted in real opportunities to see that change is possible on an individual and collective level."

For more about Henry Giroux's work in critical pedagogy, check out the following resources:

- Henry Giroux's website at https://www.henryagiroux.com/
- "Henry Giroux: 'All education is a struggle over what kind of future you want for young people'" at https://www.youtube.com/watch?v=LCMXKt5vRQk
- "Henry Giroux: Figures in Critical Pedagogy" at https://www.youtube.com/watch?v=UvCs6XkT3-o

---

certain way. It helps them articulate what may already be inside them or to shift their understanding toward empathy. Shifting out of neutral means teachers need to take a stance. It is an educator's responsibility to help students clearly see the vehicles that contribute to the systems that exploit vulnerable people, that repress rather than elevate a significant portion of humanity. Ethan, in his recognition of the role media played in Richard's case, points to places where teachers can create fissures in students' understanding of the system. And once students begin to acknowledge that seeing is not neutral, teachers can show them ways they can act on their new understandings.

Henry Giroux (1988) is a foundational scholar in critical pedagogy whose work influences much of the work we do, as well as the work of others we draw upon (Hobbs, 2020; Kellner & Share, 2007). Giroux emphasizes that literacy instruction must move beyond simply learning how to be literate and differentiating between fact and opinion. The way humans understand the world is rooted in power relations and personal experiences based upon factors such as race, gender, and class. Thus, if teachers are to truly engage in literacy instruction, it is important to teach students to read texts through a critical lens, to question how the text empowers and disempowers populations, to examine whose perspectives are present and whose are missing.

The instructional strategies that follow lay the groundwork for moving instruction beyond process. These strategies, when used across the school year, can help students develop habits that prompt them to read critically and consider the multiple voices of the story so that they can move past neutrality and toward action.

THE WOBBLE JOURNAL

What Is a Wobble Journal?

Antero Garcia and Cindy O'Donnell-Allen (2015) developed their Pose, Wobble, Flow framework by building from Bob Fecho's (2005) work around wobble. Fecho describes wobble as a state of transition, observing that "where there is wobble, change is occurring." Recognizing that change within students is integral to helping students see the world as it really exists, Wobble Journals help students articulate the poses they originally held, reflect upon instances that made them wobble, and explore how their wobbling may impact their flow.

Depending upon the needs of students, Wobble Journals can take on different forms. Starting out, it can be beneficial to provide different questions for students to consider, framing these questions around important ideas in the text. While these questions are similar to traditional reflection questions, the Pose, Wobble, Flow framework pushes students to reflect differently. Using the pose mindset, students must describe their original thinking around the topic, using examples to describe this thinking. Then, in addition to describing a wobble, they must articulate specifically what made them wobble. This step helps students to begin identifying the factors that influence their thinking, pushing them to move beyond just holding an opinion because others hold the opinion. Finally, students compare their new understandings to their original ideas, building their metacognitive skills. Once students get a hang of this scaffolded approach or if the students don't need the scaffolding, Wobble Journals take on a more student-directed approach. In this version of the Wobble Journal, rather than providing them prompts, students simply identify a moment of wobble that occurred during a lesson. Once they have identified a moment of wobble—often a moment not anticipated or planned for—students engage in a similar reflective process, describing their initial pose, what made them wobble, and how this new understanding will shape their thinking as they move forward.

How Can a Wobble Journal Help Students Understand That Seeing Is Not Neutral?

Wobble Journals ask students to identify moments of change. They are built upon those evidence-based perspectives that Kirkland (2019) described as integral to helping people make up their minds. While teachers cannot, nor should they want to, tell students how to think, teachers CAN provide students with multiple perspectives that allow them to explore whether or not their understanding of the world mirrors the realities others live within. And once students begin to wobble around these perspectives, they begin to understand why they cannot stay neutral.

In thinking about inquiry, Wobble Journals also help students begin to ask more questions. Change can be uncomfortable, and discomfort leads to more questions than complacency. Discomfort can also prompt the desire for action, which, when supported, can lead to inquiry that matters, that has the potential of impacting communities.

Before You Begin

Prior to starting the Wobble Journals, engage students in understanding the Pose, Wobble, Flow framework— especially what it means to have moments of wobble. To bring understanding to this framework, students participate in a series of yoga stretches that represent the stages.

To begin, students stand in various spots within the classroom and form a fairly easy yoga pose, such as easy pose, five-pointed star, or forward fold. Students engage in whole-class conversations around this pose, why it's easy, and how it represents the poses humans naturally take when asked to think about a particular concept or topic.

Poses are associated with the opinions or the first reactions toward ideas because they are natural and completed with ease. For this reason, presenting students with a choice of easy poses allows them to choose a pose that is easy and natural to them.

As students continue through the yoga metaphor, they are invited to adopt a more challenging stance that asks them to maintain their balance, which may not be so easy for all students. When asked to stand in the tree pose, students often begin to physically wobble, forcing them to readjust their strategies in achieving this yoga goal. For teachers, this invites a conversation around grappling, rethinking, and trying new ideas.

The discussion is wrapped up by examining the purpose and possibilities of flow. For students, flow becomes the space where they change their viewpoint on an issue, topic, or concept on a more long-lasting platform. This metaphor lays the groundwork for Wobble Journals, and it can also serve as an ongoing discourse in the classroom when relating to other topics or issues that may present multiple perspectives.

In the Moment

Step 1: Introduce and establish the routine. The Wobble Journal encourages students to write in stages. Since this is an ongoing writing, it becomes vital to introduce the journaling process, the routine that will be established around the journal writing, and the whys behind such an important writing experience.

One way to approach the Wobble Journal is to create a shared Google folder that serves as an online student portfolio that can be shared with the teacher and the individual student's parents. Within this shared folder, students create a document that will house the ongoing journal writing. To further support students, a template for the journal writing can be created so that students can copy the document and adapt it to their own thoughts and writings.

Step 2: Engage students in the POSE question at the beginning of a reading week (or a pre-reading time frame). While it may be tempting to open POSE questions to the whole class in order to invite further discussion, students may be easily persuaded to take on other poses when hearing other viewpoints. Acknowledging the personal and individual pose is a vital first step as students continue to participate within the framework.

A series of teacher-designed questions for students to choose from as a means to start their Wobble Journal writing can help students begin the reflective process. Based on the needs of students within the classroom, students may need to begin this process using the same question, they may benefit from choosing from a selection of teacher-designed questions, or they may design their own questions as they venture through this writing experience.

Step 3: Interact with texts and perspectives that relate to the initial POSE. Whether students develop their pose around teacher-designed questions or formulate their own poses based on the experiences in class, students need to continue to work with their identified question to interact with different perspectives.

The Wobble Journal was an essential strategy for helping students think through their reading of Dashka Slater's *The 57 Bus: A True Story of Two Teenagers and the Crime That Changed Their Lives.* Students began the week by identifying a question about the assigned readings for the week, developed a pose around the question, and then used the question as they read to help guide their thinking. For a Wobble Journal template and teacher example, check out https://tinyurl.com/4txnkuf3. This model text can serve as a starting point for students as they begin using the Pose, Wobble, Flow reflection framework.

Step 4: Revisit the Wobble Journal throughout the week. Encourage students to circle back to their Wobble Journals whenever events from the reading relate to their poses and prompt them to wobble. By the end of the reading week, students returned to their Wobble Journal to address the wobble and flow of their thinking by using text evidence to support their thoughts.

Step 5: Allow time for students to share their thoughts. When students can share their own personal wobbles, teachers create an environment of welcomed vulnerability.

Students often discover that they have identified similar wobbles. They can use their Wobble Journal writings as a vehicle to enrich discussion as well as ask more questions.

Making Learning Visible

While this may not seem like a large writing task, it proves to be meaningful as students voice their poses and grapple with those established thoughts. Allowing students to grapple in a safe, yet constructive environment promotes an endurance that students want (and need) to continue to read the world.

In addition to Wobble Journals, students also identify and reflect upon Well-Remembered Events (see Chapter 1) at the end of each unit. This reflective activity not only helps teachers see how students are processing the units, it also helps students recognize their own learning, building their metacognitive skills. At the end of the unit on *The 57 Bus*, Aya discussed the Wobble Journal experience:

> The Wobble Journal stood out to me like a picture in a pop-up book. It was clearly imprinted into my mind. I was able to see multiple sides of a perspective, and it opened my mind to how other people see problems. I was originally thinking, "Why can't I wobble on any of these topics?" and I was feeling as if I was a little too stuck in my opinion, but then Mrs. Bonner told me to try looking at the question from the *other* perspective. I had told my mom about them, but, like always, I was struggling for words. So, instead, I just showed her my computer so that she could see what I was trying to say. I honestly was thinking of re-doing the first week Wobble Journal so I could see if I could look at the other perspective on that one too. It taught me that I have to be understanding of other people's point of views.

The visible learning from students' writing evokes the need to keep this momentum going. As students make connections to the value and importance of understanding perspectives, it prompts the question, "How do teachers leverage student learning experiences to further explore/ understand/empathize/act in partnership with various perspectives?" The answer to this question is explored with the construction of détournements—or the hijacking or rewriting of visuals to express social and critical commentary on an issue (Debord and Wolman, 1956). Détournements allow students to take something familiar and remix it into a piece of art that invites a completely different perspective or conversation.

WOBBLE JOURNALS IN ACTION

For many students who were reading Dashka Slater's *The 57 Bus: A True Story of Two Teenagers and the Crime That Changed Their Lives*, questions related to race and gender presented themselves quite frequently.

Valory wanted to think through her initial poses around media in connection to this text. In her initial pose, Valory wrote that people generally become affected by the media in terms of forming their viewpoints and opinions around presented topics. Valory completed her Wobble Journal by addressing her wobble and flow in the example below:

Valory acknowledged that her initial pose had merit and value, but it was the reading experience that allowed her to broaden her viewpoint in connection to how much of an influence the media can have on issues. She continued to strengthen her newly developed flow by speaking to how the media uses words and images to influence the public, as well as the importance of asking questions about their portrayal of information. This experience challenged Valory to think differently about her established positions toward reading and understanding the world. By affording her time and text experiences around these issues, Valory had the opportunity to rethink her position, challenge her thinking, and construct a new meaning as she continued to develop her views.

Figure 2.1. As a part of her wobble journal, Valory reflected upon her new understanding of the role media plays in shaping public perception of events.

Flow	
How do you think differently about this topic given what you know about the different perspectives? How has this impacted your initial pose?	Now that I wobbled, I feel stronger than before. Before I wobbled, I knew that people were affected by the media, but I didn't realize *how* affected they could be at times. Now, I understand that people can become very hateful towards whomever is represented badly in certain media, even if the viewers have no personal connection to the victim or criminal. Going with my original pose, I want to add that the media can decide how they want their viewers to see a certain situation/crime, by showing either the criminal breaking the law, or at times, the police "stepping outside the lines." Therefore, I believe that the media has a *huge* impact on shaping how people see criminal cases and asking questions that are really important.

DÉTOURNEMENTS

What Are Détournements?

As part of a continuing exploration of critical media literacy with her students, Sarah draws upon Douglas Kellner's and Jeff Share's (2007) work, which they define, in part, as helping students to "critically analyze relationships between media and audiences, information, and power" (p. 60). Much of students' understanding of the world stems from media and popular culture, whether directly through their own engagement and interaction with media or indirectly through their friends' and families' opinions that are also shaped by these interactions. Constructing détournements asks students to consider other worldviews by engaging in an interrogation of media texts. By hijacking original messages, students work collaboratively to construct new messages that provide a critical lens to everyday societal issues relative to learners.

While participating in détournement development, students examine issues that are prevalent in the media through different lenses. After learning about media spin and slant, small groups of students take on a societal issue relevant to them.

Student groups take time to explore the media around these important issues and seek out media and popular culture texts they can modify in a way that allows them to disrupt the original message and construct a new message relative to the commentary they want to make on their chosen issue. As illustrated in Figure 2.2, a group of students studied media spin and misinformation among mainstream media outlets. On the surface, their détournement project mirrors Stanley Kubrick's *The Shining* movie poster. A closer examination shows the news outlets that regularly promote misinformation as well as a play on the movie's title that changes "The Shining" to the "The Dividing" as a way to represent this entity that haunts our media interaction experiences. Matthew and Kassidy explain their design further by saying:

Figure 2.2. Matthew and Kassidy hijacked the movie poster for *The Shining* in order to make a statement about misinformation.

We chose this big idea to show a visualization of how divided things are in our country and across the world. Whether it is political parties or simple disagreements there are a lot of divided opinions in our media. We chose to hijack *The Shining's* movie poster. We did this because the poster looked good and the element of horror conveyed how scary it is when our media is divided and spreading biased opinions.

Creating détournements requires students to understand all the elements of a text, the written and the visual. Not only do student collaborators have to think about the visual messages of their work but they also must understand how the visuals and words intertwine in order to convey the disruptive messages they seek to create for their readers. Once these decisions are made among the student groups, they construct their détournements, record an audio file talking through their writing decisions as creators, and display their work for others to interact with throughout the school building.

How Can Détournements Help Students Understand That Seeing Is Not Neutral?

Détournements help students uncover the power structures perpetuated by the media. By asking them to engage with media from varied perspectives and to ask questions of all these perspectives, students begin to discover how media informs the dominative narrative, to uncover ways that other outlets can stand in opposition to this narrative, and to negotiate how to read and understand conflicting narratives. The hijacking or remixing of existing visuals provides students with a way to question and challenge social issues, and once they begin to question and challenge the narratives, they begin to see that seeing is not neutral. There are humans behind every narrative, and there are humans who are victimized by many of these narratives.

Détournements require students to ask meaningful questions, and in doing so, they contribute to an inquiry mindset. More importantly, however, the constructions of these specific visuals prompt students to ask questions about the issues that shape our world. And these are the questions that can prompt the action that Kirkland (2019) describes.

Before You Begin

Before structuring and participating in détournements within the classroom setting, students must take time to unpack and process the role and influence of the media in today's world. Thinking through ideas like media spin, the connotations of words used in news stories, and accessing and evaluating the Media Bias Chart (see Chapter 4) all invite students to think critically about the role of media.

When students have the opportunity to discover that arguments go beyond a simple dichotomy and to examine the perspectives that arguments often hold, it creates questions like "who would care about this issue?"; "why would this person/these people care about this issue?"; and, "whose voice are we *not* listening to when presented with issues?" As students are primed to examine these types of questions, constructing a space where these questions can be channeled becomes the next step in moving forward. Détournements offer a constructive space for students to take on perspectives to argumentative topics found in today's media.

When deciding to implement détournements, taking time to plan for this experience becomes key. This planning process should involve engaging parents and important stakeholders in conversations around the work students will be doing as they prepare for their explorations and constructions. The nature of these visuals may push against parental/family beliefs. It is important to assure parents that we are not attempting to teach our own personal agendas, but that we are constructing experiences that invite students to formulate their own positions on critical topics based on their own views.

Additionally, take time to examine and collect resources related to current controversial topics. This could be found in places like mainstream media headlines, but it could also be found in resources that speak directly to critical media literacy. For example, the *New York Times* offers an entire list of argumentative prompts for classrooms to use.

Lastly, develop an organized plan to scaffold this style of learning for students. Students need to see the importance of examining controversial topics through credible sources, and they need processing and comprehension support as well. A series of graphic organizers can allow students to collaboratively play with a variety of visuals, think through their ideas before constructing their final messages, and discuss why those aesthetic choices are made throughout this writing development.

In the Moment

Step 1: Allow students to choose a topic that they want to explore further with research. As détournement work develops, student agency becomes a necessary element. By affording students the opportunity to choose their own discussion topics, we see students who are motivated and eager to participate in learning because they have ownership of the design.

Step 2: Invite students to brainstorm and discuss the perspectives that surround the chosen discussion topic. When exploring controversial topics, we understand that there are forces that hold a for-or-against stance; however, with those stances come specific reasons and perspectives. Allowing students to identify who would care about the issue, what's often not seen or heard around the issue, and the accompanying perspectives provides students a path to form collaborative research groups.

Step 3: Create a process in which students can "play" with ideas throughout the experience. Since student groups have chosen a topic and identified perspectives within that topic, it is important to construct a process in which students have an opportunity to play with visuals and ideas. As students think about the variety of perspectives that adhere to controversial topics, student groups need time to think about the visuals that will construct the messages they want to convey to readers.

At this point, students may create mock-ups or prototypes of their visuals to seek feedback from others. Students often make three to four prototypes before deciding on their final détournement idea.

Step 4: Facilitate learning experiences, resources, and individual roles within each construction. Students may not naturally know how to research collaboratively—especially when it comes to examining issues from multiple perspectives to create authentic social commentary. To support students, create a series of roles and goals for each research group to abide by as they research their perspective, play with a variety of visuals, and utilize prototyping as a way to better understand their messages. Graphic organizers—like the one accessed through the QR code—can assist in this work. While students work on individual (student-decided) goals, they are working together for the greater goal of presenting their visuals as they develop their prototypes. Roles within each group pertain to research around the specific perspective, but there are opportunities for students to engage in other roles such as fact-checking, opposition research, and even community outreach (networking with someone who holds that perspective in real life).

Step 5: Encourage student groups to develop their détournement into a published product and display your students' détournements in public spaces. As the détournements come into fruition, treat it like an upcoming gallery exhibition. Students can mount their final designs on a canvas so it can be displayed in various areas outside of the classroom. Additionally, as an artist's note, invite student groups to construct an audio recording that discusses at length the decision-making behind this creation as well as a reflection of learning because of the experience. These audio recordings turn into a QR code that is displayed next to the name of the art piece along with the names of the creators. This overall display not only affords students a means to share their writing with others, but it also becomes an interactive experience for readers. Seeing an argument come to life through an entire collection of visual art affords an opportunity for students to see the many perspectives controversial topics can hold in real life, making this a meaningful and important activity for students to participate in as they continue to make sense of the world. This graphic organizer takes students through a step-by-step process to formulate détournement ideas: https://tinyurl .com/mppsvz6s.

Making Learning Visible

Students constructed a series of détournement art pieces related to their understandings throughout their work with critical media literacy by addressing everything from artificial beauty standards to dependencies on social media for news and entertainment. Teegan and Karley, the cocreators of the détournement art entitled "All Natural" (Figure 2.3), spoke about their creation in connection to pushing against the media constructed beauty standards for women by saying:

Figure 2.3. Teegan and Karley constructed their détournement as a commentary on beauty standards.

DÉTOURNEMENTS IN ACTION

- Détournements are used to allow students to understand that arguments are complex in nature and aren't simply broken into "pro" and "con" positions.
- To blend argumentative writing standards with examining credible sources, engaging in the research process, and analyzing various perspectives that lie within controversial topics in today's world, collaborative student groups (seen in Figure 2.4) form authentic social commentary from already existing visual art.
- In the détournement entitled "Strings to Hold Me Down" (see Figure 2.5), students focused on taking

the ideas of Disney's *Pinocchio* and combining an awareness of the social media platforms that often keeps people tied to these spaces. Emma and Morgan reflect on their work, noting, "It was important for us to show people that they can think for themselves and see how attached they can be to the influence of the media around them."

Figure 2.5. Emma and Morgan identified social media as strings that hold people down while remixing a classic scene from Disney's *Pinocchio*.

Figure 2.4. Students work collaboratively to research the different perspectives around the social issue they seek to disrupt through détournement.

Not everything you see is real—that's just kind of the case when it comes to today's media. . . . She [the original art] looked very natural—so, we took that and we just twisted it around to make it look fake and fabricated. . . . We feel the media tries to promote negativity toward girls with all of the photoshopped pictures.

The détournement experience not only provides students with an opportunity to showcase authentic and organic understandings about today's media influence, but it also affords them an opportunity to construct something that raises awareness through writing and visual literacies. Students use their voice and knowledge to construct new messages about the media for a greater audience to see. The art pieces can inspire a discussion into the many facets layered among today's media presence and create an awareness that to navigate through so many layers, students need to ask critical questions, engage in research, and engage in empathetic thinking.

READING YOUR WORLD

While many valuable activities and exercises currently exist to engage students in understanding the role of the media in today's world, the experiences highlighted in this chapter ask students to think critically about the many perspectives that are formed in those spaces, invite them to develop questions rather than assumptions, and urge students to seek out their own voices regarding many of the world's pressing issues.

REFLECT, MOTIVATE, AND ACT

Reflect On Our Own Poses

- *What are your poses about teaching? Why do you believe this?*
- *What are your fears, doubts, and hesitations about engaging in conversations around socially sensitive issues? Why do these exist?*

Motivate to Discover Our Own Students' Poses

- *What are your students' poses about learning? Why do you think this is?*
- *What are your students' fears, doubts, and hesitations about the world? Why do you think these exist?*

Take Action to Create Possible Student Experiences

- *How can you create an experience that invites students to see the world differently?*
- *What types of support would you need to develop your student experience?*

THREE

Being Less Concerned About Whether They Can Answer Our Questions

Because who knows? Who knows anything? Who knows who's pulling the strings? Or what is? Or how? Who knows if destiny is just how you tell yourself the story of your life?

—Jandy Nelson

One day while on the way to preschool, Robyn's youngest pointed out the window and declared that the leaves blowing down the road were race cars and one was losing the race due to a flat tire. He was an inquisitive, imaginative child who filled silences with questions and chatter and loved to learn. Yet, he soon learned that school wasn't a place for his questions, and disinterested in the questions asked of him there, he eventually lost complete interest in school. School became a battleground rather than a playground for learning. Seeking to avoid such an experience for her own son, Sarah enrolled him in a private community school that implements a thematic, inquiry-driven curriculum. And his experience has been vastly different from Robyn's son's experience. He still approaches school with enthusiasm and spends hours exploring the shelves of bookstores and libraries. He shares quirky insights and poses thoughtful questions. Yet, Sarah worries what will happen to him when elementary school comes to an end. Will he also find himself in a school that devalues his questions? Questions help children make sense of the world. They inspire children to think creatively and to see the world in unique ways. And when we take away their questions, we take away their love of learning.

Studies have demonstrated that the number of teacher-driven questions vastly outweighs the opportunities students have to ask their own questions (Howe & Abedin, 2013). However, the asking of questions and seeking out their answers is where learning occurs. Elliot Eisner (2013), one of the most respected scholars in curriculum reform in the 20th century, prompts teachers to consider whether students are encouraged to wonder. Stating that question posing is more intellectually demanding than problem solving, he observed, "Perhaps we should be less concerned with whether they can answer our questions than with whether they can ask their own" (p. 317).

The art of asking questions may very well be the key to disrupting the systems that perpetuate the inequities in our society. As Eisner (2013) reminds us, we rarely encounter situations in life that come with defined problems. Issues such as police brutality, immigration, and school shootings are multilayered, requiring us to pose questions to help define the underlying problems and discover their solutions. We must offer students opportunities to make connections between what we are studying in school and the world outside of school. If we don't help students make those connections, then we fail to prepare them for asking the questions needed to impact the world.

By engaging with each other and the larger community through questions, students are also introduced to multiple perspectives. These multiple perspectives lead to more questions, questions that have the power to make true change. Such an emphasis on multiple perspectives develops a *habit of mind* that helps students see beyond the here and now and envision future possibilities. Today, in an increasingly polarized world, the ability to see beyond a single set of answers is vital to our work with youth.

In this chapter, we demonstrate how we help students develop driving questions that guide their learning throughout the school year. We focus on generating questions. We explore playful questioning. We examine how questions that stem from a genuine desire to understand can help shape the events in our classroom. Ultimately, we want our students to understand the ambiguity of our world, an ambiguity that Nelson (2015) reminds us of as she asks her own questions: "Who knows? Who knows anything?" (p. 425). By recognizing this ambiguity, we can learn how to craft questions that can get us closer to the answers.

OUR STUDENTS' LIVED EXPERIENCES

It was a crisp fall day as students engaged in conversations around their personal values. Students stated those values in verb-driven statements, tinkering with their value statements for a few moments before extending this exercise by identifying ideas, topics, concepts that made them feel uncomfortable. What could people say that made them want to turn away? What could they see or read that made them want to exit the page? Once they had identified these triggers, students considered them alongside their personal value statements. How did these reactions connect to their core beliefs? In what ways did their own personal biases frame their responses?

As students reflected upon their uncomfortable moments, Jenna (pseudonym) and her group engaged deeply in conversation. Jenna's expressions vacillated between confusion and frustration. It seemed that the rest of the group was resisting their discomfort, choosing to focus on topics such as talking to a teacher, sitting alone at lunch, or even asking for help on an assignment. And, while those can be very uncomfortable moments for teenagers, Jenna understood they were being asked to push beyond the surface-level discomforts of school and to reflect upon the roots of what makes them uncomfortable as humans.

To redirect the group toward a more critical stance, Jenna turned to Sarah, blurting out, "Mrs. Bonner . . . I just need to ask you a few things!" First and foremost, could she write down what really made her uncomfortable? Would she be judged for acknowledging that discussions related to those who identify in the LGBTQ+ community made her feel uncomfortable? Jenna explained that it wasn't that she didn't support those in the community. Rather, she felt uncomfortable because she didn't want to offend anybody by saying something incorrectly. Jenna stated that she had never been around someone from that community and that she had so many questions about understanding identity differences related to sexual orientation. Interrupted by the bell, Sarah encouraged Jenna to write about her questions and discomfort so they could continue this conversation at another time.

These questions percolated in Jenna's brain, as made evident by an event that occurred the following week. Robyn was working with a group of students at a local alternative school who were discussing ways to change the community narrative about them and their school. Recognizing the conversations that were taking place at both schools could inform each other, Robyn invited Sarah and a small group of students to the alternative school. The intent was to create a safe space where both

groups of students could ask questions of each other, consider perspectives other than their own, and use their new understandings to move forward with each group's personal goals. Sarah invited Jenna to join the group making the trip.

Filing into the classroom, Sarah's students shifted nervously as they were introduced to the students at the alternative school. Not only had they heard misrepresentations about the school, but the students at the alternative school were also generally older than them, with only one middle schooler in the group. At the same time, there was a sense of unease among the alternative school students. Would these guests judge them for attending an alternative school? Anticipating this, we had prepared empathy maps (see https://tinyurl.com/2p9fhzpm) to guide the conversation. First and foremost, we explained to the group, the intent of the morning was to allow the two groups of students to get to know each other and to ask questions that could inform their thinking. The empathy maps would serve as a starting point for their questions because its design allowed students to map out their partner's thoughts, actions, and feelings. However, students were welcomed and encouraged to extend those conversations in whatever direction they chose. And with that explanation, we divided the room into small groups, with 2–3 of Sarah's students joining 2–3 of Robyn's students.

After groups had time to interact, it was time to share with the larger group. The room quieted as volunteers were encouraged to share highlights of their conversations with the whole group. With a slight hesitation, Jenna raised her hand. It was evident that despite her willingness to share, Jenna was feeling uncomfortable. Her hands shook slightly and once again she fell into a pattern of sprinkling the word *like* throughout her sentences. Resolved, however, to get comfortable with being uncomfortable, Jenna spoke about her experiences in Sarah's classroom from the previous week.

Jenna shared the questions she had posed to her group and opened up about her discomfort around people from the LGBTQ+ community. She talked about how her group had helped her process her questions and discomfort. And the room was silent. Until Mia (pseudonym), a young lady who identified as queer, spoke up, praising Jenna for asking her questions and sharing her perspective about the topic. Over the course of 20–30 minutes, the two young women had found common ground and forged an understanding that resonated with both of them long after this morning drew to a close.

For Jenna, this experience led to even *more* questions. As she continued her schoolwork for months after that experience, she often referred to her group's conversation and the value of being uncomfortable. And Mia, too, referenced Jenna after this meeting, complimenting her bravery for asking the questions that she did. For both Jenna and Mia, as well as many others who joined us that day, learning became about asking questions, about being uncomfortable, and about understanding others' perspectives.

IN DIALOGUE

One of the ways we have helped to scaffold students' questioning skills is through a camera study. In a camera study, we ask students to wander the school and take photos that spark questions in them. Then, they record videos explaining why they snapped their photos. Here, Katie shares her thinking during her camera study:

> Okay, so you have to take three photos, and the first photo is about an artwork that I saw in the hallway. So, while I was crossing the hallway and thinking about what I wanted to take a picture of and what I was curious about, I looked at it, and I'm like, huh. How did they create it? Or is there like a deeper meaning in that artwork? How did they get inspired to do it? Did they just do it to challenge themselves or was it easy? What were the difficulties or easy parts? What do they have to overcome? And I'm also curious about is there someone that influenced them to create that, like a history, you know? I was curious about that. I was also curious about is there, I don't know, like did they put some feelings in there that they, you know, [have] feelings. I was also curious about what about other artists, talking about art, how did they, famous artists, get inspiration, or was it something they didn't think was gonna get famous but then they got famous or something like that? And I was curious about art and how they get inspired. How do they figure out what they wanted to draw and paint or create? I was curious about that and that's why I took a picture of the first one.
>
> Okay, the second photo is about a classroom. So, I took this picture because I was curious how teachers create lesson plans for individual students and what drives them to become teachers. Do they know they wanted to be teachers whenever they were in high school or junior high? How did they get inspired to become teachers? And I was curious about, because each student has different ways to learn, I was wondering how they adapted their lessons or creative lessons to help students? And I also was wondering how to connect, how do they connect to students? Is there some secret way that they communicate with students? So, I was curious overall, I was curious about teachers and how they adapted lesson plans to help students and how and why do they become teachers? Yeah, so that's why I took the second picture.

> *Katie's repeated use of the word "curious," as well as her reference to wonder, demonstrates her understanding of the importance of asking questions. Katie is developing the mindset discussed by Eisner (2013)—one that will allow her to ask the questions that will help her define problems she encounters in the world.*

> *Although her questions started by focusing on one specific painting, they eventually expanded to larger questions about art. Questions such as these larger questions can frame larger inquiries.*

> *Why do we do what we do? Katie demonstrates how in tune our students are with our approaches to instruction. Students notice when we connect with them and when we use creative ways to inspire them to learn.*

TRANSFORMING THROUGH PRACTICE: PREPARING STUDENTS TO ASK MEANINGFUL QUESTIONS

If we want to help our students ask meaningful questions, we must nurture a culture that encourages wide-ranging questions. Katie's musings point to the contagious nature of question asking. A single question can spark insights and additional questions that prepare students to identify and define the problems they will encounter in the world. Students need to rediscover their own curiosities about the world in small ways if we want them to develop the habits of mind needed to confront larger world questions. As Jenna demonstrates, sometimes the questions students have about the world will make us uncomfortable. Yet, we must invite that discomfort if we want our students to feel comfortable asking their questions. Some questions need to be asked so that we can help students reframe their thinking.

An advocate of the arts, Eisner (2013) established questioning as a vital aspect of learning about the world through the arts. As experts in the language arts, we can use our knowledge to help our students develop the skills Eisner advocated as being essential for citizenship in our world: making good judgments, recognizing that

THEORY TO PRACTICE

Elliot Eisner: As a former art teacher, Eisner was a passionate advocate for the impact the arts can have on a students' overall development and learning. In his essay, "What Does It Mean to Say a School Is Doing Well?," Eisner (2013) points to the flaws that rationalization and quantification has on an educational system. Such a system, he suggests, "undermine[s] the development of intellectual dispositions" (p. 300), dispositions that prompt curiosity and encourage students to challenge ideas. The dispositions he calls for are threaded throughout disruptive inquiry. The following are just a few of the questions he posed in his essay that align with the work featured in this book. They can serve as models for how to think about putting his work into practice.

- **Playgrounds:** "Are students introduced to multiple perspectives? Are they asked to provide multiple perspectives on an issue or a set of ideas?"
- **Know Your Surroundings (see Chapter 7):** "What connections are students helped to make between what they study in class and the world outside of school?"

- **Symbolic Connections (see Chapter 5):** "What opportunities do youngsters have to become literate in the use of different representational forms? By representational forms, I mean the various symbol systems through which humans shape experience and give it meaning."
- **Grading Practices (see Chapter 9)** "Do students participate in the assessment of their own work? If so, how? It is important for teachers to understand what students themselves think of their own work. Can we design assessment practices in which students can help us?"

For more about Elliot Eisner's work in the arts and education, check out the following resources:

- *Reimagining Schools: The Selected Works of Elliot W. Eisner* by Elliot W. Eisner
- "Elliot W. Eisner" at https://www.youtube.com/watch?v=QkPG8XZW638
- "Impact of Art on Education: Elliot Eisner and Michael Killen" at https://www.youtube.com/watch?v=QFrZI8-qIA0

problems have multiple solutions and questions have multiple answers, celebrating multiple perspectives, being flexible as situations change, understanding that small differences can have large effects, and expressing feelings as a way to connect to others. Developing these skills starts with empowering them to ask their own questions.

The strategies that follow provide avenues for students to begin to ask their own questions. While they may not prompt the deeper questions needed to confront the problems of the world, they help develop the habits of mind Eisner (2013) described as necessary if we want to open them to the possibilities of multiple solutions. This groundwork is necessary so that they are comfortable asking those larger questions, those questions that can propel them on a journey to disrupt the social problems that exist in our world.

THE INVESTIGATION MIXTAPE

What Is The Investigation Mixtape?

In the summer of 2021, Dr. Ibram X. Kendi (2021) produced a podcast entitled *Be Antiracist*. At the heart of this work, Kendi challenges listeners to imagine an antiracist society and how we each play an active role in building one. Throughout this important work, Kendi features an episode centered on the feelings, celebrations, and understandings of the holiday Juneteenth. Compiling a variety of voices—both well-known and randomly selected on the streets of New York City—this podcast episode demonstrated to listeners that even something as celebratory as a holiday can be processed in many ways. For Kendi, the question always remained the same: "What does Juneteenth mean to you?" But the answers collected from this question proved that there are many perspectives to consider when asking questions to a variety of people.

Applying this idea to the classroom, *The Investigation Mixtape* begins by asking students to look inward by identifying their personal values, thinking deeply about their personal curiosities, and unpacking an issue they want to know more about. After asking students to identify these curiosities, we invite them to watch the Vice News (2020) story clip "Is America Getting Better?" Throughout this news clip, students witness a Vice News reporter using the question "Is America Getting Better?" to speak to people in different parts of the nation. This specific news story serves as a model for students as they analyze the role of the reporter—what's being said, what's not being said, how to actively listen, the space for the interviewee to speak to the question, and the importance of collecting a variety of responses. As students begin formulating their own questions around their curiosities, it also becomes vital to talk about differing opinions. Students take time to watch Zachary Wood's (2018) TED Talk "Why It's Worth Listening to People You Disagree With" to think about opposing views and the value listening has when it comes to their important topics. Once students have had a chance to look inward, they are prompted to look outward, using an empathy map to guide a discussion with someone who can provide insights into topics they might struggle with understanding.

How Can the Investigation Mixtape Help Students Ask Their Own Questions?

The Investigation Mixtape prepares students for the questions that will arise while reading a novel that will present uncomfortable ideas. If we want students to really engage in meaningful and important conversations around socially connected topics, it has to begin by understanding our own personal narratives. Having students study rich, timely topics but not understand the narratives that led up to those topics often make disruption efforts seem artificial and superficial. As students start to explore the ideas that support their curiosities, they become more open to further curiosities, asking questions, and seeking answers from others. Once they are open to these ideas, they are more likely to share their feelings with others and continue to generate more questions, which lead to more answers.

From an inquiry stance, like the Wobble Journals discussed in Chapter 2, the Investigation Mixtape prompts students to experience conversations with others that can lead to further questions. Unearthing multiple perspectives can ultimately allow our students to become more curious and, therefore, more informed. Understanding these *whys* before heading into deep and critical exploration is necessary to the success of these conversations and carryovers. Students begin to build the empathy needed to design inquiries that go beyond the classroom walls. Examining a variety of ideas associated with our curiosities becomes one of our first stepping-stones toward building not only a class culture of asking questions that have the potential to break down stereotypes, but one that invites students to explore the multiple perspectives that are often wrapped around the ideas that make us uncomfortable in the first place.

Before You Begin

While other chapters showcase a project or learning exercises that require an amount of scaffolding, the Investigation Mixtape is more about allowing for time to process and time to share. Two tenets must be embedded into our classroom cultures prior to successfully engaging with very personal information: (1) Our classroom is a place of safety for students: Our words, opinions, experiences, and differences are shared with care and respect for others in the classroom. We embrace new perspectives, celebrate each other, and appreciate opportunities to engage in meaningful conversations; and (2) We accompany everything we do with a thick description of *why* it is important to do.

Students have faced many assignments in their learning journey that were artificial point-generators. Thus, when we ask students to begin a path of self-discovery, we need to provide support, patience, and encouragement. It is also important that we make ourselves vulnerable by participating in the exercises alongside our students. In doing so, we model for our students the value of such an exploration.

In the Moment

Step 1: Ask students to identify an issue that inspires curiosity and develop why statements. While there may be more than one issue that evokes these feelings, invite students to brainstorm their curiosities to narrow down their focus. As students home in on an issue that sparks their curiosities, challenge them to also think about why those issues inspire so much thought. Author Simon Sinek (2009) speaks to the notion of understanding our personal *whys* when it comes to examining the great leaders and thinkers of the past and present. His TED Talk titled "How Great Leaders Inspire Action" can help students identify and understand their own personal *whys* in relation to their chosen issues. As Sinek provides *why* statements throughout his talk, students can use this same method to explore how we think/feel/act/write/speak about their curiosities.

Step 2: Model crafting and asking questions. Now that students have identified their issue and constructed statements around why those issues are important to explore, it's natural for students to begin crafting their driving question for their mixtape. While asking students to develop one question may seem easy, this isn't necessarily natural for many students. Students need strong question examples, time to play with words as they construct their questions, and time to practice their questions to see if their chosen words work with the ideas they are seeking to understand. For many students, formulating several questions before landing on the question they will use for their mixtape is a common outcome. Not only does this allow students an opportunity to understand the development of their own personal questions, but it also offers insight into how words matter when forming essential questions.

Step 3: Find people to ask and actively listen. Since the purpose of the mixtape is to seek out and listen to a variety of perspectives, it's essential to think outside of the classroom space for students to gather a wide variety of voices for their questions. In addition to finding people, it also requires practice with active listening. Consider taking students outside of the classroom to a mall, a downtown area, or a park. These spaces can provide a perimeter for students to find people, ask their questions, and collect their data. Along with venturing outside of the classroom, encourage students to take recording devices so that they can focus on active listening when speaking with community members. These recordings would become a keystone to the mixtape construction.

Step 4: Mixtape construction. Using the collection of voices from Step 3, students are now ready to construct their mixtape of perspectives related to their essential question. Using Kendi (2021) as a writing model, encourage students to develop an introduction to their mixtape that highlights the construction of their essential questions, describes their thought process prior to talking to community members, and explain how their experience was overall when they stepped outside of the classroom. After that, students compile the voices they collected for their mixtape and edit their recordings together into one final recording.

Step 5: Plan and share mixtapes. Once students complete their final mixtape creations—the introduction, the reflection of thought processes, and the various voices collected around their essential questions—students can share their final works with others. Posting their mixtapes and reflection on a shared space invites students to listen to others' experiences and think about their issues in different ways by creating new questions, seeking new curiosities, and developing new viewpoints.

These guidelines outline steps that students can take to formulate and construct their own mixtapes: https://tinyurl.com/y9283mrh.

Making Learning Visible

Working through exercises like the Investigation Mixtape primes students to ask important questions knowing that they can be asked in a safe space. While, as teachers, we may fear or show hesitation toward our students' questions, it brings to the surface the *need* for these questions in today's learning spaces. Because if we aren't engaging students in meaningful issues that surround us in our current world, how will students understand how to read it? How will students learn to be critical? And more importantly, how will students become informed in the beliefs they are attempting to form themselves as they continue to shape their identities? As teachers, we can easily develop our own questions for students to explore, research, and answer. However, when students become the creators of their own questions and pioneers of discovering their own answers, they not only develop a deeper connection with their curiosities but also create agency in their journey as learners.

To play, craft, and share open-ended and curiosity-based questions beyond the classroom, students were challenged to develop their own Investigation Mixtapes. Not only did this provide a way for students to ask their own questions, it also afforded them space to seek out a collection of answers.

Lexi wanted to know how others thought about the concept of hard work. With her investigation question "What does hard work mean to you?," she ventured into her community, and had the opportunity to record a collection of voice recordings that spoke to this question. These voices were then compiled all together into a singular video (seen in Figure 3.1).

When reflecting on this experience, Lexi noted, "This challenge really opened my eyes on looking at different perspectives before jumping to a conclusion based on my

Figure 3.1. A screenshot that shares Lexi's question for her Investigation Mixtape.

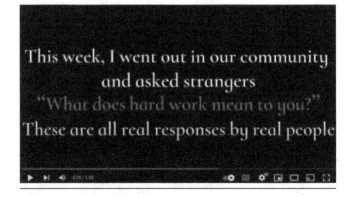

THE INVESTIGATION MIXTAPE IN ACTION

Olivia (featured in Figure 3.2)—a self-proclaimed lover of running—wanted to know about how other runners in her community felt about the activity itself. With her driving question "Why do you run?," she collected a series of voices that held a variety of perspectives related to one of her passions. Upon reflection, Olivia wrote about her experience, saying:

> Understanding others' perspectives contributes to how we are as learners and humans because it builds empathy and compassion. When you first hear someone's opinion, it may disarm you. However, when you can understand the reasoning behind that opinion, it humanizes the other person to you once more. While you still might disagree, at least now you can understand it. This challenge broadened my perspective. Since this question was very personal to my life as a runner, everyone's answers made me think and changed my viewpoint. As I previously mentioned, for me running is all about the relationship aspect. You get to spend miles with people, away from electronics or distractions, talking, getting to know each other and building amazing friendships. Before this project, I never understood people who liked to run alone or took their athletic careers too seriously. But, when they explained to me that they used running to challenge themselves or learn discipline, I understood them far better. Moving forward, I will remember never to judge a person at face value. Everyone has a story and a reason that they do things the way they do.

Figure 3.2. Olivia began and ended her mixtape using a confessional approach in order to introduce her question and reflect upon what she learned from talking to other runners.

opinion. So, from now on, I think we should all look at the world around us, talk to strangers, ask questions, and get more perspectives on things, before we decide for ourselves." Having this challenge experience, Lexi can take these understandings and apply them to other facets of her ongoing learning journey.

PLAYGROUNDS

What Are Playgrounds?

A few years ago, we attended the International Society for Technology in Education's (ISTE) Annual Conference. In addition to formal sessions and workshops, the conference also featured playgrounds. Focusing on a specific theme, such as gaming, or set of tools, such as the Google Suite, playgrounds gave participants the opportunity to visit one-on-one with a facilitator and to play around with ideas and tools. Recognizing that we learned more in these playgrounds than we did in many of the actual sessions, we began to explore different ways to integrate this concept into our instruction.

Since then, playgrounds have taken on multiple forms in our classrooms. One of the most traditional approaches has been to gather six to eight experts around a common theme such as publishing and have them introduce our students to different approaches to publishing. While the thought of organizing a playground may seem overwhelming, it can be a very low-key experience that creates a high impact for students. Experts can be found through talking with teachers in your district, tapping into community networks, or even reaching out to nearby businesses or organizations. Another approach has been to simply set up stations around the room that feature different tools. Using QR codes and short videos, we provide students with information about the tool, allowing them to access the information as needed. Once students have participated in playgrounds, we have also had them create their own sandboxes where they can share their learning with their peers. Sandboxes represent spaces in the classroom where students can independently explore, activate their curiosities, engage with their imaginations, and create with new tools and ideas. The important concept to remember about playgrounds is that they are all about play. Although they may resemble stations from a distance, they have a very different purpose. With playgrounds, students are the deciders. They decide how long they visit a sandbox or whether to visit one at all. And while they are encouraged to create while at a sandbox, there is no expectation for them to complete a project for a grade.

How Can Playgrounds Help Students Ask Their Own Questions?

Questions are a natural extension of play. Through play, our students are exposed to unfamiliar ideas and tools. This may prompt students to ask questions such as "What is . . . ?" and "How does . . . ?" These are important first questions that help them begin to define the concept. Once students have begun to define the concept, they are more ready to move on to asking the kinds of questions needed to solve problems, questions such as "What if . . . ?" and "How about . . . ?" Since questions are at the root of inquiry, playgrounds also help them develop the inquisitive mindset needed for inquiry. Larger inquiries can develop by playing with ideas and possibilities.

Before You Begin

In many ways, the idea of a playground can get muddied with the concept of station work within a classroom. Before going into a playground model, it is important to distinguish between the two for students who may have prior experience with stations. With classroom stations, there usually seems to be an unspoken (or sometimes spoken) understanding that students or student groups will move in a uniform direction, stay in each spot a designated amount of time, and attend each station. And, while there is merit to these types of activities for movement and participation, a playground takes on an entirely different mindset.

As students participate in a playground, it becomes essential for students to recall the purpose and function of a playground itself. Asking students to share their playground stories from childhood the day before hosting a playground can help reinforce the concept of play. Many of the themes taken from these invited conversations revolve around the nature of play, staying as long or as little in a spot of your choosing, and, ultimately, having fun.

As we prepare for a playground, we must keep these themes at the forefront of our minds. There must be hands on components for students to play with in each sandbox. As seen in Figure 3.3, students play with a variety of publishing tools as they enter the final stages of their multigenre writing project (see Chapter 1).

When participating in Google's playground at ISTE, they showcased more than 12 different tools educators could tinker with while they were engaged in that space. In the classroom publishing playground, more than 10 different publishing methods were showcased for students to interact with during their time of play. Whether students interact with 6–8 community experts in a playground or 10–12 tools or ideas in a sandbox, it's important to think

Figure 3.3. Students practiced using calligraphy as one way to publish their writing in a publishing playground.

about providing students with variety without overwhelming them in the process.

And lastly, a mindset of play needs to be in place. Engaging students in their own memories of play sets the tone for such an activity, but it also ensures the success of the learning environment when the playground is in action. It is important for students to understand how to play with purpose. And for us as teachers, a playground must be a place of flexibility, movement, and exploration.

In the Moment

> *Step 1: Take a moment to introduce students to the playground equipment.* When students enter the learning environment prepped for a playground, take some time to map out the various areas of play as well as review its purpose for being there in the playground setting.
>
> *Step 2: Remind students of the playground mindset.* Students often need permission to play in school. Playing is not a traditional school practice (especially once they leave recess behind in elementary school), and students may not associate these feelings with what they understand about school. Encourage students to be in play mode with all of the available texts, support the idea of trying new things, and, above all, allow them to experience and process on their own time.

Step 3: Provide a substantial amount of time for students to play and avoid micromanaging. In a classroom setting, a playground typically lasts around 35–40 minutes. As you circulate around the room to observe student interactions, avoid any type of micromanagement (assigning groups, requirements at each place setting, etc.) that could negatively influence the idea of play.

Step 4: Allow students to evaluate the playground equipment they experience. Whether it is while students are in the moment of play or affording time after the play experience, students need processing time on why these playful moments matter. For example, as students participate in the publishing playground, they can evaluate the various means of publishing writing by examining the tool for functionality and its relevance to their personal writings. Then, when it comes time for students to publish their writings, they can refer to their notes from the publishing playground to help guide them toward the tools they want to use for each of their pieces.

Step 5: Debrief and discuss the play experience as an entire class. Not only do students need time to personally connect with their play experience, but they also need to hear other experiences with the help of their peers. By igniting a discussion around the playground experience, students can share their takeaways and formulate new questions. For students, these discussions take a playground experience from just being an activity to a meaningful step in the journey of learning. For teachers, it invites a new layer to building classroom community as it promotes collaboration among students and the message that we can all learn from each other.

This graphic organizer provides an example of how we illustrate for students the potential sandboxes within a playground, as well as a think-sheet for students to evaluate the tools featured in the playground: https://tinyurl.com/4xmx2z6v.

Making Learning Visible

When we take time to frame learning in a form of play, it invites a new way to approach thinking. The notion of play allows students to try new things and experience failure through the art of fun. With play, students

Figure 3.4. Taryn visited with her classmate about her writing project during a presentation playground.

aren't concerned with assessment or performance. They simply engage in new ideas that ultimately inspire new thinking. As a capstone to the multigenre writing project (described in more detail in Chapter 1), Sarah's students participated in a playground where their personal writings became part of the play experience.

Taryn (see Figure 3.4) shared her writings, which were published using tools she tinkered with during the publishing playground. In a reflection about the experience, she stated:

> Little did I know that the playground was going to help me improve my writing and try new ways of writing. This activity taught me that there's always something new you could try and to look at the other way around doing things.

The playground offers a path to create personal meaning out of a learning experience. Rather than forcing students into prescribed writing formulas or teacher-directed notes, the playground format allowed Taryn to connect her playground experience to her own learning journey. As we ask kids to be in the driver's seat of their learning, it becomes essential that teachers allow students to steer in the direction of their own curiosities so that they may have a chance to build their own paths.

READING YOUR WORLD

In a system rooted in tradition, it may not be easy to shift into a mindset that asks you to put your questions to the side in efforts to listen to those that are being constructed

PLAYGROUNDS IN ACTION

- As a capstone to a semester-long inquiry research study, Sarah invited her students to showcase their experiences with Genius Hour (see Chapter 8) in the form of a playground. Using a variety of tables, platforms, and flexible gymnasium space, students became the facilitators of the playground (see Figure 3.5). That day, students from other grade levels, community members, parents, and administration visited the playground to experience student work on a variety of inquiry topics.

- Ava, an 8th-grader who explored Certified Nursing Assistant (CNA) work for her Genius Hour project, stated this in her reflection in connection to her playground experience:

  Being there and talking to everyone [in the playground] showed me the impact CNAs have on the residents. Without them, the elderly can start to feel alone and isolated. Not everyone has family that visits, so this is one of the only forms of interaction they get. Being an independent person myself, I understand how hard having to rely on someone for simple tasks would be. I thoroughly enjoyed my experience . . . I am so glad I got to have this experience because it really opened up my eyes to what exactly the whole industry is like and how the care is done. I feel as if it is important to understand how hardworking CNAs are and this [Genius Hour] offered me a firsthand experience into this. In the future I am going to try to see how different industries are underestimated and take the time to try and understand what they deal with every single day.

Figure 3.5. Playgrounds can also take place outside the normal school hours. Here, a student shares her Genius Hour discoveries with the community using a playground structure.

by your students. These questions can be unpredictable, unscripted, and unplanned. They may not work well in lesson plans that have been used and reused over time, but "because we've always done it like that" shouldn't be the justification when working with our students. As you can see by the activities outlined in this chapter, we're asking you to rethink and reposition yourself in your classroom to mantle the questions your students have when attempting to read the world.

REFLECT, MOTIVATE, AND ACT

Reflect on Our Practices

- *How will you model curiosity? Vulnerability?*
- *How will you create a safe space for asking questions? For students' discomforts?*

Motivate to Discover Student Questions

- *What experiences do your students have in asking questions?*
- *What kinds of questions do these experiences encourage?*

Take Action to Develop Student Questioning

- *How will you afford students time and practice with question development?*
- *What support will you need in order to do this work well?*

Part II

SEEING SMALL

Helping students learn to see the world impacts how they participate in the world. As Wesch (2018) explains, "Participation is not a choice. Only how we participate is a choice" (p. 47). As teachers, we are often told that we must be apolitical in the classroom. That's simply not possible. Choosing to not address the problems of the world is participating in politics. And this passive form of politics models passive participation for students. As Wesch states, we cannot pretend that our actions don't matter because they do. So, once we help students to see *big*, we must then turn their attention to seeing *small*. As students recognize the larger systems of culture, social norms, economics, history, and politics, we must turn their attention to the details. It is through nuances that often go recognized that we begin to learn more about the problems in society, and we are better prepared to address the problems we identify. This means students need to closely examine who is composing messages, how the messages are being presented, who the messages are targeted toward, when the messages were created, and where the messages appeared. Students need to learn context matters. Intent matters. Impact matters. And they need to look at all of the details that make up a message or action and try to determine the *why*.

For these reasons, Part II of this book focuses on strategies for teaching our students how to *see small*. Chapter 4 starts this process by exploring how to prepare students to notice the important details in the texts we study. We ask students to set aside their initial impressions of texts as a whole in order to notice the implicit messages that small details create, and we prompt them to pay close attention to the denotations of words in order to understand how each word choice shapes the overall message. Chapter 5 asks that we, as teachers, examine how we teach novels. It prompts students to examine the small (and sometimes big) moments in the texts and identify connections to the larger world. It asks students to first *see big* and identify systems that characters struggle within and identify *small* examples in the text that demonstrate instances of struggle, strength of character, and needs for surviving the system. Finally, Chapter 6 explores how collaborating with individuals within the community can help students better see the impact of small details on both the events in the texts we study, as well as on the larger world. Having access to additional voices allows students opportunities to *see small* in ways they might not be able to if we limit our learning to the classroom walls. If we want to impact the world, we must begin bringing the larger world into our schools.

FOUR

Acquiring a Disposition Toward Texts

Maybe our favorite quotations say more about us than about the stories and people we're quoting.

—John Green

In our early years as teachers, we largely stayed away from whole-class novels. Although Robyn would on occasion assign *To Kill a Mockingbird* or *The Giver* to the class, she recognized that the chances that all students would like a novel of study were slim, particularly when that novel was one that had been read in schools for years. But she would, at times, give in to pressures by teachers in her department to assign these books. Yet, she much preferred the literature circle and reading workshop approaches because they provided students with choices around the books they read. Sarah, on the other hand, never assigned one book to the entire class. She started her career in a space where the perspective of teachers was that whole-class novel instruction was a dated practice. The only texts they would study as a group were short stories and poems. Like Robyn, she felt strongly about the need for choice in reading and one novel for the entire class simply did not provide this choice.

There was, however, another perspective, one that Linda Rief (1992) wrote about in her book *Seeking Diversity: Language Arts with Adolescents*. Whole-class novels provide a common experience from which to build upon in other units. They provide common language and common understandings. And they provide spaces to explore meaningful questions. What we did not understand at the time when we were avoiding using one novel with the entire class is that there is nothing wrong with reading a novel together. The problem arises with *how* one novel is often taught to the class. While we know there is more to teaching than lecturing, our own experiences with using whole-class novels was through a very teacher-centered approach. Teachers designed the discussion questions. Teachers created quizzes to ensure students were reading (and many weren't). Teachers developed projects—or if we were dedicated to integrating choice, a list of projects—for students to complete to

share their understanding of the book, which was often the teacher's understanding of the book. In our original understanding of whole-class novel study, there was little room for students' voices.

In his work with critical literacy, Allan Luke describes a shift in instruction around texts. As a part of the New London Group, he worked with notable scholars to capture a vision of pedagogy that "oscillates or weaves through different pedagogical modes" (Garcia et al., 2018, p. 302) in response to the needs of the students. As we began to consider the stories students were encountering in the media and the need to assist students in fully seeing and acting upon these stories, we began to connect Rief's (1992) argument about the value of teaching one novel to the pedagogy described by the New London Group. By creating a common experience through the study of one novel, we could immerse students in the ideas presented throughout it and explicitly teach them about the topics needed to understand the novel. We could also provide them room to critique and deconstruct the messages they were encountering in the book (as well as in the supplemental materials we provided them) and create a space for social and civic action.

Luke notes that once teachers and students engage with "critical, inquiry-based and constructivist work" as a way to develop an understanding of truth, of text, of language, of images, "there's no going back." We have discovered this to be the case. And our students often tell us when they return to visit that they wish this was the case in the English classrooms they enter after leaving us. Through our approach to instruction, we immerse our students in critical literacy practices, which assist students in "acquiring a disposition towards texts, a learned and inquiring skepticism" (Garcia et al, 2018, p. 302). When critical literacy is eschewed in favor of what Luke describes as "ideological red herrings of phonics and 'back to basics'" (p. 299) instruction, students begin to lose their dispositions toward texts.

We know and recognize that not everything we do in our classroom will result in big actions or even in shifts of thinking for all our students. Yet, we also know that if we had continued to teach as we did early in our careers that there would be no big actions or shifts in thinking. While we might have been able to point to successful readers and writers, to successful lessons, to successful moments of connection, we would not have been able to point to moments where students acquire dispositions toward texts that can help them develop the key ethical and political understandings needed to remake the world. We now understand that we can use one novel as a launching point for bringing in multiple texts in multiple forms to help our students further understand the ideas introduced in the novel. We are not simply teaching the novel so that students can identify elements of plot or characterization. Rather, we are "setting the ground for rebuilding of community relations of work, exchange and trust" (Garcia et al., 2018, p. 303).

This chapter sets the stage for helping students to acquire a disposition toward texts that prompts them to approach texts with a healthy skepticism that prompts them to ask questions rather than accepting their ideas at face value. We share some of our approaches for preparing students to study the focal novel, providing them with the first clues that our approach to reading may not mirror approaches they have seen before. The strategies we share help push our students out of a passive role as reader into an active role that requires them to consider others' stories, as well as how they will choose to see these stories. We encourage them to consider, as Green (2008) suggests, that what we, as readers, take away from an experience with a text provides us with an opportunity to reflect upon ourselves as humans. Do we like what we see, or do we want to reenvision ourselves as someone else?

OUR STUDENTS' LIVED EXPERIENCES

Six sheets of white paper about the size of a movie poster decorated the perimeter of the classroom. One word was printed on each piece of paper: *Police, Bystander, Community, Racism, Activism,* and *Loyalty*. Students were participating in an activity called "Graffiti Walls" created by the #WeNeedDiverseBooks (https://diversebooks.org/) campaign in anticipation of the upcoming book study using Nic Stone's *Dear Martin*. The novel focuses on 17-year-old Justyce who experiences racial profiling and then later witnesses a tragedy instigated by an off-duty police officer. Students formed groups, each with a different color marker to be used at the different word posters. There, students talked, wrote, drew, and connected to ideas related to the single word presented on each poster.

While walking around the room to monitor the discussions and connections students were making as they participated in this activity, Sarah overheard a group mention her name. She walked over to the table and noticed that they were working with the word "racism." "How's it going over here at this table?" she asked. Not receiving many responses, she prompted the group about any questions they might have had as they continued to work with the words in the room. One student finally gathered his nerve, looked at Sarah intently, and said, "Mrs. Bonner, why don't we say 'colored people' anymore?" The groups stared at her intently, so she explained how *people* should always come first and how this was a term laced with historical degradation of people.

At that moment, Sarah remembered exactly why she had chosen to teach *Dear Martin*. It was as much needed as a window for her students and students like them as it was a mirror for others. What if the group had never asked Sarah that question? What if they asked that question in another context? What if they never asked that question to anyone and continued to use that term? Sarah's experience motivates us to create safe spaces for students to ask their questions because it's within these spaces that real conversations happen.

IN DIALOGUE

Prior to reading a shared novel, we provide students with texts to help them develop the dispositions needed to work with the ideas in the larger text. This transcript is from a vlog post created by Cameron in response to reading "The Ones Who Walk Away from Omelas" by Ursula LeGuin. Students read this short story prior to reading *Internment* by Samira Ahmed.

Hello. Today, I'm going to be answering the question: Is justice for all possible or will injustice always exist? My response to that was I think injustice will always exist because it is a part of our everyday lives and is a part of our mindset. I got to witness and experience injustice in Task 2 when I saw that Muslims have to experience

> *In her examination of the story, Cameron begins to understand how fear and cruelty are motivated by a human need of feeling safe and content. Understanding these as motivating factors prepares her to think critically around texts.*

it every day because they are all treated differently just because of what one person did or terrible stereotypes that people have for them. This also happened in the short story because the town had to treat this one boy differently in order for everyone else to be happy and survive. That relates back to the Muslim video because everyone else basically has to be mean to them in order to make them feel safe because they feel that Muslims are the only ones threatening them . . . the theme of this book was that their society has to keep from making people happy and being nice. They have to lock up that one boy in order for them all to be happy and feel safe and all be kind—kind of—not necessarily kind. They just have to be, feel safe, and in order to do that, they have to lock up that one boy and have injustice. And this relates to our society today because we have to, we're mean to people, and when we're mean to people, that makes us feel more secure about ourselves, and how we feel about ourselves, and makes us happier about ourselves, kind of.

> *Luke et al. (2018) state that one of the key aspects of critical literacy is helping students develop a curious and skeptical mind. In this post, Cameron demonstrates her skepticism about the reality of a just world. In reading the short story, she makes a connection to the TED Talk, "What's It Like to Be a Muslim in America?" She uses the information she saw in the video to inform her thinking about the story and recognizes that justice is likely unattainable. Grappling with this question informs her thinking when she later reads the novel.*

TRANSFORMING THROUGH PRACTICE: HELPING STUDENTS ACQUIRE A DISPOSITION TOWARD TEXT

In approaching teaching through a critical lens, helping students to acquire a disposition toward texts means more than the pre-reading strategies many of us learned in college. While it is important to build students' background knowledge around a concept and pique curiosity to increase comprehension, it is also vital that we use the time we have before reading a novel to help students adopt a disposition of critical and constructive skepticism toward a text. This skepticism allows students to approach the novel from a stance that prompts them to question the novel's representation of reality. It can, as it did with Cameron, allow them to consider whether the text is a complete work of fiction or whether it contains kernels of

truth. Acquiring a disposition toward texts also means that we provide students like Oliver the opportunity to ask questions. These questions might alarm us, but if they go unasked, they also go unaddressed. When we know questions such as Oliver's exist prior to reading a text, we are better prepared for ways to use the text to

---

THEORY TO PRACTICE

Allan Luke: Luke and Dooley (2009) define critical literacy as "the use of texts to analyse and transform relations of cultural, social and political power" (p. 856). Teachers can build upon Luke's work in critical literacy when designing disruptive inquiry by paying close attention to the texts they use and equipping students with the tools needed to analyze those texts through cultural, social, and political lenses. The following are ways that work in this book connects to Luke's writings about critical literacy. They can serve as models for how to think about putting his work into practice.

- **Deconstructing the Familiar:** "The focus is on ideology critique: exposing, second guessing and reconstructing dominant versions of the world provided in literature, textbooks and everyday texts and utterance."
- **Détournement (see Chapter 2):** "The aim is to develop learners capable of critiquing and making texts in their cultural and community interests. This involves an understanding of how texts and discourses can be constructed, deconstructed and reconstructed to represent, contest and, indeed, transform material, social and semiotic relations."
- **Collaborative Community Interviews (see Chapter 6):** "Learners become teachers of their everyday understandings and experiences, and teachers becoming learners of these same contexts."

For more about Allan Luke's work in critical literacy, check out the following resources:

- *Critical Literacy, Schooling, and Social Justice: The Selected Works of Allan Luke* by Allan Luke
- "Leaders in Educational Thought: Allan Luke Critical Literacy" at https://www.youtube.com/watch?v=UnWdARykdcw
- "Allan Luke: Rich Tasks" at https://vimeo.com/88186018

help our students achieve a broader understanding of the world, an understanding that can help us move toward positive change.

For Luke et al. (2018), acquiring a disposition toward texts meant that we help our students learn how to, as Freire (1972) described it, read the world. When students learn to read the world, they begin to develop curiosity and a skepticism that doesn't lead toward cynicism, but rather toward a desire to understand why others view the world in certain ways and to investigate and solve problems in society. Further, a disposition toward texts means that we help our students become conscious of how language works and how it shapes our perceptions so that, as they are reading, they think critically about the ideas in the novel. It means that we engage in dialogue and debate around texts.

The strategies that follow each demonstrate one way that we have tackled Luke's (2018) call for helping our students read our world and for paying attention to the role language plays. Each is a strategy that can, when students engage with it prior to reading a novel, cause students to approach the book with healthy skepticism and a critical eye.

DECONSTRUCTING THE FAMILIAR

What Is Deconstructing the Familiar?

Deconstructing the Familiar asks students to explore how words, images, and people communicate direct and indirect messages. It draws students' attention to the portrayal of identity markers such as gender, race, class, body images, and perceptions of disability. In Deconstructing the Familiar, students are asked to identify a movie or TV show that is familiar to them. They are invited to watch it with new eyes, looking for how speaking roles, actions, and words/messages frame the way the audience views these identity markers. Once students have had a chance to analyze their chosen media, they reflect upon how media has helped shape their understanding of the people and events in the novel being studied.

How Can Deconstructing the Familiar Help Students Acquire a Disposition Toward Texts?

It can be difficult to approach a text with an open mind if we don't first recognize where our old ideas originated. Too often, students (and many adults!) do not recognize the power media texts have on shaping these ideas. When students participate in Deconstructing the Familiar, students can identify the messages they have been immersed in, and by taking a step back, determine if they truly agree with the messages. Such an analysis inevitably raises questions and creates spaces to consider new possibilities.

Deconstructing the Familiar teaches students how to approach media with a healthy skepticism. They begin to recognize that authors of texts are intentional in their choices, and they learn to look for authors' purposes. Such skepticism promotes an inquiry mindset, which is essential to asking why authors have made the choices they have made.

Before You Begin

As teachers, we continuously design learning experiences for our students that are meaningful and important to them as they seek to understand the world. In many instances, examining the familiar can be a starting point to engage in such learning.

In preparation for this work, think about the time your teaching context affords. How can you allot enough time to allow students to analyze media in a meaningful way? Time is essential because students need to understand why they are engaging with this material. We are asking students to think differently, to think critically, which may not come naturally to students, so they must be given adequate space to navigate the resources and ask questions. And because we are asking students to think differently, we must ensure that we have plenty of time to talk about the experience, explore questions that arise, and reflect upon new understandings.

Take a moment to evaluate the resources provided in your teaching context. As students access support resources or seek their own media images, it becomes essential that access is available. Prior to starting this activity, test internet access and firewall restrictions to see what students can and cannot access.

In the Moment

Step 1: Form groups and invite students into a conversation about why they will be participating in this activity. This activity is collaborative by nature. Encourage students to form groups of three to four to support each other throughout this activity. Allowing time for students to critically examine media images can invite further questions and curiosities into the classroom. Additionally, this activity affords students an opportunity to examine the familiar using a variety of lenses to see things differently.

Step 2: Encourage student groups to watch and discuss the TED Talk by Colin Stokes (TED, 2012) titled "How Movies Teach Manhood." While other texts could serve the same purpose, this TED Talk is a way to introduce the notion of thinking differently about the media we might be familiar with on a daily basis. Collaborative student groups should be given time to discuss this conversation in terms of their new understandings, possible questions they may have, and how they can make connections with the text.

Step 3: Ask students to select an excerpt from a familiar television show or movie and to watch it using the Deconstructing the Familiar's Graphic Organizer. Choosing a familiar excerpt for this step allows students to focus on the graphic organizer rather than being caught up in the storyline. Within the organizer, students observe key factors like gender, race, body image, ableism, and socio-economic status of the characters featured in their selected excerpt.

Step 4: Provide time. Allow students time and space to engage with their selected text, answer the provided questions on the graphic organizer, and permit other questions and conversations to bloom from these experiences. Students within these groups may have chosen the same media to analyze, but each student brings a new sense of connection and understanding to this process. For this, students need time to process as they work through their observations by analyzing speaking roles, actions, words, and messages of the characters highlighted throughout the excerpt.

Step 5: Debrief—always. Debriefing is key to not only the continuation of promoting a safe classroom climate but also helping students unpack many of the realizations they might be making for the first time. Many students are looking to us as a model to see how we would think, feel, and speak about many of the ideas they are thinking about in this activity.

Step 6: Invite students to independently reflect on this experience. While student groups examine and analyze the clip together, ask them to individually think about their *big* understandings and conclusions because of participating in the activity. Encourage students to think about how

this activity made them change their thinking or wobble (see Chapter 2) and be present when they have questions they want to share with you and others.

This resource provides an example of how to outline and support an activity that centers on the images seen in today's media: https://tinyurl.com/562z3jvh.

Making Learning Visible

We know as adults that when we engage in any form of analysis, it takes time and attention to do this well. Encourage students to choose imagery that provides a sense of familiarity—something from their childhood or something that they have watched previously. This sense of familiarity prevents them from being distracted by new characters and plot lines so that they can focus on noticing details they haven't seen in their prior viewings.

For many students, this activity provides a new way to think about something that has always been safe and

---

DECONSTRUCTING THE FAMILIAR IN ACTION

- As student groups worked together to examine and analyze common media, the role of debriefing and reflecting became essential to this work. By reflecting on this experience independently, students took time to process this experience and place it into their own understandings of the world.

- In her reflection following this activity, Robin recognized that media such as movies and television shows can expose viewers to messages that lead to bias:

  I think that while I watched *Johnny Test*, I saw a lot of similarities. Thin, white, able, middle class people, mostly male. I never noticed this when I watched this show when I was younger, but the messages that are being put off are not something that I would want to see. For example, the only time there was a heavier person was when they needed to create some sort of problem. The only time they showed a person of any other race was when they were agreeing with the white main character. The only time they showed anyone from the higher class was to be a villain. I think this is saying that you can't have money, because it will lead you to being power hungry. You can't be heavier, or you're going to cause problems. You can't be of a different race, or you're not going to amount to anything important. And this is *so* wrong.

familiar. As outlined in Figure 4.1, Sarah's students Robin and Brady worked together to complete their organizer by watching one of their favorite childhood cartoons *Johnny Test*. While they were also asked to observe other aspects like social class, body image, race, and ableism, the example features their thoughts on gender. We can see that by focusing on gender, Robin and Brady noticed the implicit gender bias in the cartoon. Without this activity, it is likely neither student would have given much thought to how the cartoon objectifies women, nor would they have recognized the harm this message can inflict. Developing such a disposition toward this text can encourage students to approach other texts in a more critical manner.

THE WORDS WE USE

What Is The Words We Use?

The Words We Use draws upon one of the principles of critical literacy described by Allan Luke and colleagues (2018). As the name implies, this strategy requires students to pay close attention to how language is used to shape perceptions. The Words We Use prompts students to construct their own understanding of bias by analyzing the headlines from multiple media outlets.

Drawing upon the media bias chart created by Ad Fontes Media (n.d.), students look across multiple media outlets to discover how outlets on different sides of the spectrum report the same events. After selecting a specific topic being reported on in the national news, students look specifically at the headlines appearing in the media on the left, the right, and in the center. In their analyses, they are asked to focus on the emotions evoked by specific words, as well as to identify what the headlines say and don't say. Once they have examined each headline individually, they compose a reflection that looks across all the headlines, identifying epiphanies that resulted during this activity.

How Can the Words We Use Help Students Acquire a Disposition Toward Texts?

Exploring The Words We Use helps students develop a critical eye toward language. More specifically, this strategy asks them to drill down to the word level, allowing them to see how words that on the surface may seem to mean the same things carry with them nuances that shape people's worldviews. Once students understand how one word can shift an entire sentence's meaning, they begin to develop an understanding of the ethical and political importance of paying attention to language. This can

Figure 4.1. Robin and Brady shared observations about the treatment of gender in the cartoon. *Johnny Test* during their Deconstructing the Familiar assignment.

TYPES OF ANALYSES/ HOW TO ANALYZE	Speaking Roles Use the space to document the speaking roles of the specific person/persons using tally marks. Please identify your tally marks specifically.	Actions What are people doing? How would you describe their actions? For example, are they in the background? Main character? Doing something significant to the plot?	Words & Messages What kinds of words or messages are people conveying to the viewing audience?	Your Thoughts What can you learn about each of your analyses? For example, are stereotypes being perpetuated? Or is there an unfairness exhibited? Or what's not being shown? What's the impact of not seeing something?
GENDER (male, female, non-binary	Female—48 times Male—76 times	Most of the background characters didn't have lines at all. When the main characters talk the female is usually some stuck up rich girl or she's one of the scientist twins. While the male is either the main character, clueless, the person who saves the day, or the perceived villain. In this case, Johnny is the person who saves the day and the bully.	To me this shows that women are usually seen as objects because they are so often shown as what society thinks is beautiful. I also think that the show was trying to be inclusive but eventually ended up following the same pattern.	Robin—I think that they tried to show kids that they can be a scientist, even if they're a girl, but eventually it ended up going back to the "women are objects and must be beautiful all the time" pattern. Brady B — I think that during this episode they tried to show that not only the most high tech things are, the old rough looking things are also cool, and people enjoy those things too.

prompt them to approach texts more warily, so that they understand the authors' motivations for creating the texts. While students may understand the power of words, they may not recognize instances of power play outside of their own worlds. Through everyday interactions, students can interpret the tone and usage words often bring when used in various contexts.

The Words We Use naturally builds an inquiry mindset because it requires students to question why specific words may have been selected by the author. When they begin to ask these questions around intent, they also begin wondering how another perspective might approach a topic. Taking time to understand the power that words can have when it comes to communicating with one another about issues, topics, concepts, and ideas is essential to unravel for students to see the relevance this exercise plays in today's world. If we can work on our words, we can work on the ideas that connect to those words. Knowing how words play such a pivotal role in everything we do sets a course to use this power to strengthen our critical lens and evoke ideas of disruptive inquiry.

Before You Begin

In preparing for this activity, it's important to not only understand the power that words hold, but also acknowledge how your students see that power. Take a moment to observe how your students use words in everyday conversation: How do they describe themselves, others, topics, and ideas? How do students use words in spaces like hallways, lunchrooms, and even at home? As teachers, how often do we take time to listen to our students—what they say, what they don't say, and how they choose to say it? When we have a strong sense of our students' word choices, it allows us to discover ways in which we can analyze the words we choose to use in authentic and meaningful ways with our learners.

In thinking about how your students use words, it's equally important to discuss with students the why behind such an activity before starting it. Think about this activity as a mirror being held up for students as they stop and take time to analyze the words used in today's world. What do those words mean? How are they meant to be used? How do these words have the power to influence thought?

In the Moment

Step 1: Review the nature of connotation vs. denotation. Provide students with two words

that have the same meaning but are portrayed differently because of how we associate those words. For example, provide one student with the word "fib" and another student with the word "lie." Then ask them to find each other and partner together. Have the words "positive" and "negative" posted on opposite sides of the classroom and ask student partner groups to determine which partner should go to each side of the room. The whole class can then debrief on why decisions among partners were made and how the power of words evokes different meanings.

Step 2: Ask students to explore resources like Ad Fontes Media's (n.d.) Media Bias Chart to see how words are used in different spaces to thread bias into their messages. Especially in today's mainstream media, we see a variety of words being used when it comes to headlines geared toward certain readers. Not only is it vital to show students how to read the media chart but it is also beneficial for them to analyze how various news outlets choose their words when describing events. Invite students to jot their observations and discuss the variety of words they observe and what that means to their understanding. Having students examine these differences ultimately makes a case for understanding how words play a role in various narratives that exist among topics and issues.

Step 3: Engage students in documenting and dissecting the words used in various media outlets. Ask students to seek out six different news sources (all from different points of the Media Bias Chart), document the headlines of a common topic, and discuss how that chosen common topic is headlined using various words that inspire different meanings.

Step 4: Invite students to look across headlines and synthesize their observations. Allow students time to see the different headlines all together and have conversations around the ideas being communicated—what's being said, what's not being said, and what biases may be exhibited based upon the word choice. For your students, synthesizing their thoughts can come through in many ways. Graphic organizers and collaborative discussions can scaffold learning opportunities for students to play with their ideas and synthesize what they are seeing.

Step 5: Have students share their syntheses with each other as well as the class. To help students see similar themes, invite students to discuss the power and relationship words have with issues, topics, and concepts. After sharing their own thoughts from this exercise, students can move forward by not only reflecting on the words they choose to use when addressing issues but to also continue to strengthen their critical lens to the world of words around them.

This resource provides an example of how to outline and support an activity that centers on the use of words woven in today's media: https://tinyurl.com/4shnz8ha.

Making Learning Visible

One of the most powerful exercises we can engage our students in is examining how words are used and formed in today's world. This learning experience affords time to scrutinize words in different contexts to gain a stronger understanding of the various narratives that exist in real life. Not only does this exercise present a case to understand words in a general sense but it also asks us to understand the *power* and *influence* words can have when it comes to shaping our personal beliefs and understanding the world.

In connection to studying the power of words and participating in critical media literacy with the support of the podcast *Serial* (season 1, Koenig, 2014), Maggie reflected on her experience with the The Words We Use exercise by stating:

> Some people make stories sound sad, other people make stories sound dangerous, and other stories might make it seem like whatever is happening is a good thing. This made me think that things are not always so bad, or maybe they are worse than we thought. This can relate to the *Serial* podcast because both these stories and Adnan's trial didn't share all of the information that they had. In the *Serial* podcast it talks about a man, Adnan, who is on trial for the murder of a young girl (his ex-girlfriend) Hae Min Lee. But during his trial, a girl that went to his school called in with more information about Adnan's innocence. She mentioned that he couldn't have committed the murder because he was at the library. The thing is that they didn't even use this in the trial. They left that useful information out. But this relates to how people explain the news.

In a time where misinformation and bias has moved into the forefront of today's media climate, students need experience in analyzing the words being used about and around important conversations. Paying close attention to how authors use words is not just about students being informed. It also impacts how students develop their values and beliefs. If students experience learning that leans into developing a critical lens, the way we use words can potentially be changed for the better. And, as students seek to build their critical lens, it creates a space for more curiosity about understanding the complex world around them.

THE WORDS WE USE IN ACTION

- When we ask students to take notice of the words being used in today's world around the topics that matter the most to them, we invite them to activate their critical thinking in various ways. By participating in this exploration, students discover for themselves the power words can have—not only in the way they communicate but also in the way they influence thinking.
- As seen in Figure 4.2, Tyler wanted to analyze the headlines and media reports of NBA star

Kobe Bryant's untimely death. Providing Tyler time to process these various media outlets and formulate his own thoughts allowed him to gain strength and courage to be critical when it comes to being informed. And, as Tyler can see that he has the ability to think deeply about words being used in reporting, he also cultivates a sense of confidence to be able to do this on a regular basis.

Figure 4.2. During The Words We Use, Tyler examined the treatment of Kobe Bryant's death in multiple news outlets.

News Outlet State the name of the news outlet you examined your chosen topic	"Headline" & Brief Summary Record the headline from the news outlet of your chosen topic as well as a *brief* summary of the report.	Connotation Analysis Think about the words used in the headline and throughout the summary of the report. What kinds of emotions are evoked?	Your Thoughts What does the report say? What doesn't it say? How does this news outlet paint a picture of the report? How might the news report compare/contrast with others? Do you have other opinions?
MSNBC	Kobe Bryant's life and legacy	The headline was very specific in what they were going to talk about. It talked a lot about the surprise about the news as well.	This report said a bit about the grief that people felt following the death of Kobe Bryant. It was complimenting him on the fact that he was a good man on and off the court. This news video seemed very true and very factual on the life of Kobe in and out of the NBA.
Daily Kos	Kobe Bryant Reported dead in helicopter crash	This was a very Straight forward title. It was not even mentioning the other people that died in the crash.	This report was crazy, and very untrue. It went on to say that Hillary or Obama were also on the plane crash with kobe. It also said that this was a political act, and Trump may have something to do with it. Overall this report was very untrue and far fetched. This report didn't say anything about the other families that died. This article will most likely have a different viewpoint on how and why this happened. This article says it was a political act. Other articles will most likely say It was just an unfortunate event.

READING YOUR WORLD

Moving forward with this work in connection to the texts that can inspire real-life inquiry and your own teaching context, we ask you to begin thinking about how you position your professional self when it comes to engaging students in texts that evoke these questions and conversations.

REFLECT, MOTIVATE, AND ACT

Reflect on What We Think We Know About Our Students

- *What are your students' observations of the world around them?*
- *What concepts are important to explore to understand the novel? Why are they important?*

Motivate to Understand What Students Know and How to Move Forward with Support

- *What do students already know about the issues in the novel?*

- *Where do students have limited knowledge around the issues in the novel?*
- *What texts will help students explore different perspectives in connection to the novel?*

Take Action to Cultivate Positive Dispositions Toward Texts

- *What's happening in students' lives currently that could be explained through literature?*
- *What's happening in the media that is getting the attention of students?*
- *What's happening in the school culture that could/ should be addressed using texts?*
- *What possible learning experiences could connect to these experiences?*

FIVE

Offering the Freedom to Experiment With New Ideas

Never let your obstacles become more important than your goal.

—Dashka Slater

Recently, we were catching up over breakfast with Carter (pseudonym), an ELA teacher who teaches in a nearby small town. We always enjoy our time with Carter. His passion for his students, for reading, for writing, for becoming the best teacher and person he can be is contagious. Even when he is frustrated, his positivity shines through. During breakfast, Carter shared his most recent frustration with one of his classes. After spending half a class period reading Jack London's *The Call of the Wild* aloud with his class, he tasked them with using the rest of the class period to finish the chapter and write a summary. The next day, Carter was surprised to discover that most of the class chose not to do this. He felt he had set them up for success by beginning the task with them, and his request should have easily been completed. In some ways, he was right. Writing a short summary after reading half a chapter is not a lot of work, but sometimes the amount of work cannot compensate for the kind of work we ask our students to do. If we rewind this story a few seconds, we can note how this becomes problematic for students: We see "he felt" or "his request" or "his surprise," but what we don't see is anything relative to the learners in this moment.

We can—and did—empathize with Carter. We've assigned similar tasks to our students only to be frustrated by their lack of effort. Those tasks were ones that we did as students. Tasks such as reading classic novels on our own, writing summaries, and completing reading quizzes have permeated the ELA curriculum for years. It's not surprising that most of us have replicated these tasks in our own classrooms. But if we stop and think about our moments of joy around reading, those moments did not emerge because of those tasks. Further, tasks such as these only exist within schools so they lack any purpose outside of performing for a teacher. There is no joy or authenticity. And if we must rely on tasks such as these to force our students to read a book, we might need to ask ourselves why we are reading the novel in the first place.

Several years ago, we discovered the work of Daniel Pink (2011). Pink, who focuses on creativity in the workplace, points to intrinsic motivation as one of the key factors to success. School, like the workplace, relies heavily on carrots and sticks. Grades operate in such a manner. If, for example, Carter's students successfully completed their summaries, they would be awarded with a good grade in the gradebook—the carrot. However, most of his class likely got the stick, a "0" in the gradebook that negatively impacts their overall grade. In presenting this as an example, we don't mean to imply anything negative toward Carter. He is simply operating within the system that was created decades ago. And while this system may work in the short term for some students, it diminishes motivation in the long run.

Carrots and sticks—including grades, honor societies, reward programs, detentions—are considered extrinsic motivators. They take the locus of ownership away from the individual and impose an outsiders' expectations and preferences onto the individual. And while this type of motivation may work for mundane, repetitive tasks, it does not work in the long run for any kind of task that requires creative or critical thinking—the very kind of thinking we want to cultivate in our students. If we continue to use extrinsic motivators, we will be left with students who lack the internal motivation to think and perform tasks for themselves—whose performances diminish over time, who cannot think creatively, who are less inclined to act in ways that are considered good behavior, who are more inclined to cheat, take shortcuts, and engage in unethical behavior, who become addicted to external rewards, and who cannot engage in long-term thinking (Deci et al., 2001; Pink, 2011).

So, what does that mean for teaching? How can we overcome the temptation to rely on external rewards and punishments when we work in a system that is built around them? Some of this goes back to what we ask students to read, to do, to think about, as well as how we ask them to engage in these readings, doings, and thoughts. Assigning books to students that have relevance to their current lives is a first step. When Carter talked about asking his students to read *The Call of the Wild*, our first question to him was why this book? We can imagine that many of his students find little relevance in this story. However, *how* we ask students to read the book also impacts intrinsic motivation. Sometimes, we have little choice in what our students read, but we do have the power to determine how they read a novel. And writing summaries and taking gotcha quizzes won't develop the intrinsic motivation we want to build within our students.

Designing reading experiences that include autonomy, mastery, and purpose are vital components of helping students discover what motivates them (Pink, 2011). When we consider autonomy, we are tapping into the human desire to be self-directed. Very few of us like to be told exactly what to do and how to do it. We want to be able to determine the task we want to complete, when we want to complete it, how we want to complete it, and who we want to work alongside. And while we may not be able to give students the complete freedom to do whatever they want in the class, we can provide them with some flexibility that gives them some autonomy in how they reach a goal. Pink (2011) observes, "The opposite of autonomy is control. And since they sit at different poles of the behavioral compass, they point us toward different destinations. Control leads to compliance; autonomy leads to engagement" (p.108). When we assign tasks to students that they have little say in, we are inadvertently trying to control their learning. For Carter's students, those who turned in their summaries were being compliant. The very nature of summary writing rarely leads to pleasure; thus, it was highly unlikely that they found the task engaging. Even making a small shift toward autonomy such as allowing his students to determine how they wanted to demonstrate their reading of the chapter might have led to more engagement. While we don't believe such small steps should be the final destination, we do believe working toward the goal of more autonomy is a vital characteristic of a class culture that encourages disruptive thinking in students.

When we nurture autonomy in our classroom, we also begin to nurture mastery in our students. Mastery, despite what the word suggests, does not mean that we expect perfection. Rather, Pink (2011) describes mastery as the desire to get "better and better at something that matters" (p.79). When we begin to allow students to explore their own questions and demonstrate how the books we study matter to them and to their communities,

we begin to see students doing the work because they want to do the work and they want to do the work well. They take the steps on their own because *they* want to do the best work that they can—they don't do it because we want them to.

The last piece of the intrinsic motivation puzzle is purpose. Purpose, as Pink (2011) defines it, is "our yearning to contribute and to be part of something larger than ourselves" (p. 10). Our students, like us, want to make a difference in the world. They want to contribute their ideas and talents to real-world problems. And when they do this, it is an incredible thing to behold. "The most deeply motivated people—not to mention those who are most productive and satisfied—hitch their desires to a cause larger than themselves" (Pink, 2011, p. 131).

This chapter explores how to design reading experiences that are student-centered and that encourage students to find intrinsic motivation in the work they do. We share some of the anchor activities that we have used with students as they are reading our novel. These anchors have been designed so that students have the freedom to begin experimenting with new ideas and to explore connections to the world. We focus on the ways they provide student autonomy, encourage mastery, and develop a purpose. In doing so, we seek to help our students—as well as ourselves—push past obstacles that get in our way, so that we, as Slater (2017) encourages us, never let these obstacles consume us and prohibit us from reaching our goals.

OUR STUDENTS' LIVED EXPERIENCES

In the fall of 2017, Sarah's students received brand new copies of Nic Stone's *Dear Martin*. As students began reading, their experience was partnered with a series of collaborative anchor activities that supported various analyses around the book. Anchor activities prepare students to interact deeply with the novel, provide opportunities to make connections to our world, and develop skills needed for later inquiry work. Each morning, students had time to engage in their collaborative anchor activities. This gave Sarah an opportunity to sit with small student groups to converse with them about the book, to facilitate their work with supportive resources, and to answer any questions they may have as they worked with the material.

One morning, Sarah saw Caitlin sporting a furrowed brow and waving her hands in frustration. She sat down at Caitlin's table knowing that her collaborative group had been working on character analyses. As she sat,

Caitlin looked directly at Sarah and said, "Mrs. Bonner! Is it Mee-low or Mellow?" It seemed that Melo, a secondary character in *Dear Martin*, had sparked a spirited debate. With a smile and shrug, Sarah encouraged Caitlin and her group members to reach out to Nic Stone and ask her. And what started as a small nudge into the anchor activity grew into a quest to find the answer to a driving question.

Caitlin, a young lady determined to prove to her group that it was pronounced Mee-low, went to Twitter to find the answer. Skeptical that Nic Stone would even reply, they had fun continuing to debate which pronunciation would be the correct one. Then, as the bell was about to ring, Caitlin jumped out of her chair and shouted at the top of her lungs, "She wrote back!" By now, the entire class was invested in the answer, so they gathered around Caitlin as she opened her direct message. Caitlin read Nic Stone's message aloud with a small smile of disappointment. She had been wrong. Melo, Nic explained, is pronounced Mellow in connection to NBA player, Carmelo Anthony.

The bell rang and echoes of "See?" or "I knew it" rippled across the classroom for that moment. Sarah continued to observe Caitlin, thinking maybe she might be upset. Caitlin just stood there staring at her phone. Sarah approached Caitlin and placed an arm on her shoulder for encouragement. And, while her reaction still wasn't clear to Sarah, Caitlin turned to her with a huge smile on her face and said, "I can't believe she wrote me back!"

While on the surface this example might seem inconsequential, it exhibits how allowing students even small moments of autonomy can have a larger impact on their drive to learn. This small moment turned into many larger moments as it became a turning point for Caitlin who—because of one brief message from Nic Stone—became one of *Dear Martin*'s, one of Nic Stone's, biggest fans. And because of this fandom, she was motivated to fully immerse herself in the upcoming reading experience and to engage in ways that resulted in more questions that led to more discoveries.

IN DIALOGUE

Blogging is one way to introduce an authentic purpose to students. The excerpt from Madi's blog shared here was written as a part of an anchor experience during the unit that focused on *Dear Martin* by Nic Stone. The class was divided into three groups, and each group rotated through the three anchors throughout 3 weeks. For the blogging anchor, Madi was interested in learning more about racial profiling, which occurs in the opening pages of the novel. In the first section of her blog, Madi discussed instances of racial profiling in the novel before moving into a discussion around the article she discovered during their research.

"Racial Profiling" Article

Similarly to racial profiling happening in school circumstances, it also applies to minorities and highway stops. In one incident, Dr. Gerald Oliver was pulled over because he was "speeding and driving recklessly." However, these were false accusations because Dr. Oliver was not doing either of them. After arrested he was questioned and suspected of stealing a car. "Naturally" this was suspected because it was an expensive car and because he was black he "probably couldn't afford it." Once explaining that the car was his own, he was released with the only charge being driving while black. After the arrest Dr. Oliver was just glad he was still alive. . . . As you can see racial profiling plays a huge part in basic police duties. Around the same time as the court case, the Drug Enforcement Administration Operation Pipeline was suspected of teaching local and state officers to make highway stops based on race. Racial profiling happens every day, even if we don't realize it. Sadly enough, we've all probably done it at least once in our lives. However, when it occurs in the line of duty, it becomes a much bigger issue.

Connections and Conclusion

As stated above, racial profiling isn't just a fictional issue that occurs in books. Racial

> *Using quotation marks to set off the word* naturally, *the girls demonstrate how pervasive racial profiling is in the world. They don't, however, seem to understand that driving while being black is not an actual charge but rather commentary on racial profiling. Seeing such a misunderstanding in a blog provides opportunities for further conversations around why phrases such as this exist.*

> *Although students were not given complete autonomy in this anchor, they were given the autonomy to select an issue in the book they wanted to learn more about. In doing so, they were able to discover information that helped them better understand the events in the book and how they are a reflection of the larger world.*

injustice and inequality has majorly decreased over the years. But racial profiling is just as dominant as it was years ago. Because Justyce is black, he is suspected of not being as intelligent as Jared who is white. The two were not given the same opportunities growing up, yet both ended up at the same prestigious high school. Jared considers them equal because they both received the same high school education. However, he doesn't consider the racial injustices Justyce had to face to get to that point.

TRANSFORMING THROUGH PRACTICE: PREPARING STUDENTS TO EXPERIMENT WITH NEW IDEAS

If we want to provide our students with the freedom to experiment with new ideas, a must if we want to position them to make changes in our world, then we have to provide them with opportunities to engage in activities that provide them with autonomy, that encourage them toward mastery, and that give them a purpose larger than themselves. This means that we are obligated to rethink how we teach novels. As Caitlin illustrates, rather than locking down tools like social media, we can embrace them as ways to reach beyond the classroom. Although it was a small moment in the larger novel study, providing students with the autonomy to reach out with their questions to Nic Stone via Twitter changed the entire learning environment. Students were excited to make such a connection, and this excitement lent itself to a shared purpose for the class—fully engaging in the work of an author who cared enough to respond to them. Similarly, autonomy while reading allowed the girls who blogged about the book to select an issue that stood out to them rather than one preselected by us as teachers. Tapping into their interest early in the unit, provided avenues to maintain that momentum as they selected topics for later study. Their autonomy encouraged questions they may not have had the opportunity to ask in a traditional novel study, and, as a result, they had a purpose for learning more about racial profiling and stereotypes and were willing to work toward mastery.

Mihaly Csikszentmihalyi (1990), the psychologist who recognized the concept of flow described in Chapter 2, identifies purpose as essential to humans achieving flow: "I think that evolution has had a hand in selecting people who had a sense of doing something beyond themselves." We believe him. Our journeys as teachers have been up and down. We have engaged in traditional novel studies, both as teachers and as students.

THEORY TO PRACTICE

Mihaly Csikszentmihalyi: In a conversation with Samuel Whalen (1999), Mihaly Csikszentmihalyi talks about how teachers can work toward helping students achieve flow in school. Flow is closely connected to inquiry as disruption. Achieving flow often stems from setting personal goals, receiving meaningful feedback, and working within our talents and interests. As demonstrated in this book, working toward inquiry as disruption involves all of these. Leveraging this knowledge can help students achieve flow as they work toward social action. The following are ways work in this book connects to Csikszentmihalyi's philosophy of flow. They can serve as models for how to think about putting his work into practice.

- **Genius Hour (see Chapter 8):** "You own the kind of learning that you want to acquire for its own sake because you are interested in it."
- **Mentor Moments (see Chapter 6):** "For the first four million years of human evolution, which includes probably about 200,000 generations, children learned by observing and participating one-on-one with adults who taught them how to become members of that society."
- **Documenting Community Stories (see Chapter 8):** "You don't want to only teach book learning or skills, but also a kind of feeling that the universe is a wonderful place to inhabit and that somehow you love every part of it."

For more about Mihaly Csikszentmihalyi's work on flow, check out the following resources:

- *Creativity: Flow and the Psychology of Discovery and Invention* by Mihaly Csikszentmihalyi
- "Flow, the Secret to Happiness" at https://www.ted.com/talks/mihaly_csikszentmihalyi_flow_the_secret_to_happiness?language=en

We have pushed the boundaries in ways that don't look like school, many of which we describe here. And we have discovered that when we give students a purpose for learning beyond school, they respond in unexpected ways. How we teach novels makes all the difference.

While there are multiple ways to approach teaching novels, begin with the keys to motivation in mind. While students may not have complete autonomy, teachers can build paths for them to navigate toward the ideas and modes of expression that fit them best. This means building in choice, but these choices must lead to a broader purpose. Keeping purpose at the forefront ensures that we design anchor activities with the end goal in mind. Will students need to engage with multimedia during their final work? If so, we build in opportunities to experiment with media as they are reading. Will students need to conduct research? Then, we must provide them with experiences that require them to seek out other information whether via online research or in-person interviews. These experiences, paired with an understanding that their audience will be people outside our classroom, provide students with a purpose for their work. And when we give them autonomy and a purpose, our work toward mastery is well on its way. The strategies that follow are a sampling of how we have structured anchor activities to accomplish these goals. In giving them the freedom to try on multiple ideas as we read the text, we are preparing them to accomplish the incredible work that is to come.

SYMBOLIC CONNECTIONS

What Are Symbolic Connections?

The importance of making text-to-self, text-to-text, and text-to-world connections has long been understood in literacy research (Anderson & Pearson, 1984; Keene & Zimmerman, 1997). For learning to occur, it is important that our students connect new material to their prior knowledge. If we want literature to be a bridge to understanding the social issues we face, it is also important that students make connections between our novel and the larger world. Symbolic Connections help students start to make these connections.

To begin, students are asked to identify an issue in the book that they feel is also an issue in our society. They then must locate two current texts—one news article and one video clip—that connect to this issue. After locating the additional texts, they create an artifact that uses an image to symbolize the connection. In this image, they provide links to their texts, quotes from their book, summaries, and an explanation of how the new texts support or contradict the novel's stance on the issue.

How Can Symbolic Connections Prepare Students for Experimenting with New Ideas?

Symbolic Connections encourage students to explore issues in the book that speak to them. Like the other strategies designed in this chapter, this strategy provides students with the autonomy to choose an issue that matters to them. It also gives them the autonomy to find other texts that help them create meaning around the issue. Further, Symbolic Connections asks them to begin to think differently by visualizing an image that represents these connections. By combining images with written texts, students can experiment with different ways of looking at the issue.

Symbolic Connections prepare students for inquiry because they help students begin to define the problem by examining multiple perspectives around an issue. Through these perspectives, students can begin to empathize with the people who are impacted by their focal issue.

Before You Begin

When planning for an activity that invites students to make real-world connections, it is essential to design with purpose in mind. In many ways, students still view reading and interaction with texts—like reading a novel, for example—separately from their daily lives. Take time to think about the real-world connections and the seeds of discussion that can be harvested while engaging in a novel with students. In bringing together real life and fiction, students can begin to think critically not only in their own views but about how other views continue to be shaped.

It is also important to think logistically about what type of product you want students to create. Currently, ThingLink and Genially are tools that allow users to upload an image and then create hotspots that provide more information about the image and share links to other connected resources. This makes them the ideal tools for making connections with images. If you are unfamiliar with the tools and want to use them with your students, take some time to play with them so that you can answer questions as they arise. Other modes of presentation, such as slides and digital or physical posters, can also work.

In the Moment

Step 1: Form collaborative student groups. Since this work lends itself to making connections and understanding of a variety of perspectives, collaboration is essential.

Step 2: Encourage student groups to brainstorm possible real-life connections to the novel. As student groups brainstorm, they construct a focused list of real-life topics that connect to specific events or ideas in the novel. Once students have developed their list, it makes selecting topics easier for students as they move forward.

Step 3: Invite students to form partners within the larger collaborative group and use the brainstormed list from Step 2 to select a topic to investigate. Once students cultivate a list of real-world topics connecting to the novel, partners within the student group can choose a topic from the list to explore further.

Step 4: Allow time for student partners to investigate their real-life connections through a variety of media that showcases different perspectives. Ask students to identify articles and videos so that they see different approaches to sharing real events. This can lead to future conversations around the impact of a visual story versus a written story.

Step 5: Collect and construct. Once student pairs have completed their investigations, encourage student partners to use their collected texts to construct a product that shares their connections through an interactive medium like ThingLink and Genially or through infographics, slideshows, or videos.

Step 6: Debrief, share, and reflect. When students are asked to construct a bridge between fiction and real life, it's necessary to schedule time to share these connections and think about how these connections shape our personal understanding of the novel. In addition, ask students to reflect on these newly generated connections and how these connections may have inspired new questions, new thoughts, or new perspectives on real-world issues.

For an example of a Making Connections sample anchor activity related to the young adult novel, *I'm Not Dying with You Tonight* by Kimberly Jones and Gilly Segal, check out this link: https://tinyurl.com/26sp6d5k.

Making Learning Visible

Leaning into the idea of making meaningful connections, students investigated a variety of narratives that exist within their chosen topics. Using ThingLink (see Figure 5.1), students generated a collection of voices related to their topic in efforts to see threads that string these narratives together. When students can see both the depth and breadth of a topic, it presents an opportunity to understand the underlying conditions that influence these narratives, provides a path to view text critically, and offers a layer of empathy to the topic that students may not have acquired if not challenged to see these viewpoints.

Kassi wrote in her reflection about her experience examining various perspectives:

> We need to see all sides of the story like the perspective that the book gave us so that we can make the best choice possible for ourselves and our community. We need to stand together even when we are afraid.

By asking students to explore their curiosities, seek out various perspectives of critical matters, and process these understandings, we empower students to take the stands that they need as they become more active in understanding the world around them.

SYMBOLIC CONNECTIONS IN ACTION

- Affording students time to make connections between the novel they are reading and real-life experiences offer a chance to form new understandings about the world they currently live in.
- The same book can result in different worldly connections. While Kassi focused on riots, Ellie examined the impact of social class on the characters in the book *I'm Not Dying with You Tonight* by Kimberly Jones and Gilly Segal as well as its impact on citizens in the United States. Ellie constructed a ThingLink around the role of privilege and social class in today's society using a photo of an older neighborhood. She placed circular icons on the photo to connect to a variety of texts and to share quotes from the novel. The questions and research threaded within and throughout her ThingLink forged a path to new questions and connections as they continued with and beyond the book.

Figure 5.1. While reading *I'm Not Dying with You Tonight* by Kimberly Jones and Gilly Segal, Kassi examined riots (an important part of the book's plot) from the perspectives of police officers and rioters by locating news articles about real-world riots.

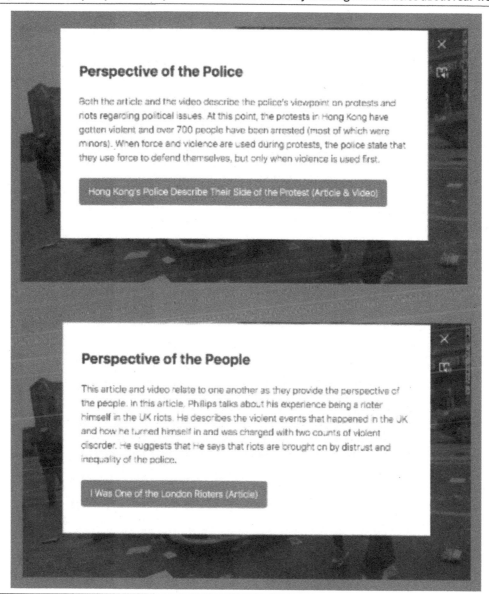

SURVIVING THE SYSTEM

What Is Surviving the System?

Inspired by the work of educators who are a part of Teaching Tolerance (now https://www.learningforjustice.org/), Surviving the System asks students to explicitly examine how the marginalized characters in the novel they are studying exist within a white-privileged system.

Often, students focus more on the plot in books rather than using the characters to help them better understand our world. Books written by authors from marginalized and underrepresented groups can teach our students a lot about the system we live within.

In Surviving the System, students are asked to identify moments in the text where characters are vulnerable and to connect those moments to similar events that happen in our world. Then, to help counter many of the deficit mindsets our students can lapse into—consciously or unconsciously—they must provide adjectives and examples from the book that capture the character's strengths. Finally, they must consider and name what their character needs to be successful in life.

How Can Surviving the System Prepare Students for Experimenting with New Ideas?

Surviving the System directs students' attention toward the inequities that exist in societal and political systems. By asking students to pay close attention to the vulnerabilities, strengths, and needs of people different from themselves, we help students develop empathy. When students feel empathy, they are more inclined to consider ideas that push back against the system they live within (Mirra, 2018).

Pushing back at the system provides students with an authentic purpose that marries learning with student agency. Surviving the System encourages students to question the system. And this mindset encourages students to ask questions that can guide inquiries that can lead to social action.

Before You Begin

For students to engage in this experience successfully and positively, think about your teaching context and the needs of your stakeholders. Topics like privilege might invite quick assumptions and opinions laced with fear. Venturing into a discussion with such weight should be approached with open communication and complete transparency.

Additionally, take time to think about how these variables—vulnerability, strengths, and needs—have a presence within your own students. Think about how students would view these variables and how they identify these variables in others. Middle school students, for example, may need more support prior to entering a learning experience like this than high school students. Identifying these variables within themselves first before seeing it in others can provide this support.

In the Moment

Step 1: Pause and de-school your students. Students entering your classroom have had years of experience being schooled. They have been inundated with tests, quizzes, comprehension questions, plot points, mundane text details, and on and on. This experience asks students to do something that pushes against how they think of

school as it seeks to look beyond the details and look broader into our world. Be ready to provide additional support to students by providing continuous flexibility, celebrations of mistakes, close listening, and the enthusiasm of learning alongside them.

Step 2: Offer time to explore and understand terms like privilege, marginalized, *and* underrepresented. Provide a time and space where students can think about and around these concepts. Allow time for questions to cultivate a safe learning space and remember that flexibility and celebrating mistakes advice from Step 1.

Step 3: Identify and outline the variables. Working with such abstract ideas does not always come naturally to everyone. Take time to work with the variable terms—*vulnerability, strength,* and *needs*—so that students understand what they are and know what to look for. Modeling what this could look like when working with a text is imperative.

Step 4: Ask students to identify evidence to support their observations. To help students learn how to use evidence to support their observations, students should locate lines from the novels to illustrate their points. This process can be enriched even more if we ask them to find images that illustrate their ideas, as well as real-world connections through nonfiction articles and media.

Step 5: Provide time to work with these variables in connection to the text. By affording students time to workshop these ideas with a provided text, you become a facilitator in the learning experience. Students can think through these ideas with your support as a coach who can provide feedback as they continue to process.

Step 6: Develop a means for sharing student work. Digital tools like Padlet or Google Slides provide students with a space to share their thinking with others in class. By expanding beyond their own examples, students are better able to see the larger system at work.

Step 7: Reflect on the experience. Reflection on big ideas can come in various forms. Threaded throughout our novel studies, reflection is encouraged by journaling, well-remembered events (see Chapter 1), and Socratic seminars. All these practices can offer rich connections as students use metacognition to process their understandings. In addition to reflecting on what has been constructed, take time to push reflection into forward-thinking spaces. As this experience has been outlined, it opens new opportunities to construct more meaningful questions and possibly inspire new avenues of inquiry or acting from students as they look ahead.

Surviving the System sample anchor activity guidelines related to the young adult novel *Dear Justyce* by Nic Stone can be found at https://tinyurl.com/2p959ccw.

Making Learning Visible

In many classrooms, it's not uncommon to hear discussions related to injustices, especially when connecting to specific literary characters or examining historical events. However, we argue that discussions that focus on the systems that construct these injustices are rarely examined. As we seek to answer *why* in many of our studies with students, we acknowledge that we must approach this question at all levels and in all layers.

In a unit that focused on examining intersectional identities, Ellie examined the vulnerabilities of the main character, Darius, in the novel *Darius the Great Is Not Okay* by Adib Khorram. Darius, who suffers from clinical depression, struggles to identify with his Persian heritage until he takes a trip to Iran to visit his grandparents. There, he begins a voyage of self-discovery, connecting to his cultural roots and finding the strength to take his newfound understanding home with him to America. Wanting to demonstrate that vulnerability looks different based upon the context we exist within, Ellie highlighted how Darius was vulnerable in America, as well as in Iran (Figure 5.2).

By stepping back and looking at the larger picture, Ellie was able to gain a deeper understanding of how issues such as politics, gender, race, and culture influence the structure of systems and how these systems impact individuals. Seeing the individual is an important step to dismantling systems that want to sort people into groups.

Figure 5.2. The book *Darius the Great Is Not Okay* by Adib Khorram gave Ellie the opportunity to look at the systems in two different cultures and examine the impacts of both systems on the main character, Darius.

Vulnerabilities (in America)	Vulnerabilities (in Iran)
Darius has his mother's Iranian dark hair, eyes, skin, and eyelashes. He is not seen as American even though he was born in Portland. "This was not the first time I was called a terrorist. It didn't happen often—no teacher let it slide if they heard it—but school was school, and I was a kid with Middle Eastern heritage, even though I was born and raised in Portland" (39). Boys at school think it is funny to call him hateful names even though he is just as American as them, he just happens to have darker skin.	Darius may look like he's Iranian, but he doesn't speak Farsi like everyone (except for his father) in his family does. This leaves him confused about many of his family's conversations, and he does not feel Persian enough to fit in. His Babou often scolds Darioush's mother for not teaching him Farsi. "It's because you don't teach him," he said. "You wanted him to be American, like Stephen. You don't want him to be Persian" (136).
Darius is a target for bullying. He is called names such as D-hole, D-wad, D's Nuts (4), and D-Bag (8). His bike tires were also stolen by his bullies. His father says he just needs to stand up for himself, but he's afraid to (13).	Darioush's family in Iran does not understand what depression is and why he is medicated for it. His Babou says, "What are you depressed for? You have to think positive, baba. Medicine is for old people. Like me . . . you just have to try harder, Darioush-jan. Those will not fix anything" (102). Many different countries do not understand that depression is an actual medical condition and not just "feeling sad." This makes Darioush very uncomfortable and ashamed when he has to take his medication.
	*Darioush is the Persian spelling of Darius.

SURVIVING THE SYSTEM IN ACTION

- When we ask students to analyze the systems that our characters live in, we invite them to broaden their analyses to connect to the world around them. As teachers, we may start with the comforts of fictional characters, but using these characters as conduits into real discussions only strengthens the possibility for deeper questions and social action.
- Kassi highlighted her thinking around Jason Reynolds's *The Boy in the Black Suit* by using Padlet to link additional sources, images, text quotes, and themes to better understand how the main character in the book related to these systems (see Figure 5.3). By organizing her thinking in this way, Kassi was able to demonstrate her understanding of a fictional character, but, more importantly, she was able to see how the vulnerabilities, strengths, and needs identified within the book exist in the larger world. By continuing to make connections and ask meaningful questions, Kassi is more prepared to engage in social action as we work toward using novels to prompt further inquiries.

Figure 5.3. *The Boy in the Black Suit* highlights ways the main character is impacted by the system he lives within. In exploring these vulnerabilities, Kassi was able to connect the impact of the social system in the United States by finding other media connections.

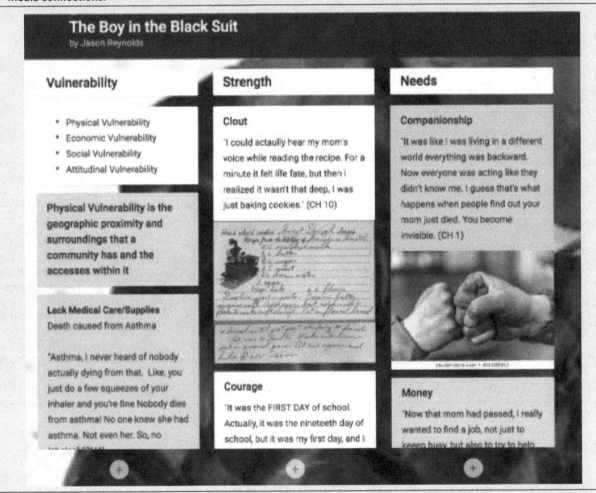

READING YOUR WORLD

The activities within this chapter give evidence on how we help our students make meaningful connections and go beyond the existing mainstream narratives. With the opportunity to explore perspectives and unearth the systems that influence these perspectives, we know that our students begin to see the world in ways that prompt them to experiment with new ideas.

REFLECT, MOTIVATE, AND ACT

Reflect on the Freedoms We Provide Our Students

- *Where might you find opportunities for students to play with their ideas?*
- *Why is it important for students to play?*
- *Why might students fail? How will you support failure?*

Motivate to Investigate Your Students' Strengths and Obstacles

- *What strengths do your students feel they will bring to the reading of the novel?*
- *What obstacles do your students see that might get in their way? Why might these exist?*

Take Action to Create Learning Experiences

- *What experiences can you create that will invite students to experiment with new ideas as they are reading?*
- *Who and what can support you in creating these experiences?*
- *How will these experiences help ignite meaningful connections with your students?*

Having the Courage to Do What We Know How to Do

You have to know what you stand for. Not just what you stand against.

—Laurie Halse Anderson

Robyn went into teaching for a combination of the above reasons. She had a passion for reading that she wanted to instill in all students. (She still does.) She watched her brother struggle in school not because he wasn't bright enough, but because he didn't see why what he was learning mattered. She wanted to help students see why it matters. (She still does.) She wanted to change the world. (She still does.) In the formative stage of her career, she offered a book as an option for students to choose for a literature circle. It grappled with how decisions can change lives. It grappled with apathy. It grappled with drugs. It grappled with the impact of divorce. But most importantly, in some parents' eyes, it grappled with sex. For this group of parents, it didn't matter that this was just a small part of the book or that this wasn't the focus of the conversations around the book. It only mattered that it existed. Calls were made to administrators and the school board. Whispers of outrage were shared among parents. Flyers were handed out at little league basketball games. All these pressures were enough to make a young teacher walk away from the profession. They almost did. And while Sarah doesn't have as big a story about pushback from the community, she, too, has been challenged by parents, administrators, and other teachers, in smaller but also deeply cutting ways.

So, when we hear fear from teachers when they consider adopting the approaches we advocate, we understand. We have been there, too. But, we've come to realize that teaching in a way that matters, that impacts students' current and future lives, takes courage. Through our work with teachers, we have witnessed, as Ernest Morrell (2015a) described in his NCTE Presidential speech, the *daily genius* taking place in classrooms. Some of these genius teachers include Craig, an experienced teacher who challenges students to critically examine our past to understand our future; Becca, an early career teacher who constantly seeks out opportunities for students' voices to

be heard; and Patrick, another early career teacher who is questioning his traditional curriculum and finding ways to create dissonance in his students through alternative texts. Each of these teachers bring the power Morrell described to their classrooms. And we have witnessed their revolution in practice when they shared their approaches and philosophies with each other.

Our work with these teachers, as well as our conversations with others, is what prompted us to write this book. When we seek to disrupt student thinking, we are advocating for their futures. In doing this work, however, we share Morrell's (2015a) observation: "Advocating is not complicated. The complicated part is having the courage to do what we know how to do . . . the hard part is doing it alone. . . . It is much easier when you are walking with people" (p. 325). In compiling our stories as educators, as well as the stories of our students, we hope to create a community that will empower more teachers to do the meaningful work with students that they deserve.

Many of the strategies in this book aren't new. They may have been updated or tweaked slightly, but if you stop and think about it, taken individually, you know how to do them. Like Craig and Becca and Patrick, you have the genius inside of you. What may be new, however, is how you frame them. The framing we ask of you does take courage. But to continue with Morrell's (2015a) words: "We have the power to act. We have the moral obligation to act" (p. 325). And when we show courage and act, we also model for our students how to tap into their own courage—which they often have more of than we do—and act to make our world a better, more just place.

As we have continued to develop this framework, we have come to appreciate the importance of transparency, as well as partnering with members of our community. When we do this, we are not working alone. Rather, we have invited parents, administrators, and other stakeholders to partner with us as we help broaden our students' understanding of the world. Thus, when we experience moments of wobble (Garcia & O'Donnell-Allen, 2015), we have others to turn to who bolster our courage to move forward. When we need resources to help students act on their ideas, we know who can help us access these resources.

This chapter shares ways we work with our community. It seeks to demonstrate how we, as teachers, communicate with parents and other stakeholders. It also illustrates how our students interact with members of the community. These interactions are part of our students' journey of discovering what they stand *for* and not just against.

OUR STUDENTS' LIVED EXPERIENCES

A new school year invited the idea of engaging students in grittier conversations around the role of police and racial stereotypes with the use of the book *Dear Martin* by Nic Stone. Prior to open house night, Sarah sent out a parent survey, as well as background information about the book *Dear Martin*, to her parents and constituents. In this message, Sarah did not phrase this experience in a form of permission but rather as an inquiry into what she needed to know before going into real-life discourse with students. By pairing the timing of this parent communication with the district open house, she hoped that those who wanted to discuss the learning experience would come speak to her in person.

As the night continued, Sarah welcomed many familiar faces into her room as she had worked for the community for more than 10 years. The Long (pseudonym) family was instantly drawn to *Dear Martin*. While they continued to explore Sarah's classroom, they seemed to almost linger as if they wanted some personal time with Sarah. When the room cleared, Mrs. Long gained Sarah's attention by saying, "You know, Mrs. Bonner . . . I'm not too sure about this book you're going to read. We've had a long talk about it at home, but one of the reasons we'll let this happen is that we trust you . . . we know you'll do it right."

Honored by the amount of trust the Long family instilled in this moment, Sarah remembered that Mr. Long was a high-ranking local police officer and sensed that a book like *Dear Martin* may have created some pause for this family. Channeling the trust of the Long family, Sarah provided a copy of the book to Mr. and Mrs. Long so that they could preview the text before their daughter engaged in the class reading experience. A week later, Sarah's student returned the borrowed book with a note from Mrs. Long attached to it that simply stated, "We loved it!" And it was with that message that Sarah knew that students are not alone in their need for support when unpacking reading experiences. Parents and community members need support too.

IN DIALOGUE

While reading the novel *Internment* by Samira Ahmed, a group of students interviewed Dr. Rahil (pseudonym), a political science professor who is Muslim, and Pastor Brown (pseudonym), a pastor at a nondenominational church. The following is an excerpt from their discussion:

8th-Grade Students: In the book *Internment*, Muslims are being pushed out of their homes and given 10 minutes to pack their items and relocate to a government-created camp. Can you give a better understanding of being Muslim, and while we know that the author identifies as Muslim, why do you think the author chose Muslim and not other religions beyond her personal connections?

> *In their interview, students wanted to better understand the role religion played in the events of the novel.*

Dr. Rahil: First of all, just by the fact this book is about the Muslim community. For a moment, just forget they are Muslims. Try to understand that it could happen to anybody. That is the message, actually, that is coming from the lady's experience. Why did she choose Muslim? Because it should be easily relatable to what has been happening. Particularly since 9/11, we have seen that, and let me tell you a very personal experience that you might be able to understand. I have moved into this country in 1987. . . . I have never been asked, looking at my name whether I'm a Muslim. Either people took it for granted and didn't think it's an important thing or thought it is immaterial whether I'm a Muslim, or a Christian, Jew, Hindu or atheist, God knows what. Nobody cared until exactly September 12th, the day after 9/11. I was teaching at a university in South Carolina at that time. Interestingly enough, one of my colleagues from another department, whom I met the day I moved there in August, the middle of August when the semester started, and we talked about our family, we talked about a lot of things. Never,

ever did he ask me if I was Muslim until the 13th of September 2001. So, my identity became I'm a Muslim first, which I never thought of; I never thought myself as a Muslim first and then something else. To me, I am who I am. That's why this experience is, when the author is putting these things, you know, if you look at the book, the cover and everything, particularly the characters, she took Leila's character because we will be able to understand. . . .

Through their conversation with Dr. Rahil, students were able to see how society attempts to flatten identities in order to better fit people into single stories.

8th-Grade Students: So, in the text *Internment*, the main character, Leila who is a Muslim, has been put into an internment camp with her mom and dad, and they were taken out of their homes because of their religion. What can you do and what can't you do in America because of your religion?

Pastor Brown: What type of restrictions do we have based off of what we believe?

8th-Grade Students: Yeah.

Pastor Brown: Well, you guys are in school, obviously, so you know that there is a law that's been passed that is separation of church and state. So, as a pastor, I could not come into this school and I could not try to indoctrinate all of you to follow a certain belief system, right? And it's kind of, to my colleague's discussion here, it's important to

By asking this question across religions and listening to two men from different religions, students were able to expand the narrative around religion. Pastor Brown also emphasized the importance of their questions and how their search for answers furthers their understanding of people.

understand that it's how the world identifies you and there are a lot of biases that take place within the country in which we are living and many of those biases are based off of ignorance. They're not based off of laws, they're based off of people's perceptions, okay? So, although I could not come in here and try to indoctrinate anybody, you, certainly as a student, could come in, and

you could bring a Bible with you, for example, to school. You could have a student-led prayer. You could come together and do that. That's well within your rights. . . . I like the question because the question means you're trying to absorb some education. What can we and can we not do? I think it's important for us as individuals to really get past perceptions and get past how people perceive us or identify us and really get to the root of who am I and what is my role? What are my intentions? That's just kind of scratching the surface, but, in all reality, we have to educate ourselves . . .

8th-Grade Students: Have you ever been treated differently because of your guys' beliefs?

Dr. Rahil: Personally, I haven't experienced much. Maybe there is the latent thing, but I've heard, I've seen, including in some cases I have had to interject, you should not be treating this individual like that. There have been, unfortunately, instances like that. One thing I tell everybody, which I am going to tell you, too, or two

Both pastor Brown and Dr. Rahil spoke to the students about the role fear plays in shaping society's views of the world and the people in it. They encouraged students to take the steps to find the courage to move beyond this fear.

things, maybe. First thing: let not other people define you. You define yourself. When we define ourselves, similarly when you are looking at someone else, don't define them by only one thing, whether it is religion, skin color, education, social status. Don't define. One individual is not made of one thing. We are many things.

TRANSFORMING THROUGH PRACTICE: HAVING THE COURAGE TO INVITE THE COMMUNITY TO LEARN WITH YOU

Morrell (2015a) reminds us that when we are walking alongside others, we can tap into the courage we need to teach students how to critically examine the world we live in. Teaching a novel that confronts race and police brutality can be frightening. But if we shake off that fear, we realize that we know how to teach students to think about the message being shared within the pages of the novel. We teach students to understand character motivation and larger world themes in every novel we pick up. It's just easier when the topics within the novel are not a part of an intensely polarizing and politicized debate. But, having open conversations with parents about why we are reading the book and inviting them to read the book alongside their children can shift the narrative. By including parents into our learning community, we can promote meaningful conversations at home and at school.

And we cannot stop communicating clearly and openly with the parents of our students. The larger community also sees the work we are doing. This can be frightening, as well. Yet, when we invite multiple voices to share their experiences, our students are exposed to viewpoints they might not otherwise have had the opportunity to learn from and about. As the interview with Dr. Rahil and pastor Brown demonstrates, students were able to ask questions that occurred to them as they were reading, but they were also reminded, by Dr. Rahil, that we cannot treat any group of people as monolithic. The more people we invite in our learning journey, the more our students can reject the temptation to stereotype a group of people.

As we introduce the following strategies, we return, once again, to Morrell's (2015a) reminder that we know how to do these things. We, like most of you, learned about Lev Vygotsky (1978) in our educational course work. Vygotsky understood that learning is social. Before our students can individualize their thinking, they must first interact socially with others. Our students are cognitively ready for this work, but we must provide them with social interactions to help them develop a deeper understanding. And while those social interactions *can* occur within the school walls, limiting interactions in this way restricts their understanding. Like Morrell, we believe that we have the moral obligation to engage students in a larger dialogue. If we don't, we run the risk that others won't, either.

The strategies that follow are not isolated to one-time learning events. Rather, they are approaches we thread throughout our units to help our students reach the maximum potential described by Vygotsky (1978). They remind us to make our work transparent to our students, our parents, our larger community, and ourselves.

THEORY TO PRACTICE

Ernest Morrell: Although most of Morrell's work focuses on urban youth, his emphasis on designing around students and using the language arts as tools for social action applies across contexts. Much of his work focuses on student-driven inquiry, including his work in Youth Participatory Action Research (YPAR) with Nicole Mirra and Antero Garcia (2015). In a short column for Texas English, Morrell (2015b) presents four challenges to ELA teachers who want to shift instruction toward changing the world: (1) develop powerful readers of multicultural texts; (2) develop powerful authors of multimodal texts; (3) connect classroom production to social action; and (4) build the discipline around the students. Selecting multicultural texts to spark inquiry answers the first challenge. The following provide approaches in this book that answer the other three. They can serve as models for how to think about putting his work into practice.

- **Media Campaign (see Chapter 8):** "When we consider the dimensions of advocacy and social and environmental justice, the new century will require students who can create eloquent and informative texts that provide commentary on their world; in our classrooms, they should develop the capability of creating multimodal texts that aim to inform, educate, and entertain wider audiences in the hopes of illuminating possibility and enacting positive change upon their world."

- **YPAR (see Chapter 8):** "By participatory action research, I refer to research projects where students investigate and report on issues that matter to them in the real world. Research, in this guise, becomes more than a chance to let the teacher know how well a student has accessed information on an existing topic; research becomes a tool to provide critical information about the world around them."

- **The Investigation Mixtape (see Chapter 3):** "As English teachers, we are challenged to find ways to honor what communities value while practicing and imparting the best of what our discipline has to offer."

For more about Ernest Morrell's work, check out the following resources:

- *Critical Media Pedagogy: Teaching for Achievement in City Schools* by Ernest Morrell, Rudy Duenas, Veronica Garcia-Garza, and Jorge Lopez
- "Powerful Teaching, Powerful Schools: Engaging Youth in the Digital Age" at https://www.youtube .com/watch?v=gRuitlh3jvE
- "Powerful Literacy-Ernest Morrell" at https://www .youtube.com/watch?v=_qObcdvwRgQ

COLLABORATIVE COMMUNITY INTERVIEWS

What Are Collaborative Community Interviews?

As the name implies, Collaborative Community Interviews require students to work together to create interview questions for members of the community. We use these interviews to give students the opportunity to ask real people questions around the topics we are studying. In novel studies, this means we identify roles and events within the novel that we recognize may be unfamiliar, controversial, or in need of further exploration. Then, we invite community members who can share insights into these character roles or events to visit our classrooms.

Prior to the community member's visit, a group of students (usually one-third of the class) researches the person or their profession. As they are researching, they make connections between the profession and the novel. These connections help form the foundation of their interview questions. The group creates a Google Docs page to compile their questions before checking with the teacher for final tweaks. Recognizing that writing good questions is a skill that must be developed, it is important to work with students to ensure that each question mirrors their intent, digs into the topic, and is respectful of the person being interviewed.

How Can Collaborative Community Interviews Help Students (and Teachers) Have the Courage to Do What We Know How to Do?

For students, talking to adults can be scary. Asking questions around sensitive social topics can be even more frightening. Their lack of experience in the world means they naturally have a lot of questions about these topics, but many feel reluctant to voice these questions aloud because they hear the voices of friends, family members, and the media outlets they use telling them how they *should* answer these questions. Collaborative Community Interviews can help students overcome their fear of asking questions important to them because they have their peers working alongside them. The questions they are asking are not any one person's questions. This can be liberating for students because the group owns the questions, not the individual. Once our students recognize the importance of engaging with others around their questions, they are more likely to have the courage to continue to ask these questions and to begin to formulate their own understanding of how *they* feel about a topic rather than relying on the opinions of others.

Collaborative Community Interviews prepare students for inquiry-centered learning because they learn that answers to questions aren't always simple ones. Rather, through interactions with others, they begin to discover that each perspective raises more questions. They also learn the value of seeking out answers beyond Google. And because they feel more confident in speaking with experts, they will search for these experts to aid in their understanding—sometimes with our help but sometimes on their own.

Watching students develop the courage to stand up and ask their questions is also empowering for us as teachers. When we see our students engage in these ways, we know we are on the right path, making it easier to stand up for ourselves when challenged. Community Social Interviews also give us courage in other ways. It's natural for our community to be wary of our motives if we do all our work behind closed doors. When we open the doors to our classroom, we demonstrate a transparency that diverts suspicion. Inviting the community in to share their perspectives helps to develop a trust that fortifies us in moments of uncertainty. And the more parents and stakeholders we add to our learning community, the more allies we have who will support us when questions around our motives arise.

Once teachers take a moment to engage in self-reflection and know why community voices matter to the learning experience, it is essential to gain classroom allies. It is often wise to begin with members of the school board, as well as building administrators and parents, because these are the community members most vested in what is happening in the school. Asking for these voices to speak to the issues being explored provides transparency, which can lead to more momentum among students, as well as support from the community. It is this support that brings a sense of courage to keep moving forward.

Before You Begin

When thinking about the act of bringing community voices into your classroom, there need to be moments of teacher self-reflection. This reflection helps us understand why community voices can become the catalyst to changing traditional practices. First, we must reflect upon getting comfortable with disrupting the roles we may traditionally play in the learning environment. For teachers, part of the struggle with bringing outside voices in may come from giving up the control of being the only voice of knowledge present in the classroom. In many ways, it becomes essential for teachers to step back and acknowledge that we aren't (or maybe can't) always be the expert in every learning space. Additionally, it becomes equally important to understand that this control *must* be released because we may not have the voice to speak on the topics presented in the texts we use with our students.

Another point of teacher self-reflection connects to the notion of letting students be in control of the learning experience itself when speaking to outside voices. As students begin to construct their questions for the community experts, recognize that many students have limited experiences with formulating strong questions for outside figures. As teachers, we need to become comfortable with allowing our students to draft their own questions with our help. Guiding the construction of questions becomes a collection of teachable moments as we help our students reflect upon the words they choose to use with others. Ultimately, giving students the agency provides an opportunity to model, design, and reconstruct questions that fuel deeper student learning experiences.

In the Moment

Step 1: Take steps to gain allies and make connections. Prior to starting a learning experience like this with students, reach out to key people who can provide support, add additional ideas, and bolster students' confidence when moving forward. Such allies may include parents, community stakeholders, school board members, building administrators, and more. As you know more about the insight of these stakeholders, it becomes easier to be responsive to student needs and to determine which voices should be brought into the reading experience itself.

Step 2: Create a platform for parents to share their voice. As you begin to implement a unit like this, it is vital to construct a space where not only parents are informed of the unit topics themselves, but also have a space that encourages them to voice suggestions, topics to think about, invite questions, and more. Remember, our parents play a very important role in this process, as well. *Not* having our parents and primary stakeholders involved only cultivates a sense of confusion, assumption, and lack of transparency. These elements become a storm of distrust and may set back this experience before it even starts.

Step 3: Evaluate the text for real-life voices and connections. In thinking about the text

experience, what voices stand out that students can experience in real life? Take time to construct a list of potential roles that could deepen the value of the reading experience for students. These might be professions like a police officer or an attorney, but they could also be people with experiences, activists in a specific cause, or mirror a character's position for further insight into understanding the text.

Step 4: Communicate your needs with a wide audience . . . and, don't be afraid of rejection. Once a list of voices is established, share your message and need with a wide range of connections. Construct an email sharing a summary of the primary text, a list of voices that could be used to support the primary text, and a list of potential dates and times for others to pass along. You never know who might know someone who can contribute to the conversation.

Step 5: Schedule Collaborative Community Interviews to correlate specifically with text plot points. In efforts to maximize the curiosity of readers, timing is key. As a book study may often take a few weeks with students, allow the interviews to be scheduled in conjunction with key areas of the text so that direct connections can be made and explored further.

Step 6: Coach students in preparing for their interview experience. While the interview questions, the interview itself, and the documentation of the interview to be shared with the entire student population rests on the shoulders of students, we need to consider how to support students so they are successful. Encourage students to participate in research about the interviewee to gain a better background understanding. Students can also watch interviews to analyze interview techniques, as well as to make note of the types of questions to ask. Additionally, consider providing question stems to help students play with the structure of their questions. And, lastly, conference with the student team to ensure that their questions use respectful language and promote answers that enhance the overall learning journey.

Step 7: Create a space for students to familiarize themselves with technology and share their expert voices with others. Because only a portion of students participate in interviews, ask guests for permission to record the interviews so that the rest of the class can watch them later. This means that prior to the interview, students need time to plan their use of technology. They may need to think through camera angles, what technology is best in an interview setting, and who specifically will be managing the interview recording. Additionally, they must know how to share the interviews with their classmates. One way is for students to upload their interview videos to an established Google folder that can be accessed on the classroom website. Then, students can access these interviews anytime.

Step 8: Allow student interview groups to make meaning of the expert voices. From understanding the expert to designing questions to participating in the interview itself, students become heavily invested in the interview process—but how can the community expert impact the understanding of the primary text? It is essential for students to process the information provided from the interview to construct connective tissues between the primary text and real life. For many students, the interview supports their understanding of the events within the primary text, but, for some students, it may prompt them to consider the text through a stronger critical lens. There are multiple ways for students to make these connections, including structured discussions, reflective writing, and creating products such as infographics. Whichever way you choose, it is important to take this last step so that students engage in deeper learning and, often, feel inspired by a new level of curiosity.

Taken from an anchor activity related to Jeff Zentner's *In the Wild Light*, this resource takes students through the process of preparing for a community interview: https://tinyurl.com/bp3f7j26.

Making Learning Visible

As teachers, we do not have to be the only voice within the classroom setting. In fact, the more opportunities that students have with a variety of perspectives, the more students engage in asking meaningful questions and continue strengthening their understanding of the world.

The opportunity to share this information in a meaningful way becomes an essential component because it serves as a powerful conduit for deeper understanding. After completing the interview, students developed a series of infographics to synthesize their new information with a greater population. Students can use these infographics to visualize their understanding as well as spread the messages of the community voices.

As part of an ongoing reflection titled "Well-Remembered Events" (see Chapter 1), one student reflected on the interview process by stating:

> I think that the interviews with the people really helped give us a better understanding of the book. For example, when I talked with Dr. Rahil, I never experienced a conversation with a person whose religion is Muslim. After talking with him, I could visualize Muslim practices more clearly, and I had a *way* better understanding.

COLLABORATIVE COMMUNITY INTERVIEWS IN ACTION

- Using a collaborative approach to understanding specific topics and concepts invites students to ask questions that can often lead to breaking stereotypes and dissolving ignorance.
- Student groups collaborate with community experts to gain a better understanding of the primary text read by the class.
- Many student interview experiences become opportunities to challenge the ideas between fact vs. fiction. It also allows space for greater reflection and connection into the real world. For example, in an infographic designed after speaking with a nurse practitioner in connection to the physical and mental health of humans stationed with an internment camp (inspired by Samira Ahmed's 2019 young adult novel, *Internment*), students stated:

> We have learned our world can be a judgmental, unjust, place, and there are/were a lot of people who make it that way. Our past, and, even present, hasn't been the greatest role model for people. Think about it, in the past, we have had slavery, racism (still a thing now), deforestation/pollution (also a thing now), people with too much power harming innocent people, and so much more. . . . We need to fix these issues to make a better world for our future.

Seeing the power outside voices can have on student learning enabled us to think of other ways to incorporate community perspectives within lessons. Knowing how these voices contribute to a greater understanding of the world, the mission to include more voices increases as it connects to student interest and learner agency.

MENTOR MOMENTS

What Are Mentor Moments?

Mentor Moments are moments in instruction where, like the Collaborative Community Interviews, learning is facilitated by someone other than the teacher. Once students have participated in Collaborative Community interviews, they are more comfortable talking with other adults about our topics of study. These moments are not one-time occurrences in our classrooms. Rather, as we create larger assignments, we build in spaces where students are asked to seek out other opinions and knowledge to have a deeper understanding. Unlike Collaborative Community Interviews, when we engage in Mentor Moments, students are working singly or in pairs. They are also responsible for identifying the adults who will best guide their learning and contacting those adults via email to arrange for a time and place to talk. Ideally, students will visit with their mentors face-to-face, either physically or virtually. We have found that this engenders a stronger relationship between mentors and students—one that can, at times, extend beyond a one-and-done experience. However, if needed due to a mentor's schedule, we have also allowed for email correspondence. Ultimately, we want our students to learn from others and to learn how to communicate in writing, as well as through speaking and listening.

When we first introduce Mentor Moments to our students, we typically do so on a small scale. We might require students to seek out feedback on an idea from a former student who has participated in similar assignments, or we might require that they contact at least one expert to guide their thinking while doing research. As the school year progresses, however, we try to extend these moments by asking students to engage with a mentor multiple times during a larger project. This is most common during Genius Hour, which is an instructional approach that devotes one day of the week where students develop inquiries around their interests—not ours. We will discuss this approach in more detail in Chapter 8.

How Can Mentor Moments Help Students (and Teachers) Have the Courage to Do What We Know How to Do?

If we consider Collaborative Community Interviews as the first step in scaffolding students toward forming questions and engaging in meaningful conversations with adults, then Mentor Moments are the next step. Through Mentor Moments, students begin to rely less on their peers and more on their own questioning and conversation skills. This allows them to further define their own understanding of a topic and to gain confidence in their abilities to articulate their understanding, as well as to find experts who help them further their learning. When students recognize they can articulate well-researched understandings, they begin to find the courage to speak up when they hear or see statements that contradict these understandings.

Mentor Moments assist in inquiry-centered learning in much the same way as Collaborative Community Interviews. Through talking with experts, students begin to understand that the world is complex and seeking out others who have studied their topics of interest can help them better see these complexities. Mentor Moments demonstrate to them that seeking answers to complex questions often means talking to people because through dialogue we can better understand the gray areas that exist in the world.

For teachers, Mentor Moments demonstrate that we do not have to build our communities alone. Rather, students can identify people who can be allies to our classroom, and often these are people we may not have found on our own. And by empowering our students to seek out new voices to add to the learning community, we are continuing to demonstrate that the learning our students are engaging in is, and should be, visible to everyone. Having the courage to expand learning beyond the classroom walls, students and teachers can begin a journey of discovery into experiences that have the potential to last a lifetime.

Before You Begin

Implementing Mentor Moments with students begins with acknowledging the importance of the mentor role within the inquiry as well as providing student support in searching for a mentor. When reaching out to a community, students do not generally have strong skills in communicating their wants and needs to a greater audience beyond their own sphere of everyday contacts.

Not only is it vital to support students' communication efforts beyond the classroom, it may also present an opportunity for teachers to explore possible mentorship connections as well.

To help students network with people outside of the classroom, encourage them to first reach out to other district teachers and staff. As teachers, we work with and are connected to many people. These connections can greatly benefit student goals in securing a mentor for their inquiry designs.

Courage to reach out to others isn't always present within our students when they are first asked to reach out to a mentor. As teachers, we can play a pivotal role in awakening an inner strength in our students. As students venture into an experience that continues to deepen their understanding, it is the opportunity to network with those beyond the classroom that enriches student learning, presents a sense of agency, and empowers students to channel a sense of courage they never knew they had before.

In the Moment

Step 1: Allow students exploratory time with their topics. When it comes to finding a mentor, students must understand a chosen topic. Allow students to participate in general, surface exploration of their ideas, attempt to find answers to curiosity-based questions, and seek to discover potential roles found within those topics.

Step 2: Think local. As students understand their chosen topics in broader strokes, afford time for students to seek experts in their own community. Who might be identified experts within the community? Who might be qualified to share their knowledge and experience with students? Encourage students to investigate their communities by asking family, friends, school stakeholders, and even local business or leadership holders.

Step 3: Encourage students to make contacts with potential mentors. As teachers, we often think we should be making these connections between students and outside mentors, but to promote student agency and integrate teachable moments around formal communication strategies, encourage students to make these first moves.

Step 4: Weave in discussions around online safety and always be in the "know." As students begin contacting outside experts using online spaces (e.g., email and social media spaces), explain to students that tools used should be school approved, no personal information should be shared, and that all communication outside of the classroom should also be copied to you. While encouraging students to make these initial steps into contacting potential mentors, you should also provide a safety parameter that can be communicated to parents, administrators, and other school stakeholders.

Step 5: Take extra steps to help students connect with mentors. For many students, finding a mentor may take more effort than finding and connecting with someone in the community. Seek out additional help from within the school or the district. Construct a list of the topics being researched by students who are still searching for a mentor and send an all-district email asking if anyone might have any connections. From these simple moves, students can connect with mentors all over the nation to construct meaningful learning experiences.

Step 6: Create schedules and supports for students to maintain ongoing contact with mentors. While many students may be fortunate to find mentors that naturally sustain an ongoing partnership throughout the learning journey, this isn't always a natural progression for all students. Require students to contact and communicate with their mentors a minimum number of times throughout a semester—we have found five times is a good number. Contacting and communicating may include face-to-face experiences, but it could also represent email communication, FaceTime, social media correspondence, and more. Additionally, provide resources for structuring questions for their mentor, mentor texts for written communication, and opportunities to discuss how to navigate social norms when meeting with others outside of the classroom.

This example comes from Sarah's Genius Hour experience (see Chapter 8) and highlights expectations for both students and mentors: https://tinyurl.com/mr32t7nf.

MENTOR MOMENTS IN ACTION

Students who have the freedom to connect with experts outside of the classroom not only gain rich learning experiences connected to their personalized study but also have an opportunity to create positive relationships with others who care immensely about their personal success. Faith wanted to pursue her passion for animation and art for her Genius Hour inquiry. Sarah's student teacher shared that she had a good friend who worked for Disney Pixar in California. With the help of Sarah's student teacher, Faith was able to connect with this expert and continue a series of email messages that supported her curiosities, answered her questions, and provided animation technique strategies throughout the semester.

In Faith's blog, she reflects upon her experience with her mentor:

> I asked her how to make an animation smoother. I'd begun to practice and work on frame by frame, but they were choppy and looked bad. Leah responded by talking about how to maximize smoothness, and told me

that 24 frames per second would be the best possible for me. So, I sped up the drawings per second and it turned out a lot better. When I discussed how I'm talented at procrastination, and it's hard for me to get things done, she recommended making a schedule, which now has me animating an hour on Wednesdays, Saturdays, and Mondays. This plan has definitely sped up the process, and made things a lot easier.

As Faith's blog indicates, the specific and tailored learning experiences she received could only be constructed from a relationship built between a mentee and a mentor. And while these examples are drawn from a larger project and expand across a longer period of time, similar moments with mentors have provided insights for students around smaller projects. For example, when constructing media texts, students have sought out mentor feedback to help them push their thinking. It is in these moments that students begin to understand that meaningful learning can occur at any time—we just need the courage to ask for assistance from others.

Making Learning Visible

When students can connect with an outside mentor, it provides an experience that almost becomes tailored to their own learning. As teachers continue to battle large class sizes and fight to connect with students on a personal level, mentor experts in the learning space creates a culture that turns a classroom of one teacher into an entire classroom full of teachers.

Emily is just one example of a student who worked with a mentor outside of our local community. She wanted to learn more about becoming a psychiatric–mental health nurse practitioner (PMHNP), but living in a small, rural town meant that it was not possible to find a local mentor. Rather than asking Sarah to be the primary contact person to help network Emily with a mentor, Emily took it upon herself to research and locate a PMHNP in New York.

Over a series of weeks throughout the Genius Hour process, Emily and her mentor from New York had an opportunity to email with each other. As Emily would ask her questions, her mentor would often not only respond but also provide additional resources that supported (and even encouraged) Emily's thinking around her inquiry questions. And, while this mentor was not someone from Emily's community, it proved to be a beneficial experience that allowed Emily to make connections beyond the

classroom setting and proved that mentors can be found anywhere.

READING YOUR WORLD

The experiences described in this chapter are just two examples of how we help our students understand the role of community experts in the learning process. Through various opportunities to network with those beyond the classroom, we have found that our students begin to strengthen their own inner courage to seek meaningful learning experiences that supersede the classroom context. This shift is a pivotal support in our larger work of helping students develop inquiry mindsets and engaging in thinking and experiences that lead to developing social awareness and action.

REFLECT, MOTIVATE, AND ACT

Reflect on Our Fears to Find Our Inner Courage

- *What gives you the courage to overcome your fears and doubts when working with controversial topics? Why is this important?*

- *What experts can support you and your students in this learning journey?*
- *How will you encourage parents and community members to be a part of the conversation?*

Motivate Students to Discover Their Courage

- *What gives students the courage to overcome their fears and doubts when working with uncomfortable ideas?*
- *What do your students want to ask parents and the community?*

Take Action to Bring Community and Classroom Together Through Teacher Practice

- *What experiences can you create that will invite parents and community members to engage in the conversation? Who should be a part of these experiences?*
- *How might you communicate experiences to students? Parents? School stakeholders?*

Part III

SEEING IT ALL

Assisting students in *seeing small* allows them to better understand what motivates humans. Providing them with opportunities to *see big* helps them see how these actions and beliefs form the larger systems. As teachers, we must help them put it all together and *see it all*. Wesch (2018) describes the following as tools that are a part of the anthropologist toolkit: communication, empathy, and thoughtfulness. These tools help anthropologists *see it all*. They can also help teachers and students—all humans—*see it all*. As teachers, we can assist students in engaging with all these tools. The experiences described throughout this book emphasize communicating with teachers, with each other, with the larger community. Through this communication, we learn the stories of others, and in doing so, we learn to accept people as they are, developing our empathy muscles. Once we can empathize with others, we can practice thoughtfulness as we reimagine what our world can look like so that it serves everyone, not just a few. These tools, along with the data we've gathered while *seeing big* and *small*, allows us to *see it all*.

Up until this point in the book, we've focused on preparing student mindsets and studying texts. Part III brings all this work together so that we can use the information we have gathered to help students *see it all* and move past just the study of literature. Reading literature and other texts should be the starting point. To truly change the world, we must demonstrate to students how inquiry grounded in communication, empathy, and thoughtfulness can lead to action. Chapter 7 begins this work by showing students how to bring everything together. We push them to see their surroundings in a different light, examining how the small details we take for granted exist within a larger system and looking at the questions that are raised when we take a step back and truly see an object, place, or idea that we take for granted. In doing so, we begin to identify problems that can be approached through design thinking, an approach to problem-solving that involves empathy, communication, and thoughtfulness. In Chapter 8, we offer approaches that allow students to *see it all* by using the experiences in our classes to develop questions and identify social issues that matter to them. We demonstrate how we can help students act, whether it be by raising awareness in others or by going out into the community and creating a change they want to see in the world. Finally, Chapter 9 helps teachers *see it all* by stepping back and exploring the role assessment plays in the bigger picture of our own teaching and community contexts. How can we all start to move the work forward? How can we all help our students accomplish the incredible?

SEVEN

Fence-Testing the Conditions of Learning

You can't change how other people think and act, but you're in full control of you. When it comes down to it, the only question that matters is this: If nothing in the world ever changes, what type of man are you gonna be?

—Nic Stone

Every day, each of us enters a teaching context that is bounded by fences constructed by the community. If we have taught in multiple schools, we understand that those fences look different in different communities. At times, they are low, white picket fences that allow us to see out and others to see in. Fences like these provide us with flexibility as they allow us to visit with neighbors and take information we glean from those conversations back to our instruction. These fences give us a sense of freedom in our classroom, yet there is no mistaking that we're still bound by community expectations, which sometimes encourage traditional, sometimes whitewashed, teaching. Other times, we are bound by privacy fences. No one can see what we are doing in our classrooms, and we cannot see what others are doing either. We might construct these fences ourselves, shutting the world out and doing our own thing, or they may have been constructed by schools or districts. Teachers have the flexibility to talk with each other within its perimeter, however outside voices are discouraged. But at least those of us who exist within the privacy fences are not facing the barbed-wire fencing that encloses some of our colleagues. We can identify these colleagues (and their students) through the scars created by the sharp spikes of district mandates that are not student-centered.

Over the course of our careers, we have worked within all these fences. Currently, Sarah has more latitude than some. She can reach over her fence and collaborate with teachers in other districts. She has the freedom to design her own curriculum. She has the space for creative movement. But while her fence is attractive in many ways, she is open to the examination of a community that has certain expectations for what teaching should look like, for what their children should do, and for what their children should believe. Robyn, on the other hand, escaped from a barbed-wired reading program into a district bound by a privacy fence. Robyn's curriculum director kept professional development in house and mandated that ELA teachers teach from the textbook 80 percent of the time, leaving little space for novels or other important texts. Intimidated by *the* test, teachers were expected to give standardized skills-based quizzes each week and to only teach material that was deemed to be at the 7th-grade level. Yet, teachers had enough autonomy within buildings to find ways to design student-centered lessons.

While we understand the factors that have motivated the building of these fences, we also recognize that when we fence ourselves in, when we fence students in, we restrict worldviews. And it is through such narrow views of the world that we, as a society, have created many of the social problems we are currently battling. If we want to broaden our students' understanding of the world, we must begin to examine the fences we live within, fence-test the learning conditions that exist, and search for ways to push beyond those fences. *Fence-testing* is a term coined by Antero Garcia (2019) and was inspired by a scene in the movie *Jurassic Park*. While describing the intelligence of the dinosaurs, Muldoon, the park's game warden, explained how they worked together to escape their confines: "They were testing the fences for weaknesses, systematically. They remember." As teachers, we have the power to fence-test. We can, as Garcia (2019) describes it, use fence-testing "as a means of speculating about alternatives to a mundane present." Working together, collectively, we can systematically find the weaknesses in our fences so that we can expose our students to the larger world.

Through fence-testing, we must look beyond our own backyards and examine others'. We must forge pathways that lead to equitable pedagogy. We can't flatten the world into two sides. We must recognize, as author Randy Ribay (2020) states in his book *Patron Saints of Nothing*, that the world is full of the hyphenated, those of us who identify as more than one thing. If we embrace the hyphenated, we can no longer exist within fences designed to keep half of us out. We must find those weaknesses to, one day, dismantle our fences altogether.

This work also requires us to, as Garcia (2019) states, "reconcile the hyphenated when we ask: What kind of future are we designing, co—constructing, coauthoring, co—dreaming?" (para. 5). If we let our students be our copilots as we push back against the boundaries we have in place in school, as we look out into the community for ways to make learning more meaningful, we not only teach our students how to fence-test themselves, but we also help them reimagine the world as a different place. This chapter shares strategies we have used to help our students embrace the questions that emerge during their novel study and use these questions to fence-test the boundaries of their worlds. While we cannot, as Nic Stone (2017) states, control or maybe even change the way others act, we want our students to understand that they can determine who they want to be. And maybe, just maybe, in the process we create a world that celebrates the hyphenated.

OUR STUDENTS' LIVED EXPERIENCES

Miguel (pseudonym) was the best Rubik's Cube solver in Sarah's junior high school. He could navigate those blocks with ease, quickly lining up color blocks to the amazement of his friends. Not only did Miguel enjoy solving the puzzle, but he also saw it as a way to connect with students in the small, rural, predominantly white community after moving there from Mexico the previous year. At the beginning of his 8th-grade year, he brought his collection of Rubik's cubes to school so that he and his friends could tinker with them during lunch.

That spring, another year of Genius Hour began (see Chapter 8). Genius Hour is passion-based and student driven, so Miguel's inquiry project was easy to predict. As students started to design their project proposals, Miguel had the idea to start a Rubik's Cube club for their junior high school. Thinking that this would be a great addition to the school, Miguel started working on a plan that would outline what the new club might look like.

Miguel was also very interested—and very talented—in art. Miguel continued to develop his Genius Hour inquiry, and he was disrupted one day by a neighboring computer teacher who introduced Miguel to the New York–based

artist, Giovanni Contardi. Miguel's eyes widened while he viewed the video—his growing smile signaled that his Genius Hour inquiry was going to drastically change. Giovanni Contardi is an artist who uses Rubik's Cubes to design pixelated murals—specifically of famous celebrities and athletes. After the encouragement of the computer teacher and Sarah, Miguel decided to contact Contardi using Instagram direct messaging.

For almost an entire class period, Miguel communicated back and forth with this artist as he asked every question he could think of in relation to the artist's work. It was with this communication that Miguel's thinking shifted. Not only did Miguel want to implement a Rubik's Cube club, but he also wanted to design his own mural that integrated both the school's mascot and a Mexican flag—all out of Rubik's cubes. Miguel wanted to create something that never existed before but also find a way to represent his own heritage in our school culture.

Miguel knew that he not only needed a plan, but he also needed funding, time, and help. He needed to create a budget for all the Rubik's Cubes he needed to achieve his goal. With the help of the computer teacher, Miguel researched how to purchase Rubik's Cubes in a global market. With the help of another high school teacher, Miguel constructed a pixelated prototype of his design. And, with Sarah's help, he wrote a grant supported by the alumni of the school to gain the funding for his club and mural. His excitement and determination were palpable.

We wish this story had a different ending. Miguel never received his funding, and he never had a chance to see his vision come to life. His family decided to move back to Mexico so that he could attend high school there. While this decision was disheartening to both Miguel and Sarah, this experience is still worth celebrating. Miguel took a risk by reaching beyond his fences and contacting an expert in New York to help him think about his questions. He developed those answers into goals that superseded anything he had ever attempted before in school. He learned how to use his voice and talents to reenvision his world. And he is better prepared to climb future fences because, as Sarah reminded Miguel, sometimes it's the journey that helps make us become who we're meant to be, not the end result.

IN DIALOGUE

After finishing *The 57 Bus* by Dashka Slater, students composed questions they had about the book for a Socratic

Seminar. This conversation was prompted by a question posed by Valory: "People call themselves your friend. They say they were there, but they weren't. Say they are coming, but they don't show. Say they have your back as they get their knives out. What is the significance of this poem to this text and how can you relate to it?"

Valory: Moving on to the second part of this question, I think teenagers in general could relate to this poem because often in junior high school people are left behind by their friends because either somebody is changing or they just decide that they're not cool enough for them anymore. Because when you're a teenager, everybody is making changes in their lives and how they want to be seen, so often other people have to try and find new friends because they're getting left behind by other people because either they don't want to change or the other people don't think they could change.

Valory: An example of this is in the ISU Queer Edbirds interview. One of the interviewees, I believe her name was Stacy (name changed), said that some of her friends were pretty cruel to her whenever she came out as bisexual, which was upsetting to her, since I mean her friends were supposed to be supportive of her and they were not doing what their job was as a friend.

Wyatt: To go along with the second part, I think one part is, it's kind of like when you're close to someone and not when *you* do it but when *they* make a decision, how you feel about it. It's kind of like I said before, how does their action affect you, but I remember watching an interview on the psychologist, what was his name again? It was, it was the nurse's husband?

Wyatt: Bond, that's what it was! Mr. Bond. In his talk—I had a little talk before he actually was

> *During the first part of the question, students played it safe, sticking to examples from the book. As they turned to how they could relate to the poem, students drew upon community members who had been interviewed while they were reading the book. These outside voices allowed students to begin fence-testing ideas, bringing in perspectives they may otherwise not have considered.*

going to speak with a group of people—was talking about how the peer help that can be helped with major trauma is kinda like your soul and your body are one. So, you almost, it's not magic, but he said it's almost as if, if you have someone who cares about you and that you care about, say that they care about you, just say and be there for you, it almost helps with the soul and transfers into the mental recovery.

Kate: Valory said that sometimes you don't want to change to be still friends with friends that are changing and sometimes you do try to change for them, which is kind of even, maybe, worse for yourself because you might not even realize it or you might realize it, but I just thought that it's weird because sometimes you don't want to change and sometimes you do, just to stay with your friends . . .

Clara: Like in junior high, people are trying to get on the popular side so they ditch their friends or leak their secrets and start gossip just so they can be considered one of the cool kids and so . . .

> *As members of a small, privileged white community, our students had no experience with the kinds of traumatic events that happened to the main characters: Sasha who identified as nonbinary and Richard, a young Black man who lit Sasha's skirt on fire. One way to help them develop empathy, however, is for our students to recognize how peer pressure and peer relationships can impact decision-making. This allows them to better understand why injustices like the ones in the book can occur.*

Abby: I feel like these are the years where you can recognize who your real friends are and who are the friends you can tell are just there. I feel you can be able to find out who you are going to be able to be with and deal with and just the ones who are not always there for you.

Reese: Kate was saying about change and stuff and how people are changing but sometimes they feel like they're forced to change to fit in or something. So, I was just thinking, what are your guys' thoughts on changing? Do you think it's good for people to change, or do you think we should all stay the same, and not be forced to?

Jacob: I think it depends on what kind of change. But, me, I feel like you shouldn't have to change yourself to roll with your friends. I don't know. I feel like you should always be yourself and not have to alter that.

Valory: Sometimes change is okay.

Jacob: Yeah.

Valory: It just depends on, you have to think is this what you want to be? Like when you were little, is this who you looked up to yourself as an adult or high schooler or anybody? And is this who you wanted to see? Is this who you want to become for the rest of your life, or do you want to stay the same? It's really just your decision as to who you want to go as.

Wyatt: Yeah. I think you guys make a great point. Change will happen. I think it's kinda like a progression. You're always going to be changing, but like I said, the good changes, and Val made a great point, who you want to be. I think Sasha is a good example of choosing the person who you want to be, your true identity.

> *While Valory had not read* Dear Martin, *here she echoed Nic Stone's words about the importance of understanding who you want to be. Through the reading of* The 57 Bus, *as well as the supportive strategies they experienced while reading, Valory and the other students were beginning to fence-test their world. Do they want to be confined by the fences constructed by others, or do they want to seek out other possibilities while staying true to themselves?*

TRANSFORMING THROUGH PRACTICE: LEARNING BEYOND THE FENCES

To fence-test with students, we must introduce them to the world beyond our fences. And we must help them recognize the role that the world has in their learning. As they move to and from school, they understand they are in different spaces, but they, like many in society, treat those spaces as separate from each other. This should not, and cannot, be the case if we want to shift our students toward a deeper understanding and appreciation of the world, if we want them to gain the experiences needed to make change. As Miguel demonstrates, using social media to reach beyond not only the school fence, but the community fence, can expose students to new ways of thinking, cultivate student talent, and inspire them to create for a larger audience. Literature and other texts can also help students fence-test their boundaries. In traditional novel units, students are not always given the space to test their fences. Rather, they see these units as just another part of school, a part that some enjoy as they read and discuss books and that some avoid as they bluff their way through the reading, worksheets, and projects. But when we approach literature through an inquiry-driven social-justice lens—whether overtly through literature and discussions that focus specifically on social issues like LGBTQ+ rights or more subtly by offering opportunities for students to create spaces that celebrate their cultures—students begin to see how books can open their eyes to a world beyond school. It is through these experiences that students like Valory can begin to question who they want to be. This means we need to create experiences that support their questioning, not only before and during the reading of the book but also, and perhaps more importantly, after they complete a book. Our work has not finished when we read the last paragraph. Rather, it is time to start climbing those fences.

Kris Gutiérrez (2008) has long advocated for what she and other educational researchers call the third space. Gutiérrez describes the third space as "a transformative space where the potential for an expanded form of learning and the development of new knowledge are heightened" (p. 152). Third spaces provide ample room for fence-testing in that they merge two spaces that are often treated as separate—most often the spaces of home and school. Advocates for approaching education through a lens of third space recognize that people live their lives in multiple settings, forcing educators "to consider the significant overlap across these boundaries as people, tools, and practices travel through different and even contradictory contexts and activities" (Gutiérrez, 2008, p. 150). In our work, we have witnessed the heightened development of new knowledge that Gutiérrez describes when we look to the overlaps. We see students developing new ideas that may not otherwise have been considered. It is through these new ideas that our students begin fence-testing their worlds, and as they push at the boundaries of their fences, they push us to consider ways to expand our own.

The upcoming strategies demonstrate just two of the ways we have helped students learn beyond the fences of school. One strategy embraces the third space by asking students to examine an aspect of their lives outside of school to help them create meaning within school. The other prompts them to pose questions that allow them to think about ways they can impact society.

THEORY TO PRACTICE

Kris Gutiérrez: Although much of Kris Gutiérrez's work focuses on language learners, insights from working in this field apply across contexts. Teachers can build upon Gutiérrez's work on expanding spaces for learning by considering how students' learning and experiences in out-of-school spaces can influence how students shape their inquiries. The following focuses on a discussion between Gutiérrez and Joanne Larson (2007) that explores expanded spaces for learning. They can serve as models for how to think about putting his work into practice.

- **Mentor Moments (see Chapter 6):** "[T]he point that we're making is that the transformative spaces and transformative learning that we're talking about can't be reduced to a specific curricular program. It's about designing a particular kind of ecology that is saturated with tools, forms and networks of support, and a variety of ways of organizing learning."
- **Genius Hour (see Chapter 8):** "We believe that the notion of repertoires of practice captures both vertical and horizontal forms of expertise; this includes not only what students learn in formal learning environments such as schools but also what they learn while participating in a range of practices outside of school."
- **Documenting Community Stories (see Chapter 8):** "As critical educators, however, we have a responsibility to help students find hope and possibility and imagine new futures for themselves and their communities."

For more about Kris Gutiérrez's work in literacy and with language learners, check out the following resources:

- *Voice of Literacy* podcast: "Third Space with Dr. Kris Gutiérrez" at http://www.voiceofliteracy.org/posts/28304
- "CLRN Interview–Kris Gutiérrez" at https://www.youtube.com/watch?v=Bzv_po-ra-0
- "Ed-Talk: Expansive and Consequential Learning for English Teachers—Kris D. Gutiérrez" at https://www.youtube.com/watch?v=pKoVuKIsYd8&t=52s

---

KNOW YOUR SURROUNDINGS

What Is Know Your Surroundings?

Another challenge adapted from Michael Wesch's (2018) work Know Your Surroundings asks students to push beyond their typical approaches to seeing the world. Students are prompted to question their assumptions about what they see when examining an aspect of their worlds. For example, students focused on topics such as the impact of color on mood and how money shapes their lives. When examining these aspects of the world they take for granted, they are encouraged to consider how their larger culture impacts their interpretation of this aspect and to notice how small details matter. This emphasis on seeing big and seeing small helps them to see the world differently.

When engaging with the Know Your Surroundings strategy, students are tasked with identifying something in their life that is familiar to them, something that is so ordinary they take it for granted. Once they have identified this phenomenon, they are asked to look at it like someone who has never encountered such a practice. What aspects would seem strange? Students examine the role society and culture place in this practice, looking for new insights into what this activity might suggest about the world. Once they have begun to look at the phenomenon differently, they create a photo essay that captures their new thinking.

How Can Know Your Surroundings Help Students Fence-Test Their Learning?

If we want to be able to fence-test our boundaries, we must have a clear understanding of what those boundaries are. While school itself can play the role of gatekeeper, other invisible factors such as social and cultural norms can also bind our approach to learning. Know Your Surroundings helps students consider a phenomenon through a broader cultural lens and urges them to look at the smaller details that often dictate how the phenomenon takes shape. When students learn to look within their fences in this way, they are better prepared to see the weaknesses that exist in their understanding of the world.

Seeing the world more clearly and understanding that we all exist within certain fences better prepares students to ask the questions needed to rearrange their fences. These questions can lead to larger inquiries that have the potential to tear down the fences that separate them from a socially just, equitable world.

Before You Begin

Prior to engaging in this experience, it is important to understand that this challenge asks students to practice the art of seeing. Skills like observation and interpretation have been practiced throughout many classrooms in a student's learning journey but maybe not as often in connection with the human condition. Recognizing that students will need practice with these skills to construct thinking around their personal seeing experiences independently needs to be a priority when planning for this challenge.

Take time to reflect on your students' experiences with observation, especially when thinking about abstract observations and viewing concepts divergently. One approach is to develop a series of model descriptors for students to analyze in a schema-building, whole-class discussion. For example, ask students to examine an iPhone. Rather than seeing it as a phone, help students construct a new observation that eliminates what they already know about the phone (it's an iPhone) and focuses on what it actually is: an inanimate box that collects moments of time and freezes them in place. Having fun with observations around concepts or tools that students see in their everyday lives provide a sense of comfort and motivation toward this challenge. Using familiar concepts or tools can also provide opportunities for students to practice their critical literacy skills, recognizing that the iPhone is a status symbol that signals an interest in communication.

In the Moment

Step 1: Discuss what it means to practice the art of seeing. Take time to break down what this means in connection to real life. This may come in the form of teacher-led examples like above, but it could also mean class discussions around defining the term, as well.

Step 2: Model the art of seeing for students. In many ways, this type of observation can be considered abstract and asks us to look at things differently. This may not come naturally to all students as they continue to stretch these types of thought muscles. You may want to prepare several examples in anticipation of this step. Use a think-aloud strategy to model the questions you might ask while seeing an everyday object, demonstrating how to make observations about the object while answering the questions.

Step 3: Allow student groups to practice these observations with teacher support. After taking time

to model this type of observational thinking, allow student groups to play with their own thoughts in testing their own observations. While you could construct these group observations in the classroom, you may want to also think about what kinds of observations can be conducted outside of the classroom environment. Consider venturing outside of the classroom and participating in a community walk. Collaborative student groups can visit sections of the community and capture photos to bring back to the classroom so that they can be discussed.

Step 4: Ask student groups to share their analyses from their collected observations (like photos from the community walk, for example) with the entire class. Having students see their peers share their observations and practice the art of seeing provides more of an opportunity to stretch and shape their own personal skills. It may also inspire students to think about their own personal observations that they will conduct for the challenge work as they move forward to participate in this thinking independently.

Step 5: Invite students to conduct observations independently and use the questions and resources that support their experience. As students venture on their own to participate in the art of seeing, take time to break down the previous experiences into steps for this experience to be more manageable as an independent learner. Provide students with the steps to the process, which were adapted from Wesch's (2018) work at Anth101.

1: Think about things that you see others do that might communicate to other people outside of your culture as different. For example, you could think about things people collect or traditions people uphold.

2: Take time to list all the elements associated with this belief, behavior, or action. For example, if you think about how someone might own an extensive collection of something, brainstorm ideas that explore this in various ways such as—why does this collection exist? Where is it stored or displayed?

3: Using Wesch's term, the ability to "see big," think about why these ideas and practices continue to exist among people. What is it about their surroundings that might produce these practices? Why, for example, are they drawn to building a specific collection?

4: After you have come to a few key insights about these ideas or practices, capture four to five photos that would best portray your new understanding. Use these photos to show a compelling story related to your observations.

Step 6: Encourage students to write about their observations using the classroom support materials. In the breakdown found in Step 5, students are invited to think about the nature of their observations in connection to the human condition and explain these observations to an alien from another planet. These writings ask students to take something they have observed and stretch into seeing the purpose of these practices. By stretching this thought process in a variety of ways, we invite students to question these practices and promote a curiosity into why things exist in the ways that they do in our everyday world.

Step 7: Invite students to reflect on their observations and writings. The nature of this work has the potential to cultivate new questions, curiosities, and perspectives. Allow students to reflect on their observations and the art of seeing experiences to think about their world differently. These questions, curiosities, and perspectives can lead to further action as student-learning journeys continue throughout the school year.

The gathering-observations support guide is a helpful graphic organizer for students to use while participating in observations: https://tinyurl.com/5n7yt4c4

Making Learning Visible

The nature of this challenge affords students an opportunity to view the world around them in new ways. As we invite our students to view the world through different lenses, we must also encourage our students to keep this momentum moving forward by providing time to process these new thoughts and welcome students to channel these efforts into new understandings and possibly new actions.

Emma participated in this challenge by observing the concept of collecting or having a collection. On her blog, she posted several examples of collections she noticed in her observations and added a reflection to support her thoughts around this experience. One might think that

observing the act of collecting may not make an impact on student learning, but as seen in an excerpt outlined below, Emma constructs new wonders about the human condition that manifest into new personal understandings about viewing the world around her:

This challenge helped me see our culture and everything we do in a new light. I now notice that many things people do, such as collecting things, don't necessarily have logic behind them. How many activities do humans do that are ruled by emotions instead of reason? It makes me wonder how these habits in our cultures came to be, especially when some make little sense. However, it also makes me think about how humans can apply meaning and purpose to things that didn't have a reason to exist before. When we decide that we want or like something, it has value, even if it's not "useful." There's also other things in our culture that are useful but still can seem just as different, like the way the bell before class "controls" our movements through the school. These things developed so slowly over

---

KNOW YOUR SURROUNDINGS IN ACTION

- Anthropologist Dr. Michael Wesch (2018) encourages those who practice the art of seeing to not only look for the big but also find wonder in the small. Even starting with the small and familiar, students can use their observations to think critically about the motives and actions of others within those spaces.

- Sage observed the Christmas tree in her house and the other houses she saw at the time. From her short experience, she synthesized her findings in bigger ways by stating:

  This challenge made me realize that lots of things we as humans do are very weird, and many people do them in fear of being an outsider or being left out. It made me ask myself, "What other things do we do as humans so that we are more accepted? Why do we want to be accepted so much that we will go extremely out of our way to do something that may not even make sense to us?"

As Sage continues to develop her thoughts around conformity and social acceptance, she increases her chances of making connections like this with other concepts related to this in her world. If our students are formulating the questions, then they are certainly ready to explore the answers.

time that we can't imagine a time without [them], but there are different ways to do things that we just don't use.

If students can be given the freedom and the tools to view their world differently and the outcomes of that experience produce new perspectives, as teachers, it invites another wave of thought into the classroom. Imagine if Emma had those thoughts but then reverted into traditional, dated classroom practices and did nothing to move these thoughts forward into change-agent acts? Emma—the highly logical, self-proclaimed introvert—channeled her observational experience into becoming a leading voice in her class YPAR project (see Chapter 8) related to working with administration to develop a supportive mental-health space for junior/senior high school students. As this challenge provides a readiness to the next level of learning, it becomes the responsibility of teachers to channel these thoughts into next steps.

DESIGN THINKING

What Is Design Thinking?

In 2009, design thinking pioneer Tim Brown described design thinking as a framework to "solve complex challenges" (TED, 2009). While global heavyweights such as Apple, Google, and Airbnb have implemented design thinking into their product development and services, its purpose is to provide human-centered solutions. According to the Hasso Plattner Institute of Design at Stanford University (or known as d. school) (2018), the design thinking framework supports a five-stage process. And, while these stages may present themselves in a linear order, their implementation often ebbs and flows based on the needs of the challenge.

Stage 1: Empathize. For this stage, researchers seek to empathize with the target audience of the challenge to think about solutions that would connect in practical ways. Stanford d.school (2018) states that empathizing is "crucial to the human-centered design process such as design thinking because it allows you to set aside your own assumptions about the world and gain real insight into users and their needs."

Stage 2: Define. Once researchers understand the target audience, it becomes essential to define the problem or the issue. Another way of thinking about this may be in terms of the groups' needs. This identification is key when moving forward into solution-based thinking.

Stage 3: Ideate. With solid background information and a specific need defined, ideation asks researchers to brainstorm multiple solutions. This brainstorm can lead to innovative and personalized ways to fulfill a need.

Stage 4: Prototype. From the generated brainstorm, researchers can now begin taking their informed ideas and develop them into real-life products. In writing, we may consider this the first draft—it's not a complete product but it serves as a representation of what could be a final resolution to the need or problem.

Stage 5: Test. Oftentimes, testing a prototype can lead researchers into new considerations for the need or problem. This stage can also allow researchers to flow back to redefining the problem or constructing other prototypes to strengthen their designs.

How Can Design Thinking Help Students Fence-Test Their Learning?

As illustrated in the beginning of this chapter, fence-testing can come in many shapes and forms. When teachers desire fence-testing for their students but are unsure of how to step into these various fences, design thinking principles can serve as that entry point. Design thinking is important in helping our students develop inquiry mindsets. It encourages students to nurture curiosity together and seek solutions using a human-centric approach and helps them understand how our questions could have a variety of answers. If we use design thinking to help students begin with the why—why the questions exist in the first place, why the issue is important to the well-being of society—we empower students to develop inquiry studies that matter. We invite them to put aside their assumptions about people so they can empathize to brainstorm innovative solutions. In addition, we also foster a celebration for "failure" as they prototype and test their solutions in the real world. Ultimately, students begin to see how inquiry can help them fence-test their own conditions of learning by allowing them to design meaningful studies rather than just engaging in inquiry for the sake of inquiry.

Before You Begin

Design thinking not only allows students to identify goals and actions in their thinking, but it also provides a steady stream of feedback and insight from peers outside of the collaborative group—especially when it comes to developing prototypes and testing those ideas with others. Before participating in this activity, there ultimately needs to be a few elements in place to establish the ebb and flow of the design-thinking framework itself.

In preparation for working with design thinking, students participated in the research process centered on their questions after reading their whole-class novel. The novel provided a springboard of questions and curiosities for students to ask and categorize into a collaborative research outline. From there, students collected, curated, and annotated credible sources related to their focused topic. This collaborative research conducted by students serves as a bridge to working with design thinking. Using the beginning stages of the design-thinking framework, students worked together to think about the target audience and played with the question, "Who would care or need to know more about these big ideas collected in our research?" This question afforded students the ability to identify a target audience and start empathizing.

In addition to identifying target audiences (like for the awareness campaign described in Chapter 8), students also needed support in giving and receiving feedback in safe spaces. For this, students need practice in providing constructive feedback so that when it comes to prototyping and testing, students feel comfortable sharing their ideas and remain open to rethinking their designs. Trust Circles, as described in Chapter 9, can help students. As students begin the design-thinking stages, they can also begin to think about the pieces of their work they want to bring to the Trust Circle to get feedback and move their prototypes in new directions.

Along with preparing mindsets for this work, students may also need physical materials to ensure success throughout this process. One way students can manage the stages of design thinking can be in the form of field notes. Whether these notes are provided in a tangible folder or housed in a digital space, having one place for students to gather and keep track of their work throughout the design-thinking journey allows students to maintain ownership of their learning.

In the Moment

Step 1: Allow collaborative student groups to empathize with their target audience. As stated above, one of the first stages to design thinking is empathizing. Students should be afforded time to think about their target audience in a variety of ways—even if this means going beyond the classroom walls. To analyze their target audience, students should critically examine thoughts, feelings, actions, and words used within these groups. This formative stage permits students to use this critical examination as they move forward in their designs.

Step 2: Define the needs of the target audience and establish a focused goal. Defining these key areas not only becomes important for student work as they continue to navigate the design-thinking framework, but it also establishes the *why* behind their designs. For students working with research, for example, defining the target audience that will be informed by student-curated research can also shape the decisions around how this research will be communicated to a larger audience. Defining what research will be used and who will benefit from understanding it provides students with a path that focuses their writing as they move further into the framework.

Step 3: Seek mentor texts to help encourage and spark the ideation process. Strong mentor texts offer helpful guidance to student writers—especially as they first enter the writing process and need to formulate a variety of ideas. Curating and analyzing quality mentor texts invite students to think critically about the need or problem they are attempting to solve by seeing how others create similar solutions.

Step 4: Construct an authentic prototype—or first draft. Ideally, students should have a solid grip on their ideas toward developing a solution. At this point, they empathized with their target audience, defined their purpose and goal for their work, and analyzed other works that create similar solutions. This step encourages students to begin constructing authentic solutions that connect to their specific need or problem.

Step 5: Provide time for sharing, feedback, and revisions. Just like Disney animators share their constructive feedback in trust circles (see Chapter 9) when developing new animation concepts, students can test their prototypes among their peers. The ebb and flow of prototyping and testing happens readily within this final step. Encourage students to participate in trust circles often to shape and fine-tune their designs.

This graphic organizer from Sarah's awareness campaign work (see Chapter 8) walks students through the design thinking process and how to act: https://tinyurl.com/3psnrpw2.

Making Learning Visible

Design thinking allows students to play with ideas, seek out other perspectives, and shape new thoughts into more definitive plans of action. As students complete the design thinking framework, they continue to shape their ideas and construct deeper questions around their central issues. It is this framework that becomes the catalyst in how students act in effective and meaningful ways.

Design thinking played a pivotal role in the development of our student awareness campaigns (see Chapter 8). As they identified a focus for their campaign around normalizing mental health, they used the empathizing stage to determine that both teens and adults would benefit from their work. The defining stage in their campaign development became a natural next step as students reviewed and coded their collaborative research to match the information they wanted to share with their target audience. Once students knew who they wanted to talk to and what they wanted to talk about, ideating, prototyping, and testing different campaign products started to form among smaller groups.

Figure 7.1 features a logo created within this awareness campaign that purposefully shows a butterfly with a broken wing to represent the stress and trauma that can affect one's mental health while the other side represents positive health. The student group first constructed their idea around a set of wings along with the campaign's name "From Broken to Spoken." When presenting this prototype to the class trust circle (see Chapter 9), other students provided feedback that inspired the creators to shape their work into a butterfly. To them, the butterfly signified a meaning of growth and change—themes they had also seen across their initial research as investigators. While this student group continued to construct a series of prototypes of their logo, design thinking allowed them to create a final product that served as the face for the entire campaign.

Figure 7.1. Students created a logo for their awareness campaign that normalizes mental health care using design thinking.

DESIGN THINKING IN ACTION

As students started their collaborative awareness campaign (see Chapter 8) around breaking stereotypes connected to the perceptions of drug addiction, design thinking played a pivotal role in the development of the group's infographics. Prior to stepping into this work, this group of students worked to empathize with their identified target audience—teenagers ages 13 to 17—as well as defining the key information discovered in their research that would be applicable to their goals in educating others about their topic. When working through the defining stage of their plan, students in this group noted some of the characteristics that they needed to consider when formulating their writing. From their defining stage, they stated, "They [the target audience] need the info to be broken down so it's easier to understand and they need good visuals to capture their attention—like graphs, charts, and tables."

As seen in Figure 7.2, the collaborative group continued their thinking by ideating possible designs for their infographics. While it may seem like a collection of pencil sketches, it serves as a bridge to creating a series of prototypes related to infographic design. The notes highlighted in Figure 7.2 show the group thinking through their defining stage using visuals to support their decisions as creators. The illustrations constructed in the ideating stage afford students to think about how to present their content to their target audience and outline the ways in which they can visually speak to their research and help build prototype designs. To bring these prototypes to a larger audience, this group created a series of infographics based on their sketches to share with the class Trust Circle (see Chapter 9).

Figure 7.2. Students sketch out their ideas during the ideating stage of design thinking.

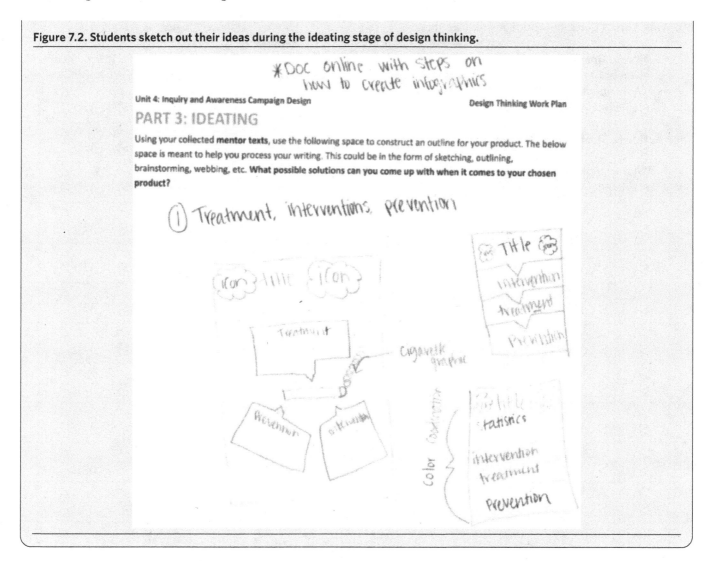

READING YOUR WORLD

While the experiences in this chapter begin and continue to be nurtured in the classroom setting, it is the action students take connected to those experiences that allows them to apply these thoughts to their world beyond school. Many of the activities outlined in this chapter provide a readiness to thinking differently about our students' surroundings and how learning is meaningful if we can experience it in real time.

And, while there are many other means with which we can engage students to think critically about the world around them, we hope that these activities help you think about how we can move learning into spaces that become real and tangible for students. When students are inspired to take action to make change, learning transforms into a greater power. But, to get there, our students look to us as they seek guidance and support along their learning journeys.

REFLECT, MOTIVATE, AND ACT

Reflect on a Path Beyond Your Own Fences

- *What kind of teacher do you want to be?*
- *What fences exist within your teaching context?*
- *How can you test these fences?*

Motivate You to Consider Your Learners' Fences

- *What kind of learners do your students want to be and what do they want to explore?*
- *What would look different in your classroom to help them be these learners?*

Take Action to Stretch Student Learning Boundaries

- *What experiences can you create that invite students to fence-test their learning?*

- *How will these experiences push learning boundaries?*
- *In what ways will you celebrate the successes of these movements? How will you celebrate the failures of these movements?*

EIGHT

Preparing to Accomplish the Incredible

Scrolling will never be enough. Reposting will never be enough. Hashtagging will never be enough. Because hatred has a way of convincing us that half love is whole. What I mean by that is we—all of us—have to fight against performance and lean into participation. We have to be participants. Active.

—Jason Reynolds

Confession time. When Robyn was in high school, she was an honor student who went on to become the class valedictorian. This was the golden ring to be won at the end of the game known as school. It was so coveted by those of us who embraced the game that we would, at times, stray away from doing what was right and do what was needed to win. One such time (and to be fair, there were only a couple of times) was during her sophomore chemistry class. The class was led by Mr. Watts (a pseudonym) who was, no doubt, a very smart man. He was not, however, a teacher. This was his first year in the classroom after a long career in science. He had no teacher preparation, and it showed. And he was faced with a group of very high-achieving students who wanted to ensure they still had a chance to win the game. So, what did this group of students do? They cheated every chance they got. Small alliances were formed around the room with different students tasked with figuring out the right answers on the worksheets, and more importantly, on the tests. Robyn left that class with her coveted A but very little scientific knowledge. After all, it wasn't about the learning. It was about winning the game.

For students like Sarah, the game was also of great value. Every day, she worked hard to understand the game that she desperately wanted to play. But since she was labeled early on as a lowly robin that couldn't keep up with the cardinals, she was constantly reminded of her deficiencies in the game. So, Sarah became obsessed with the game for a very different reason. She wanted to stake her right to be a part of the game. Later in high school, Sarah became overly focused on her grades, desired the "A," and took every advanced course she could. While these choices afforded her a college acceptance letter, Sarah missed out on the classes and content she wanted to learn because she never wanted to be labeled as "less

than" for the remainder of her school career. And learning, once again, became second to schooling.

Yet, there was another aspect of school where we both participated for the right reasons: extracurriculars. As president of her senior class, Robyn harnessed her passion for families in need by spearheading an adopt-a-family effort around the winter holidays. After spending hours on the phone soliciting donations from local businesses, she was able to multiply the number of adopted families who could be included well beyond the original goal. Sarah had a similar experience when she served as president of the Student Council. Also concerned about families in need, she helped raise enough money to serve more than 40 local families breakfast with Santa and distribute gifts to each child in attendance. Like the students we work with today, we had the capacity and drive to make a difference in our worlds. Yet, we had to find the guidance for how to do this on our own. We weren't learning how to budget for large shopping trips in math class. We weren't learning how to persuade businesses to donate in English class. We weren't learning how to civically engage with our communities in social studies class. Can you imagine what we could have accomplished if we had been learning all these things in our classes?

Maya Angelou once said, "If children are given the chance to believe they're worth something—if they truly believe that—they will insist upon it" (Azzam, 2013). We see this in our classrooms every day. When we stopped checking curricular boxes and drawing upon impersonal projects and began to really see our students, to value their voices, we unearthed sparks they had long ago buried as they participated in the game of school. When nurtured, these sparks can create fires that burn away the insecurities that often lead to societal injustices.

Although we may not like to admit it, the structure of traditional schooling labels our students as inferior. As students have fewer *years* of experience in the world, we tend to devalue the actual rich experiences, talents, and questions they do have. When we do this, we deprive them of their dignity. Dignity, as Angelou (Azzam, 2013) described, is "a belief in oneself, that one is worthy of the best. . . . Dignity really means that I deserve the best treatment I can receive. And that I have the responsibility to give the best treatment I can to other people." The approach we describe in this book is intended to instill dignity within our students. In doing so, we help them recognize the importance of that last aspect of dignity—the realization that others in the world—even those who may look and believe differently—deserve to be treated well.

Angelou also said, "All men are prepared to accomplish the incredible if their ideals are threatened." Our students are currently in the stage of formulating their ideals. As teachers, we can let them blindly replicate the ideals of their families and communities, or we can offer them opportunities that allow them to push back against ideas (their families' as well as our own), explore alternative perspectives, and try on new ideas. We can allow them to approach learning with dignity. In doing so, we can help them develop a foundation that they are willing to fight to protect, a set of ideals that will prompt them to accomplish the incredible.

Teaching and learning are not easy tasks. But they can be soul-filling tasks when we stop approaching teaching and learning, as Angelou (Azzam, 2013) says, "by rote and by threat and even by promise" (p. 13). If we keep teaching by rote, we have no chance of conquering the social problems that perpetuate the systems school and society have created. If we keep teaching by threat, we strip students of their dignity and their desire to engage in the world in a way that leads to the incredible. And if we keep teaching by promise, we risk losing credibility by offering rewards we cannot deliver. So, instead, we must teach with care, with empathy, with love. And if we lead with care, empathy, and love, we will find that our students will reciprocate with care, empathy, and love. And then, they *will* accomplish the incredible. How can they not? Because when we approach the world in this way, we begin to see the importance of fighting against performance, against feigning that we are doing what is right, and the importance of becoming active citizens who can change the world.

OUR STUDENTS' LIVED EXPERIENCES

By Sarah's second year of implementation, Genius Hour, an instructional approach that devotes one day of the week

where students develop inquiries around their interests, had already gained a reputation in her school. Students would approach her early in the school year with ideas for projects that would not commence for weeks, excited about the opportunity to be in control of their learning. Inquiries around potential careers, new hobbies, or topics of interest permeated students' discussions. And given the nature of Genius Hour, these inquiries made sense. But Sarah realized Genius Hour could accomplish even more when a small group of students came to her with an idea that had the potential to transform school culture. This became the day when Sarah understood the power of disruption and student action.

Elijah, Ginny, and Becca (all pseudonyms) had an idea they were thinking about in connection to LGBTQ+ acceptance in their school environment. They had noticed that students within the school often carelessly tossed around demeaning and offensive words that targeted those in the small LGBTQ+ population within the school and they wanted to stop this. They wanted to focus their inquiry on changing the way students spoke to each other, create a safe environment for all students and staff within the school, and promote acceptance of differences.

And so, these passionate students' mission to accomplish the incredible began. They researched methods for promoting awareness. They identified and consulted with a mentor who had graduated from the school and who had transitioned from female to male in his years since his own 8th-grade year. They designed a series of prints and videos to help educate the general student population about their cause. By late April, they were excited to finish polishing their work for the community presentation, which would occur in a few short weeks. But it soon became evident that not all members of their small community shared in their excitement.

This first became evident when Ginny's parents asked for a meeting to share insights about a conversation that had occurred at a softball game. Several parents had approached them with concerns about the group's project. Ginny's parents were unclear as to why the project caused alarm among many of their friends. One parent even voiced her concern about the project's posters that promoted support and acceptance toward the LGBTQ+ community. This parent didn't want her daughter to see or believe in anything connected to the LGBTQ+ community. As Ginny's parents shared their experience, it became clear that their conversation with the other parents troubled them. Their friends' views contradicted their own in ways they had never expected. They were there because they *wanted* this project to continue.

Their meeting was timely. Later, that same week, Sarah received a classroom visit from her building administrator and the parent who had raised her concerns to Ginny's parents. Both voiced the same concerns about the project and its message to the student population. Sarah was asked to take down her students' work. Worried about her students' upcoming community presentation, she contacted the students and their parents, asking them to consider whether the students would be safe to share their work with a community audience. Undeterred, the students and parents wanted this presentation to happen. Elijah, Ginny, and Becca were prepared to present their research, resources, and videos with the community—regardless of the community response. Their parents would be there to support their children's efforts in this semester-long journey.

On the night of the presentation, not only did the student group walk into a room to see their parents, but they faced a standing-room-only classroom. To their surprise, they discovered the room was filled with students and adults who wanted to support them. These 8th-grade students had found the courage to stand up to the very adults who perpetuated fear about the LGBTQ+ community, and they discovered allies in the community. Elijah, Ginny, and Becca found their dignity, and in doing so, they accomplished something pretty incredible. They walked away from their presentation that night feeling accomplished and empowered. Their parents, who had despaired over the community's reaction, walked away with a reignited sense of hope. And, Sarah walked away with a renewed determination. The drive and agency in her students pushed her to stay the course and encouraged her to develop a new lens toward teaching: When students are in the driver's seat focusing on issues that matter to them, they can, and often will, take meaningful action.

IN DIALOGUE

As a part of their semester-long YPAR project (described in more detail later in the chapter), students in Sarah's 1st-hour class determined that their community was in need of an outdoor space where everyone in the community was welcome and could come together and socialize and learn. This excerpt from Abby's blog shares her thinking as she begins the planning process with her group.

> *By articulating her hopes for her class's project, Abby gives herself goals to strive toward.*

> *In working toward her goals for the project, Abby recognizes that she needs to articulate specific actions that need to be taken in order for the project to be successful.*

Hopes and Expectations

I have many hopes for this project. For example, I hope that our idea will be approved by The Village Board and we will be able to create our space. Additionally, I hope that it will turn out to be a good-looking space that many people within the community and school will go to. I also hope that the space will be kept up and treated with respect so we don't have to worry about fixing the space up again.

There are some things that we can do to help us get The Village Board to let us create the space. First, we need to make a professional, well thought out design that will show how serious we are about building this space. If they don't think we really want to create this space, what will convince them to let us use it and possibly make the space [better]? Additionally, we could make it apparent that not many people use it and that it is becoming worn down without insulting them. If we insult them while doing this, I doubt they'll be very happy with us. We could also talk about the fact that we were funding it so they would know that we weren't expecting them to pay for the project. Knowing that they wouldn't have to pay for it would probably further convince them that this

> *Abby's ideas for moving forward with the project stem from many of the smaller strategies she engaged in earlier in the semester. Participating in the Media Campaign (described later in the chapter) taught her about the importance of research and design, and Mentor Moments helped her recognize the value in seeking out experts.*

> *The YPAR project allowed Abby to visualize learning differently. This new vision for what school could look like motivated her to think differently about space and time in school.*

> *In another blog post, Abby reflected upon what she had learned about YPAR: "I have learned a bunch so far with YPAR including the fact that us students can actually change a lot more in our environment than I thought we had the power to do. I also learned more about some of the things we have in our community that we can be proud of and what stuff in the community that could be changed.*

is something very serious to us and that we want to make something good for the community.

To make a space be good-looking that many people in the community will go to will be challenging, but I have some ideas that could help us. First, we could talk to design experts or people who have done things like this before. This could possibly give us feedback for our project, examples to look at, and information that we need to make our space great. Additionally, we can look up popular spaces online to take notes on and learn from. This would give us real-life examples that we could use towards our own project. We can also talk to the community and see what they would like the space to look at. This would help us know what would attract people to the space, and it could make people feel more involved.

I also have many expectations for this project. Some of those expectations include it being a space where many people can go hang out, learn, or (hopefully) play basketball. Additionally, I expect the space to be functional and utilized. Last but not least, I expect the space to be built in time for us to use the space next year.

We can build a space where many people can go hang out, learn, or (hopefully) play basketball. We can do this by making it inviting and putting our full effort into making the space work. This would help people feel comfortable and happy in the space which is our goal. We would also have to be budget cautious to make sure we have enough money to build the project and possibly make the basketball court safer and more playable. We will also make a space big enough for teachers and their class to go out and learn in a different space.

We can make the space we build functional. We can make the space functional by having a nice appearance that isn't too crazy or too dull. Having a neutral space will also contribute to the ability to make it a learning space. Additionally, we can include good seating that will allow people to talk to each other while also being practical.

TRANSFORMING THROUGH PRACTICE: ASSISTING STUDENTS IN ACCOMPLISHING THE INCREDIBLE

This chapter begins with the words of Jason Reynolds (2020). His powerful words remind us that we cannot

sit idly by, nodding our heads. Teachers and students must be active participants in reshaping our world. As we continue to examine ways to help provide our students with agency, we keep more of his guidance in mind: "There's no way you can want to do away with injustice unless you want to do away with all of it. Remember that. You can't be anti-racist, but tease people about their weight. You can't fight for women's rights, and talk about your classmates who learn differently. I know, I know, you can't fight every fight. Except . . . you can. Accept . . . you can" (Reynolds, 2018, Item number 2).

Teaching with the greater good of the community in mind is one way that we can accept our responsibility to fight injustice. At times, this means we tackle social issues such as racism, sexism, classism, homo- or transphobia head-on, creating opportunities for our students to explore the roots of the issues and to, as Elijah, Ginny, and Becca demonstrate, come face-to-face with their communities' prejudices in hopes of changing the larger community narrative. At other times, this means we design experiences that allow our students, as Abby illustrates, the agency to identify the problems they see in the community—even if those problems may seem minor on the surface—and create solutions that bring hope and beauty to their neighborhoods. Both approaches have room to exist, and should exist, in our curricular design because both approaches nurture empathy for others and demonstrate the reverberating effects of taking action. They move students from passive learners to active creators. They instill dignity within our students. And to combine the ideas of Angelou (Azzam, 2013), when we have dignity, we can accomplish the incredible.

Teaching through inquiry is our path forward. But we cannot teach inquiry just for inquiry's sake. Too often, we see inquiry conducted around inconsequential matters. We get it. We've designed such units ourselves. We recognize that there is something to be said for designing units such as this because they can help our students develop habits of mind. And we understand that our students, especially those who have embraced the game of school, cannot jump into heavy inquiries. There need to be scaffolds along the way. Yet, we cannot stop with these types of inquiries. To do so would be equivalent to the scrolling described by Reynolds and Kendi (2020).

To develop students who are active participants in their education and in society, we need to embrace the philosophy of John Dewey (1903), who emphasized

---

THEORY TO PRACTICE

John Dewey: John Dewey was a strong advocate for education as an experience, emphasizing the role of democracy and social reform in schools. He argued that schools should not be separate from the world outside of school, but that students should learn how to live in schools—not just focus on content. Excerpts from his book *Democracy and Education* (1923) follow, highlighting how disruptive inquiry fits within Dewey's philosophies. They can serve as models for how to think about putting his work into practice.

- **What We Keep (see Chapter 1):** "Just as the senses require sensible objects to stimulate them, so our powers of observation, recollection, and imagination do not work spontaneously, but are set in motion by the demands set up by current social occupations. The main texture of disposition is formed, independently of schooling, by such influences. What conscious, deliberate teaching can do at most is to free the capacities thus formed for fuller exercise, to purge them of some of their grossness, and to furnish objects which make their activity more productive of meaning."

- **The Investigation Mixtape (see Chapter 3):** "Except in dealing with commonplaces and catch phrases one has to assimilate, imaginatively, something of another's experience in order to tell him intelligently of one's own experience."

- **Deconstructing the Familiar (see Chapter 4):** "We rarely recognize the extent in which our conscious estimates of what is worthwhile and what is not, are due to standards of which we are not conscious at all. But in general, it may be said that the things which we take for granted without inquiry or reflection are just the things which determine our conscious thinking and decide our conclusions."

For more about John Dewey's work in democratic and progressive education, check out the following resources:

- "Stanford Encyclopedia of Philosophy: John Dewey" at https://plato.stanford.edu/entries/dewey/
- "John Dewey's 4 Principles of Education" at https://www.youtube.com/watch?v=y3fm6wNzK70
- *How We Think* by John Dewey

---

democracy in education and the importance of self-critical communities of inquiry. The self-critical, we believe, is a vital piece of our work. If we are to answer Reynolds's (2020) call to be active participants in the dismantling of injustices, we must teach our students to examine the systems we live in, as well as their roles within those systems. This means our classrooms must become the communities of inquiry that Dewey promoted, rather than maintaining the traditional passive role of learning that schools often perpetuate. We cannot contribute to, as Dewey described it, the stifling of autonomy in our students. Inquiries developed through social consciousness can help our students bring about the social change described by Dewey, by Reynolds, by Angelou.

Unlike in previous chapters, what follows are not strategies. Rather, they are larger approaches to teaching and learning that build upon the strategies we have outlined previously. Each takes time. While we have typically implemented at least two of them in a school year, you may prefer to start with just one. Each approach is built with the intent of helping students become more self-critical and socially conscious. And each is intended to help students understand their potential for accomplishing the incredible.

MEDIA CAMPAIGN

What Is a Media Campaign?

A Media Campaign is exactly what it sounds like—a series of public service announcements designed to convince a larger public to think differently about a topic. Through a Media Campaign, students take what they have learned through their explicit examination of media and apply their understanding to an issue inspired by the novel we studied.

Media Campaigns are developed after students identify an issue in the book that they feel passionate about. Together, they research the issue, develop a message designed to reach a larger audience, and create original media to convey their message. Whether it is a commercial, a print ad, a social media post, a mural, or even a T-shirt, students compose photos, plan and record video, utilize graphic-design programs, and consider the statements different fonts make.

How Can Media Campaigns Help Students Accomplish the Incredible?

Media Campaigns provide students with an avenue to leverage their own voices around an issue that matters to them.

They encourage students to examine the issue from multiple viewpoints and to build empathy with others. They give students a concrete way to act. And while finances may limit some of what they can create, they learn how to use their available tools and resources to reach beyond the classroom walls. In the years since we began implementing the campaign, students have had the opportunity to have their voices validated by the authors of the books that inspire their work. In this day of social media, the possibilities for creating messages that can be seen and shared are endless. When their work is valued by others, they gain the confidence needed to continue to push themselves toward the incredible.

Media Campaigns are rooted in inquiry. Students take the experiences they have had before and while reading the novel and consider the questions the text evoked in them. Meaningful experiences lead to meaningful questions. And this leads to doing inquiry for a greater social good rather than just going through the motions (Beach et al., 2022; Juliani, 2014; Mirra et al., 2015; Vasquez et al, 2019). Further, campaigns demonstrate one way to share their new understandings with others, one way to, perhaps, make a difference in how others think.

Before You Begin

Prior to students collaboratively constructing media awareness campaigns, student groups need time to explore the answers to their questions and gather research from multiple sources. After completing a whole-class novel, students ask questions about and around the text. Student-constructed questions may be directly motivated by the novel, but they can also come from the variety of text experiences students participate in throughout the first half of the unit–schema-building activities, anchor activities, community interviews, and more.

As students construct a generous list of questions, they record their curiosities on a master list so that, as a class, they can synthesize these questions into bigger themes. The themes generated from this experience become the catalyst to the students' collaborative research and underpinning focus of their Media Campaign work.

In working with these established themes, student groups continue to formulate questions and annotate research around their newly developed questions. Collaboratively, students develop a Research Bank—a shared document that houses key research, links to credible research, and connections to the bigger themes. Once students compile their research, encourage students to think about how this collected information could be shared with others. And, while the Media Campaign serves as the general direction in sharing student collected research, student groups ultimately choose the information they want to share, who they want to target as they construct media, and how this information will be presented.

In the Moment

Step 1: Build a schema around the concept of awareness campaigns. Take time to introduce this concept by examining effective campaigns on a national level. Allow students to explore the characteristics of awareness campaigns such as those created by the AdCouncil. Once students examine these campaigns, ask them to share their findings as a whole class. This moment of sharing can serve as a foundation to the decision-making collaborative groups face later in the development of their own campaigns.

Step 2: Encourage student groups to evaluate the research they collected prior to starting the project and identify an aspect to focus on in their campaigns. A lot of research can be collected as a collaborative group but not all the research may be relevant to the focus of the campaign. Providing students time to think about the information they want to share in the form of their campaign becomes an essential step in this construction.

Step 3: Establish a target audience, develop goals, and assign roles. Once students have determined the key points of research and focus for their campaign work, student groups must decide on the target audience of this information. This is also a good time to introduce the rhetorical devices of ethos (asserting authority), pathos (appealing to emotion), and logos (appealing to logic). Demonstrating how these devices work to persuade audiences can assist students in understanding their developing campaign work through a more holistic lens. As students identify their target audiences and use modes of persuasion to think about the types of products that should be constructed within their campaign, it becomes important for students to develop goals around these products and determine work roles. Ask student groups to formulate an action plan that outlines the details of their campaign to help them conceptualize and manage all the pieces of the campaign. This plan helps students assign roles and identify specific goals as they work toward achieving the bigger goals of the campaign. A sample action plan guide can be found here: https://tinyurl.com/5n9a5h3p. It is also helpful to remind them about the design-thinking process (see Chapter 7).

Step 4: Seek out mentor texts to support campaign construction. Mentor texts provide a series of guidelines to students in connection to their assigned media construction. Invite students to think about elements their chosen mentor text highlights and how those features can inform decisions within their own authentic creations. Provide students with a series of support resources housed on their class webpage that showcases a variety of examples for students to use as potential mentor texts. These are a few sample support resources Sarah provides for her students as they begin designing their own campaigns: https://tinyurl.com/2p98kv5s.

Step 5: Provide students time, space, and feedback when it comes to constructing their media. Many of these experiences are new to students—especially when it comes to constructing quality work for greater audiences beyond the classroom. Allow this time to follow a workshop model and facilitate students' needs as they surface. Creating a workshop culture also invites students to seek out peer-supported feedback as well as feedback from those outside of the classroom. Students will need time to formulate and reformulate their ideas as they continue to take shape into their final products.

Step 6: Celebrate awareness campaigns by hosting a campaign launch. Collaborative student groups come together and present their work as a cohesive unit. Their launch presentation to the class offers an opportunity to share their products with peers as well as invite classmates to follow/like/bookmark student-created campaign resources. Provide a presentation outline that supports student groups in developing their discussion around their campaign. This resource is used in Sarah's classroom to help students collaboratively present their awareness campaign: https://tinyurl.com/2p93pe7z. It not only focuses on the au-

thentic products created for their campaign, but it also invites students to talk about their decision-making and process of their construction.

Making Learning Visible

Affording students the opportunity to take action related to topics and issues they care about in their world magnifies a powerful moment in teaching and learning. As students become more comfortable in the learning driver's seat, they seek to explore new ideas and push themselves to go to new places in their thinking.

Karina's media campaign about the responsibilities teens have toward media use today illustrates this. Her collaborative team constructed the "You Choose" campaign to inform teens about the positives and negatives of media with a specific emphasis on social media. Her specific role in this process connected to the website design. Karina speaks more about her experience in a reflection by stating:

> Throughout the process of making a website, my partner and I had to figure out which formats would work, what we should say on different pages, and how we can get our viewers involved in such an important topic. Also, we had technical difficulties. This included my computer crashing twice in one day and a glitch in the database editor of our website. Despite all these problems, we were able to make a satisfying, intriguing website that people would enjoy looking through. We were proud of our work and even more so when we presented our campaign to the class and to the community.

Not only does Karina acknowledge the importance of her campaign to others, but she also addresses the skills that go beyond the guidelines of the learning experience. Students are willing to stretch their abilities and try new things if they are given agency in their learning. Karina not only experienced trying something new with constructing her group's website, but she also developed skills far more valuable than learning standards: perseverance, advocacy, collaboration, creativity, digital communication, and design, to name a few.

MEDIA CAMPAIGNS IN ACTION

- From prints to logos to social media and public-service announcement videos, students can construct a wide variety of authentic writing pieces to promote change.
- In the "Reconnect" campaign shown in Figure 8.1, student creators wanted to highlight the use of personal information and negative experiences in cyberspaces. Their campaign focuses on how to participate in online spaces using both caution and safety.
- As seen in the "Be the Change" campaign pictured in Figure 8.2, the focus of this group relates to abolishing stereotypes and labels teens often place on others in school.

Figure 8.1. In the "Reconnect" campaign, students wanted to educate their peers about being safe online.

Figure 8.2. Through the "Be the Change" campaign, students prompted their peers to push against stereotypes.

GENIUS HOUR

What Is Genius Hour?

Genius Hour was modeled after the approach of innovative technology companies like Google that structured company work time in an 80/20 format. Eighty percent of the time, employees were expected to work on company-dictated projects, while the other 20% of the time, they were free to explore innovations that were connected to the mission of the company. Through this approach, many of the innovations such as Gmail and Google news have become mainstays in our lives. In the last several years, this concept has been taken up by educators (Juliani, 2014; McNair, 2017; Purcell et al., 2020). Students who are engaged in Genius Hour develop inquiries around their interests—not ours.

There are multiple books devoted entirely to Genius Hour, and we know we cannot break it down as thoroughly as they do. But what we can do here is demonstrate how we structure Genius Hour so that it not only captures students' passions and helps them learn to structure ongoing inquiries, but so that it also helps them develop social-consciousness and social action as they engage in their work. One of the ways we do this is by integrating Mentor Moments (see Chapter 6) within the Genius Hour structure. But more importantly, as we help our students select their topics of study, we do so with the caveat that whatever they choose, they must be able to articulate how this will impact the larger community, and they must be able to develop a give-back as a part of their final work.

How Can Genius Hour Help Students Accomplish the Incredible?

Perhaps Hayden can help us illustrate this. One morning, Hayden passed Sarah in the hall. As he walked by, he stopped in front of her, stating: "I'm not going to be in class today, Mrs. Bonner. I have a meeting with the mayor." Hayden had a passion for dogs, so as he was designing his Genius Hour project, he knew he wanted to focus on them. He realized that although a lot of community members enjoyed interacting with their dogs, they didn't really have a place outside their homes to do so. Thus, his idea for a community dog park was born, and his visit with the mayor was his first step toward attempting to make this a reality. And while his efforts ultimately were not successful, he learned a lot about the channels of making change in a community as he interacted not only with the mayor but also in a monthly town-hall meeting. Hayden, like many of our students during Genius Hour, channeled his passion into something that was bigger than himself. And while a dog park might not address the larger social issues we face, the process of identifying a problem within a community and taking steps to make a change taught him about the importance of action. And when our students get out of their seats and shake off the passiveness that school often instills in them, they *can* accomplish the incredible.

When we approach Genius Hour through the lens that their inquiry needs to be something larger than themselves, we help them see why inquiry matters, why it can make a difference. And when we stress to them the importance of finding mentors in the community, they learn about the collaborative nature of inquiry. Genius Hour is no longer simply something we do in school. Rather, it is something that we do together with our community. And that's pretty incredible in and of itself.

Before You Begin

While Genius Hour presents a number of logistics to work through as students prepare for their individualized inquiry experience, it also offers an opportunity for teachers to undergo a shift in their professional mindset. Welcoming Genius Hour into the classroom experience requires that teachers let go of lessons, units, and texts to make room for this new student learning journey. In addition to letting go of aged practices, it also begs teachers to let go of the teacher-centered mindset as students enter the driver's seat of the learning process.

Agreeing to Genius Hour means a shift in identity that places teachers as a guide or a facilitator to student learning. It also means that teachers are not the sole expert in this framework. We must be supportive of students as they seek outside help from community experts. Furthermore, the nature of Genius Hour means that teaching and learning practices will look different from traditional practices and, for this, it becomes vital that transparency with parents as well as other classroom stakeholders is present.

When introducing Genius Hour to students, communicate key points around why this framework is being implemented to parents, what it will look like for students, how community mentors play a significant role in this process, and how assessment will be addressed throughout this journey. From there, the gradual release from teacher-driven to student-centered begins.

In the Moment

Step 1: Explore why students participate in Genius Hour, review general logistical steps, and invite students to brainstorm. If Genius Hour is a new concept to your students, providing time to explore what Genius Hour is and why students participate in these experiences becomes an important first step as students formulate their own reasonings for embarking on such a learning journey. As students continue their exploration, they often generate their own questions related to how it may look within their classroom environment. Therefore, reviewing the bigger goals of Genius Hour provides a vision for the work they will be engaging in throughout the learning time frame.

After students investigate the many facets of Genius Hour and discuss many of the questions that surface from their investigations, it is necessary for them to participate in self-investigation. Students cannot always naturally identify what they want to learn more about because the teacher often primarily directs what will be learned, offering very little opportunity for students to engage in their own curiosities. Allow time for students to assess their personal values, identify hobbies and talents, and inventory issues they might be interested in exploring with more depth. This needed time ensures that students make an informed decision on choosing their inquiry topics.

Step 2: Create project proposals and pitch ideas for feedback. As students settle on their inquiry topics, have them develop a project proposal, which identifies their initial steps in formulating their inquiries. Within their proposals, students can think about why their project matters, list possible community mentors, construct a suggested timeline for their inquiries, and explore how their projects will support civic engagement goals. Encourage students to pitch their ideas to others (peers, school staff, community members, etc.) to collect feedback to strengthen the vision of their projects.

Step 3: Find an expert and establish mentorship. Following the development and finalization of project proposals, students need to seek out mentorship from experts related to their inquiries. Experts offer a unique voice to Genius Hour as they provide another layer of learning for students. Within this step, encourage students to stretch the boundaries of community when seeking experts. For example, Kierstein wanted to explore what it meant to be an author for her Genius Hour inquiry; she remembered her previous interactions with YA author Nic Stone and decided to contact her. Much to Kierstein's surprise, not only did Nic Stone agree to be her mentor, but also gave feedback to Kierstein's writing, met with her on several occasions to answer her questions, and even made a school visit to talk to her as well as others about writing. Remember that experts exist everywhere and many of those experts want to help students as they continue their learning journey.

Step 4: Encourage students to develop action plans and weekly schedules to strengthen self-advocacy. As students slide more concretely into the driver's seat of their learning, they also need to develop an action plan that establishes learning goals. Since all inquiry projects become so vastly differ-ent from one another, creating a generic weekly schedule or plan of action often does not work. For this reason, students design and construct their own weekly schedules in conjunction with the goals of their project.

Step 5: Provide time for students to construct weekly blogging or writing experiences around their projects. Blogging alongside the development of Genius Hour projects not only offers a way to weave in different writing genres into the classroom, but it also provides a layer of metacognition for students to process their thoughts around their topics. The weekly blogging experience models the thinking of researchers and reflexive journaling. While blogs may focus on research elements, they may also offer insight into student thinking as they experience various phases of their projects— such as working with mentors, gaining feedback from peers, and commenting on research that supported the actions of their project.

Step 6: Strengthen student inquiry projects to include civic engagement components. Students spend so much time thinking, questioning, researching, and writing about their inquiries that it begs the question, "What can we do with all of this information?" With this driving question in mind, students seek out ways to give back the collected information to a greater audience. For some students, it may be an opportunity to work closely with their mentors in hands-on experiences but, for others, it may be a chance to promote change (in the school climate, policies, procedures, or more). Any opportunity students can have that goes beyond the classroom walls, engages with the community, produces content for a greater good, and nurtures student agency is a win for any learning experience.

This support guide breaks down Genius Hour into smaller goals to make bigger goals easier to obtain: https://tinyurl.com/5s8hm9wa. Throughout this guide, there are resources related to all the steps outlined in this chapter.

Step 7: Celebrate the final products by hosting a pre-sentation forum. Genius Hour can be one of the most impactful learning experiences for students and, therefore, calls for a celebration. While many presentations are confined to the classroom during class hours, celebrate Genius Hour by inviting the community into the school to experience student learning experiences. One way to do this is by creating a forum modeled after TED Talks. Students develop presentations about their projects and the journey of the project to share with others. These presentations often include artifacts like pictures, hands-on activities, or primary sources. Sarah uses this document with her students to better support their presentation efforts and ensure that students discuss key points from their inquiries: https://tinyurl.com/yck8shyu.

Making Learning Visible

Genius Hour not only offers an opportunity for students to practice a variety of learning standards, but it also centers many valuable life skills that supersede anything that could be found in a textbook. In connection to her experience with Genius Hour, Abby wanted to explore travel writing. Upon reflecting on her experience, Abby stated:

> With Genius Hour, I wanted to make sure that my give-back would be something that was actually important to my project and would really help something out. When I found out about Global Volunteers, I knew that this was something that I wanted to do. With my giveback, I talked to Global Volunteers, and they helped set up a page for me on their website. Global Volunteers is an organization that helps people raise money to go on trips around the world to help people out. Since I was not old enough to go on a trip, they helped me set up a page, and the money I raised for that would all just go back to them. So, I made a page, and I also made luggage tags and sold them.

In another instance, Katie challenged herself to learn conversational phrases in Mandarin Chinese. Being bilingual (Spanish and English), her aspirations to work in business led her to explore other globally predominant languages. Noticing the lack of language studies her school offered, she developed a document for the district's school board to consider expanding the foreign-language department to offer more language studies for all students. Even though she wasn't successful in her efforts with the school board, Katie speaks about her Genius Hour experience in connection to learning by saying:

> I learned that learning is a hard process, you have to fail to actually learn. Failing is a good thing in learning, what I'm saying is, failing can be hard but you have to learn from your mistakes and use them to help you learn; don't let them get the best of you.

As these students reflect on their Genius Hour projects, they both emphasize their thoughts on learning and how learning played a significant role in their overall experience. Looking carefully at their testimonies, you begin to notice that their learning awakening connects to concepts like taking risks, asking questions, understanding different perspectives, and viewing failure as a positive stepping-stone in the learning journey.

These reflections are possible when teachers afford trust to their students. So often, we protect our students from failure and cushion them from the practices of the real world. Students own their Genius Hour experience from the very beginning and dedicate themselves to the very end. Students contact experts, outline research, develop questions, act, and give back to their community. And, while not all projects work out the way they are intentionally designed, celebrating failures is a way for students to do better in the future.

YOUTH PARTICIPATORY ACTION RESEARCH (YPAR)

What Is YPAR?

Youth Participatory Action Research (YPAR) extends the idea of Participatory Action Research, which is research centered in a community, with community members participating in research that focuses on community-identified issues and uses research to find solutions for those problems. YPAR adds youth to the equation, partnering youth and adults in a quest to identify issues in their lives and communities and engaging youth in the research that leads to solutions. Through YPAR, students learn how to systematically research to improve their lives and the lives of others in their community (Bautista et al., 2013; Mirra et al., 2015). Students work with adults, in this case the teacher, to identify and define a problem, pose a research question, design plans for data collection, and analyze the data collected. And then, rather than writing up a report for the teacher, they take the next step of putting their researched ideas into practice.

Like Genius Hour, YPAR is a pedagogical approach that is larger than what we can fully explore in this chapter. Berkeley's *YPAR Hub* (http://yparhub.berkeley.edu) has been invaluable in our work to begin to integrate the principles and practices of YPAR into our practice. But while we cannot dig into it as deeply as the Berkeley Hub, we can illustrate how we have begun to modify the approach so that it has a place in the classroom. We can also explore how it extends the work described in this book.

GENIUS HOUR IN ACTION

- Integrating Genius Hour in a classroom can become one of the most important studies students experience throughout the school year. In addition to the student agency it provides in the moment, Genius Hour also seeks to practice long-lasting skills that carry forward beyond the classroom.
- Corey constructed his Genius Hour around computer coding (see Figure 8.3) and the need to integrate more coding within the school curriculum. Rather than presenting in a TED Talk format, this group facilitated a community playground to share their work (see Playgrounds in Chapter 3). In Corey's reflection about his project and presentation experience, he stated,

> [W]hen they came over I had my whole speel about my project and what it was about, but I also compared coding to the act of knitting, in how the two are intertwined (pun intended). They could understand and relate to what I was saying because it was something they were familiar with, something their grandparent, parents, or even themselves had tried at some point in time. After my short chat, I then set them free to try and code something on their own on the Chromebooks. Most failed, but they still were excited to try it out and give it their best shot through exploration. I think that while they were learning about my topic, I was learning right alongside them. This project grew my understanding not only in my topic, but also how to stand up and present/show off what I had learned. I learned more from this presentation that any old paper or blog could've taught me.

Figure 8.3. Corey identified coding as a necessary skill that was lacking in their school curriculum. He used Genius Hour to learn more about coding and to create a tutorial for others to learn how to code too.

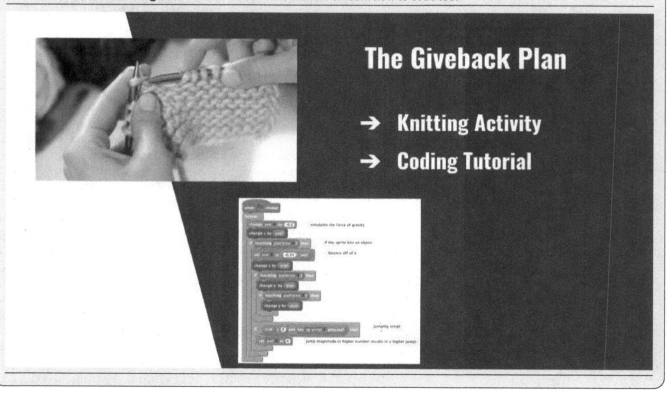

How Can YPAR Help Students Accomplish the Incredible?

By situating students as experts in their communities, YPAR provides students with the tools to understand the issues they face daily and to determine solutions that are supported by data. Participating in YPAR equips students with skills that will serve them beyond their time in our classrooms. Importantly, YPAR teaches students how to be active participants in solutions, enabling students to find their dignity and learn to privilege the dignity of others. Through active participation, students learn the power of the collective and begin to value the perspectives of others. When they can do these things, they are primed for accomplishing the incredible.

Further, YPAR is built upon a foundation of inquiry as it turns the classroom into a community of inquiry that is engaged in the problems of the larger community. Like the approaches described before, this ensures that students are not doing inquiry for inquiry's sake but rather for the sake of themselves and larger humanity.

Before You Begin

When taking the plunge into YPAR, it's important to immerse yourself in understanding what this framework is, how others have approached it, and how it can be seen in action with your students. YPAR serves as a next step to Genius Hour. Once students become comfortable with individual inquiry, YPAR can evolve the work to be more collaborative and in tune with the community.

In the initial stages of YPAR, familiarize yourself with the *YPAR Hub* (http://yparhub.berkeley.edu/) created by the University of California Berkeley and the resources they provide to start YPAR with students. Evaluating these resources to meet the needs of students, viewing examples, and sketching a game plan for the semester all become necessary practices before inviting students to engage in this inquiry practice. As seen in both the overview and the support guide, the design thinking framework can help students map out their YPAR work for the semester as they experience each stage of design.

In the Moment

> *Step 1: Empathize with surroundings, understand YPAR, and reimagine community.* Before introducing this concept to students, Sarah created an overview to help students understand the "why" behind bringing

YPAR into the classroom as well as some of the bigger goals that connect to the inquiry design itself: https://tinyurl.com/5yyyjery. Modeling the first phase of design thinking (see Chapter 7) helps students empathize with their surroundings by going on a community walk to capture a variety of elements that make up their community. Students bring that information back to the classroom so they can brainstorm a list of issues and assets found in both their school and town.

In conjunction with the community walk, introduce students to YPAR by examining the nature of the words within the acronym. Suggested by UC Berkeley's *YPAR Hub*, give students time to dissect the meaning of each of these words to start making connections between what they were seeing and how they could take steps to promote change.

Lastly, engage students in an exercise designed by the YPAR Hub that invites them to reimagine their community—policies, systems, practices, and habits can all be redesigned within this activity. This reimagining step welcomes students to think about the changes they would like to concretely see in their communities and work to create a plan that turns make-believe into reality.

In addition to constructing an overview that can be used with students along with other classroom stakeholders, students can also benefit from a support guide that showcases each of the bigger steps they will take when venturing through YPAR: https://tinyurl.com/9kkwkkb6.

> *Step 2: Define the key elements in the inquiry design.* After examining the communities through a variety of lenses, students can narrow their focus on something they want to act on as they seek to move forward in the inquiry process. Throughout the definition phase, it's important to work with students to facilitate their thinking around specific topics. During this time, ask students to formulate an extensive list of questions related to their focus, create a pitch presentation around some of their forming ideas to gain feedback, and begin collecting credible sources that help support their vision.

> *Step 3: Ideate a plan of action and talk to experts.* Once students have defined their target focus and identified goals associated with that focus, allowing students to formulate a plan of action

that highlights roles and goals becomes an essential next step. At this point, students are not only shaping their plans to move forward but they are also finding ways to network with potential experts or mentors in this process and strengthening their ability to collaborate with one another. Encourage students to use a collaborative group think-sheet to identify primary goals and assign specific roles to students so that everyone can move forward. This think-sheet captures a series of roles and goals students established while developing plans to revitalize a rundown tennis court space in the community to envelop more practical and modern uses: https://tinyurl.com/ycyytuhk.

Step 4: *Allow students time to construct prototypes around their thinking as they attempt to connect their research, design, and expert voices all together into a working concept.* By prototyping a variety of concepts, student groups can invite others in to provide feedback as they continue to shape their thinking. Prototypes afford a time of play for students before moving on to finalizing their designs. One of Sarah's YPAR classes focused on refurbishing an abandoned tennis court area in their community to reflect a more modern, practical use for the space. After meeting with one of the school's architects, students constructed a series of prototype designs to be surveyed by the community.

Step 5: *Move forward with details and act.* Now that students have a focus, a plan, and a design in place, moving forward with the details of this project becomes a key component to seeing student vision come to life. Student collaboration magnifies as students work together in implementing their overall plan of action. At this point, students must often be reminded that this is not just a school project—this is happening in real life as students still doubt the magnitude of their YPAR work. Throughout this step, student groups may be contacting their mentors or various other experts to help them organize the details of their project. They might be creating a media presence for their work, fundraising, or budgeting as they move the project into its final stages—the possibilities are endless and ultimately student-driven.

Step 6: *Celebrate and reflect.* Given the magnitude of this work and how students collaborated to do something impactful for their community, celebrating their efforts is a well-deserved step in the YPAR process. Whether you invite parents and community members to an unveiling or contact a local news outlet to create a story around the movement, it's essential for student work to be highlighted in positive ways. In addition to celebrating, encourage students to reflect on these experiences in connection to their learning journeys and big take-away moments.

Making Learning Visible

Seeing students take ownership of both their learning and their community is nothing short of breath-taking in the world of learning. YPAR invites students to go beyond their own personal lives to become change agents for the world around them.

Alex discusses one of his experiences with YPAR in his blog. Working to secure funding for the tennis-court space, Alex worked with the district money manager to understand the nature of budgets. Additionally, he narrated the gravity of funding a project like the one he and his peers have worked to construct. He indicated that his role in the project was vital and that his peers were counting on him to deliver his identified goals. It's this agency in learning that evokes a strong sense of intrinsic motivation for students like Alex. He understands that his role in the YPAR design is essential to the entire concept.

Interview Experience and Moving Forward—YPAR Blog #6

In our most recent weeks of YPAR we have found an expert to interview and contacted her, set up a date and time, formed interview questions, and completed the interview. We interviewed the finance manager for the Heyworth Jr./Sr. High School, Mrs. S. She gave us valuable information on starting a budget, and how to manage it throughout the project. She also offered to set up an activity account for us to store our funds, but we would have to speak to Mrs. Hicklin (the principal) to get the details for setting it up.

We also asked Mrs. S. to guide us through the project and provide help if needed. Overall, this interview was very helpful and important to our progress through this project. But we aren't done yet; we still have to research and seek out

YPAR in Action

- Alongside the phases of design thinking (see Chapter 7), students also participate in a weekly reflection journal that focuses on various aspects of the YPAR journey. Students brainstorm potential writing topics at the end of their YPAR workshop time and spend the week constructing a reflective blog post that asks students to analyze specific pieces of their part in YPAR.
- Maggie discussed the importance of community experts in her project. She continued her thoughts by celebrating the work that has been accomplished in the YPAR journey so far but also understood that their journey was far from over. Maggie's writing supports the need for reflection as she acknowledges the next steps her project must face as it moves forward. These identifiers lay the groundwork into her goals for the next YPAR workshop.

YPAR Blog #6: Hopes and Goals

For this week of YPAR, we have continued to contact people and prepared to contact people. Not many people have gotten back to us, and I think that is one of our biggest hopes, is to get word back from everyone we have contacted.

GOALS:

1. Reach out to everyone on our list, such as teachers, students, and community members.
2. Talk to experts (specifically experts in design).
3. Get our survey out for students to take.
4. Continue preparing for interviews with experts, teachers, Mrs. Hicklen.

HOPES:

1. For students to take the survey and answer the questions honestly.
2. For everyone we contact to get back to us.
3. For the Village Board to approve what we are doing.

This week we have been really trying our best to reach our goals. We have reached out to close to everyone on our list; also we have researched some experts that we contact. For some experts we have considered even some people at our school because of the kind of designs they created in the school or community.

ideas for fundraisers. We need to have a way of letting people know about the fundraiser, a way to actually persuade them to come, a place to hold the fundraiser, what we're actually going to do at the fundraiser, a backup plan if things don't work out well, volunteers if needed, how we will get the things required for the fundraiser, there's *a lot* of things to factor . . .

It does look like a lot of work, and this is just a part of the grand scheme of money/budgeting in this project. It is very important that everyone is doing something at all times in this group, or else we could fall behind and bring down the entire group with us. Without funding, we can't move forward once we get to the part of construction.

DOCUMENTING COMMUNITY STORIES

What Is Documenting Community Stories?

When students venture outside of the classroom, they are exposed to a world of untold stories waiting to be seen and heard. Often, we seclude our learners from the community and focus solely on the tasks, standards, and objectives prescribed by stakeholders. Documenting community stories invites students and teachers to branch out beyond the classroom and discover voices that continue to shape these shared spaces. In this experience, students become the writer, director, and producer of stories that exist in their communities. Not only can learners tell these community-based stories, but they can also use their platform to process important issues and understand multiple perspectives.

HOW CAN CREATING DOCUMENTARIES HELP STUDENTS ACCOMPLISH THE INCREDIBLE?

Imagine the agency, significance, and empowerment that comes with being the director and creator of an untold story. Storytelling allows us as humans to provide insight and perspective into our own lived experiences to be shared with a greater audience. As students place themselves as creators, storytellers, and directors, documentaries supply students with experiences that not only connect them to each other collaboratively but also forge a connection between them and their community. It is with documentaries that students begin to see the value and importance of connection, communication, collaboration, and community. This active participation encourages students to see learning beyond the classroom and create something that they never thought they could possibly do.

In many ways, our students' lived experiences with learning have been singular, short-term, and artificial. When constructing something of magnitude like a documentary, students not only participate in developing the product itself, but they experience a journey in learning. As with any journey, there are obstacles, new inquiries, mentors, failures, and successes. As facilitators, it becomes essential to provide a path for our students to walk this journey and embrace these qualities. Providing structure to engage in this work but also space for students to make their own decisions makes this experience something that challenges our students to think bigger beyond the classroom walls.

Before You Begin

It may be true that students have experienced documentaries as readers but, as educators, we can't assume that learners have analyzed documentaries for creator purposes. Before stepping into the creator role, it's important for students to understand how professionals research, interview, and tell stories. Prior to having students think about their own community stories, allow them to watch a variety of documentaries presented in different writing styles. Easing into this work, take time to plan a watching experience with students so they can see and learn about how other creators tell their stories. This example unit guide invites students to watch, discuss, analyze, and conceptualize documentaries in various ways: https://tinyurl.com/yazumpar. Creating a watching experience like this also provides common language to use within the class environment despite the assorted stories that will be developed later in their own collaborative documentaries.

Moving from viewer to creator when it comes to documentaries requires some mindset work. Before teachers can assist students in stepping into a creator space with students, it's important to be in a teaching mindset that supports facilitation, seeks outside expertise, and provides a responsiveness to the needs of learners embarking on this learning journey. For students, it's important to understand that this is a long-term journey of learning and creation. Ideas, questions, and flexibility need to ebb and flow throughout this process. Coaching students in this mindset—cultivating ideas, asking questions, seeking new solutions when faced with problems, soliciting feedback from others—prior to the documentary-creating process permits them to apply this coaching in real-life learning scenarios.

It is also essential to afford students time to play with potential stories that could develop into future documentaries. For many students, the idea of creating a documentary can be overwhelming but when we ask students to find a story in our community worth telling, the sense of storytelling seems manageable and engaging. When approaching a big task like creating a documentary, it's vital for students to develop multiple stories. If we ask students to focus only on one story at the beginning of this process, it's likely that our learners will lose interest or find other stories that they would rather tell instead. Taking time to find those important stories within our communities will afford students more agency, dedication, and compassion in their documentary development.

In the Moment

Step 1: Spend time analyzing expert documentarians and their craft. If we want our students to think/act/speak/write like documentarians, then it only makes sense to study experts that have demonstrated this craft well. Allow students to explore various types of documentary structures—how they are formed, what stories they tell, how documentarians present their information to larger audiences. By taking time to critically analyze the decisions documentarians make throughout a finished product, it invites students to think about their own upcoming decisions as they move forward as creators. Rather than having a rubric or a bulleted list of to-dos, provide guidelines to students that not only offer what should be included in documentaries but also the support needed on how to demonstrate those guidelines in their own creations: https://tinyurl.com/2p8rrxmj.

Step 2: Allow students time to brainstorm and play with different stories. When it comes to discovering untold stories within our communities, students need to brainstorm individually, in small groups, and collaboratively as an entire class uncovers a vast array of choices for students. As writers, the act of brainstorming or playing with potential writing ideas affords time to strengthen and specify ideas until something worth spending more time on emerges more concretely.

Step 3: Provide time and space for questions, research, and storyboarding. To conceptualize one central documentary idea, student groups need time to think about their driving questions that inspire the purpose of their storytelling. While students continue to develop their central questions, this may lead them to areas where they need to become more informed through research.

This quest for knowledge not only influences their guiding questions but also how they might intertwine that knowledge into their presentation and gives strength to their credibility as creators. In addition to questions and research, student creators need to spend time thinking through their vision for their documentary. Storyboarding is a strategy that can invite students to think critically about the people, settings, messages, and order of their overall creations.

Step 4: Think outside the classroom walls. Asking students to construct documentaries also comes with a mindset of flexibility knowing that its construction will ultimately take place outside of the classroom. Be mindful that students will need time and space to gather the footage they will need to bring their stories to fruition. Throughout this step, students may need additional support in connecting with adults (e.g., sending emails, arranging meeting times and locations, structuring

---

MAKING LEARNING VISIBLE

Empowering students to develop their voices through writing is one of teaching's greatest gifts. While students embody the work of documentarians, they also experience a level of learning that will ultimately impact them as humans. Aaron, an avid student athlete, wanted to showcase the story of when sports and activities were abruptly shut down due to school closings. His documentary *Without the Crowd* highlighted the stories of students, coaches, and administrators who commented on the direct impact this had on players. After creating and sharing his documentary with others, he reflected by saying:

> We learned *a lot* about this unit. We learned about how everyone was affected in some way by the pandemic. All types of people, ages and places were affected by it. Athletes in specific had hard times as well. A lot of athletes based their whole lives around sports practices and games and when all that got shut down and canceled, a lot of athletes including me were a bit lost in what to do with our lives and newly found free time. A new idea I had from this unit that we are wrapping up currently is how much the pandemic impacted peoples' lives. I thought at first it just cancels school a little bit and sports we still had just not all the way (mask mandates and such). But it really affected people's mental health and well-being.

Ellasyn, another student documentarian, accomplished the incredible with her work highlighting the untold stories of teachers shifting to remote learning spaces to better understand and empathize with teachers in her school. Her documentary, *Online in an Instant* (Figure 8.4) provided her community with an inside view into teachers' struggles, worries, and successes under this abrupt change. She reflected on her experience as a documentarian by saying:

> I learned a lot about stepping outside of my comfort zone and self-advocating by asking questions. These are all valuable skills that I can use in the real world. Whether it's in a job or sticking up for something I believe in, these skills can all be used. These skills that I have learned this year can be used to better my community and the rest of this world.

It is these experiences that shape our students as they move beyond the classroom and into the spaces where they can continue to do incredible things.

Figure 8.4. A scene from the documentary *Online in an Instant* that highlights teachers' shift to online teaching during the COVID-19 pandemic.

interview questions). They may also need your support with physically going outside of the classroom—such as creating an itinerary of places students need to gather footage and using school resources (e.g., buses, vans) or walking in the community. Allow yourself to be part of the learning journey as well alongside students.

Step 5: Create a culture of trial, error, and constructive feedback. Let's acknowledge that going through the process of creating a documentary can be hard—especially for our adolescents! However, if we place value on the process or the journey of this work, it can ultimately create an empowering moment for students to showcase their voices. Throughout this process, it becomes especially important to create a classroom culture of trial and error. By affording students the space to "fail," they can learn from their mistakes and strengthen their creations. As described in Chapter 9, trust circles offer a way for student groups to share their ideas, storyboards, and developing footage with peers in a way that both supports and stretches students in new directions.

Step 6: Provide structured guidance as students construct their final documentaries and celebrate! By now, student creators have spent a considerable amount of time conceptualizing their untold story, selecting how they want to tell that story within their documentary, gathering footage from outside the classroom to support their work, and shaping their thinking with the help of their peers. At this point, students need support tying everything together (remind them of the guidebook from Step 1). When these final stories come together, take time to celebrate the creative journey with students (e.g., a viewing party or a film festival).

READING YOUR WORLD

At a time when students are attempting to understand what happens around them, we can't afford for our students to just be bystanders. This logic invites us to think about learning in new ways as we seek to empower our students to become active participants in their world.

Throughout this chapter, we highlighted several experiences that placed students in control of their learning, challenged them to spread their wings, and formulated action for things that mattered. Whether it's cultivating awareness around important causes or constructing a journey of inquiry to promote change in a community, students can push our world in new, innovative directions. We owe it to our students to design meaningful and important learning experiences that are active and motivate them to be the best version of themselves.

REFLECT, MOTIVATE, AND ACT

Reflect on Our Personal Inspirations to Move Toward Change

- *Who inspires you?*
- *What changes would you like to make to the world?*
- *How do these aspirations influence your approach to teaching?*

Motivate Students to Accomplish the Incredible

- *Who inspires your students?*
- *What changes would your students like to make to the world?*
- *How do these aspirations influence your students' approach to learning?*

Take Action to Accomplish the Incredible with Your Students

- *What experiences can you create that invite students to accomplish the incredible?*
- *What do you need to support these experiences?*
- *What do your students need to participate in these experiences?*

NINE

Celebrating the Teeth Marks on Our Tongues

The world's been waiting for your genius a long time.

—Elizabeth Acevedo

Biting our tongues does not often come naturally to teachers. Whether we are excited to share the questions that reading books raise in us or eager to demonstrate to our students why the language arts are important to learn, we have a lot to say. Sometimes, we have so much to say that we leave very little room for our students to ask their own questions or raise their own ideas. For Robyn, the potential for student-centered teaching and learning became more apparent when she began to implement Socratic Circle discussions, student-led discussions that task students to develop a series of questions, prepare for discussion by collecting evidence, and lead a discussion together without teacher prompting. At first, structuring a circle that relied primarily on student questions was frightening. What if they had nothing to say and the whole lesson flopped? What if they had too much to say, but it didn't follow the lesson plan? What if they talked over each other? What if they stared in silence? Yet, we tried it anyway. And it worked. It wasn't perfect at first . . . or ever. In fact, Robyn's coteacher at the time struggled a bit with the silence of the early circles. This meant that it was tempting to step in when students were silent. But what she didn't understand at first was that sometimes we find joy through struggle, especially if that struggle leads to questions that matter to us, to autonomy to learn about what we want to learn, to a feeling of accomplishment for thinking for ourselves. Fortunately, after a few gentle reminders, she was willing to give them this space for struggle, and soon, Socratic Circles became the highlight of the class with students frequently asking if that was on the day's schedule. Turns out, our students had a lot to say and a lot of questions to ask—they'd just never been given the chance.

Through these experiences, as well as through the lessons we've learned since then, we recognize why Alfie Kohn (2013) stated, "In outstanding classrooms, teachers do more listening than talking, and students do more

talking than listening" (Item number 5). This is why we aspire to be that terrific teacher that Kohn describes as having "teeth marks on their tongues" (Item number 5).

Starting this work is daunting because it pushes against the kind of teaching and learning most of us have experienced, most of us have witnessed, and most of us have practiced. If we want to assist students in thinking for themselves to move toward solutions to the world's problems, we *have* to do the work. We know that, as Kohn (2013) states, "thinking is messy; deep thinking is really messy" (Item number 2). Yet, it is so necessary. If we continue to do the thinking for our students, to ask the questions for our students, how, when, and where will they learn to think? For this reason, we have worked to shift our practices around designing learning experiences that focus on problems and students' questions, answering the call Kohn has been sending out to educators for most of his life's work.

Kohn (2013) also pointed out that, "Children learn how to make good decisions by making decisions, not by following directions" (Item number 6). We find this to be true, as well. Much of our early days and weeks working with new groups of students involve deprogramming students who have learned how to follow directions very well but who struggle to make decisions. This is why this work spans a school year rather than a single unit or semester. Making decisions means that we must learn who we are and why we are that person. It means that we must consider how our actions impact others. It means that we must trust ourselves and others who exist in the learning space with us. And it means that we, as teachers, must embrace the pain that can come when we bite down on our tongues.

How we do this will look different for each of us. We each exist and work in different contexts, so where we start and how fast we can move will exist across a spectrum. For some, the approaches we've shared will be replicated with just a few tweaks. For others, these approaches will simply be the ideas you need to spark your own classroom evolution. But once you start, once you commit to allowing students to shape the work in your classroom, you'll notice everything starts to shift, including the way you structure your time, your interactions with parents and community, and even your grading. And in doing so, you'll discover not only the genius within each of your students but also the genius within yourself.

OUR STUDENTS' LIVED EXPERIENCES

It was nearing the end of our first year centering inquiry as a way to disrupt student thinking. Students had spent a semester identifying a topic of study, working with mentors, and developing a giveback to the community through their Genius Hour projects. Now, they were preparing for their final presentation, which would be in the form of TED Talks given to the community on the same night as the science fair.

Students were excited, although a little nervous, to share their learning with their parents and other community members. Topics of study ran the gamut. Some were geared more toward personal interest like Dave's and Jake's project on basketball, which resulted in a series of videos designed to help young players in the community learn different moves and plays. Others, like Stephanie's, were more focused on larger social problems. Stephanie had spent the semester studying and looking for solutions geared toward a problem she had witnessed in their school. She had noticed that students had difficulty relating to Jason, a classmate who was on the autism spectrum. Thus, she had spent the semester investigating autism and creating a resource to help her classmates better communicate with Jason and other students who were on the spectrum.

On this day, Sarah was sharing details about the presentation with her students, and as is so often the case in school, the question about how their presentations would be assessed was raised. As Stephanie listened to Sarah describe each element of the rubric, her eyebrows raised and she gasped out loud, stating, "You mean to tell me that my passion is only worth 50 points?" In that moment, Sarah felt paralyzed, knowing Stephanie was correct. She couldn't change her grading approach at the last minute, but Stephanie gave Sarah something to think about as we continued to develop our work.

Although this moment was a short one in terms of time, Stephanie's question continues to resonate all these years later. Stephanie verbalized a concern Sarah had been grappling with the entire school year. How can we boil a semester's worth of questioning and social action into a single rubric, into a mere 50 points? The work students were doing represented their curiosity and passions—and each student's was vastly different. The rubric being shared with the class simply could not do justice to their work. Stephanie's question is the reason our grading practices continue to evolve, and it's the reason we share some of what we've learned with you in this final chapter of this book.

IN DIALOGUE

Each week, Sarah's students write an email to their parents or guardians. Weekly emails assist students in developing their writing by providing them with an authentic purpose and audience with whom to communicate. In this excerpt from Emma's email, she provides them with an overview of what students worked on in class, providing the transparency that is necessary when using a disruptive inquiry approach.

> *Emma's recognition of the benefits of better managing her time demonstrate that she is learning skills beyond just those emphasized in ELA standards.*

Hi Mom and Dad,

Here is my weekly update for Language Arts. This week, we had to change our plans a little bit because of remote learning but we were still able to move forward. On our agenda this week, we had a chance to do some writing into the day, participate in a one-on-one meet up with Mrs. Bonner, work on any missing assignments we might have had this quarter, and move forward on our next Lesson/Challenge #3—The Investigation Mixtape.

This Wednesday I met with Mrs. Bonner to discuss my progress, performance, and participation so far this quarter. Mrs. Bonner says that she is happy with how I have done so far, but she wants to see me continue to progress and wants to see me start taking risks. For example, for the second half of Unit 4, we will be making a Social Awareness project and she would like to see me make something like a vlog or podcast rather than something like a poster. Something we discussed is how I can manage my time better between other classes to allow more time to dive deeply into this class. This will help me to be less stressed.

One way I made progress this week in my learning was by really taking time to get ahead. This was easier for me to do because I have been quarantined allowing much more time for me to work ahead so I can ask questions and get feedback.

> *Emma connects her own efforts to the progress she has made in class, which is an important mindset for lifelong learning.*

TRANSFORMING THROUGH PRACTICE: BITING OUR TONGUES SO STUDENTS CAN LEARN TO SPEAK

Providing a space where our students can learn to speak may seem unnecessary. After all, most of us have numerous experiences working with students who aren't afraid to tell us what they think. But do they know how to speak in spaces and ways that matter, that prompt change? Often the answer is no because as teachers we tend to want to speak for our students. We fill the silences with our own voices. If we want to really help our students learn to speak, we need to learn how to bite our own tongues, letting them engage in productive struggle when they are not sure what to say and listening to their ideas and opinions when they *do* know what they want to say. When we do this, we can learn from students like Stephanie about gaps in our own practices. We also provide opportunities for students like Emma to identify their own roles in the learning community.

Recently, we have been engaging with the work of Gholdy Muhammad (2020) who has studied historical Black literacy societies to understand how to cultivate the genius within all of our students but particularly within students who have been (and continue to be) underserved by schools. Her work focuses on a more balanced approach to literacy instruction. Rather than using pedagogy that focuses solely on students' skills—and to a smaller degree intellect—Muhammad argues that we also need to help students pursue their identities and criticality within our curriculum. And while our work is primarily with white students, we see this framework as one that not only helps our students develop their skills, intellect, identities, and criticality but one that also helps our students recognize the problems in the social world that seek to stifle other voices and cultivate the empathy needed to make changes to these systems.

As we wrap up the pages in this book, we do so with Muhammad's and Kohn's voices in mind. We seek to cultivate the genius in our students, but also in all of you. Knowing that we each begin this work in different contexts, with different experiences, through different lenses, we provide you with some ideas on how to start this work. We encourage you to find balance as you consider the traditional curricular demands of skills and content and weigh those against the need to help students pursue their identities, their intellect, and their criticality. We also encourage you to bite your tongues during times when it may seem difficult to do so, particularly when we consider how to assess and grade our students as they engage in this complex work.

THEORY TO PRACTICE

Gholdy Muhammad: In her book *Cultivating Genius* (2020), Gholdy Muhammad shares that in historically Black literacy societies, "literacy was connected to acts of self-empowerment, self-determination, and self-liberation." She noted that Black people did not wait for others to determine who they would be but used literacy as a way to determine their lives' trajectories for themselves. Historically, literacy was used to disrupt racism, and by using the tenets of Black literacy societies, teachers can help students disrupt racism and other social problems in today's world. The following are ways work in this book can help answer Muhammad's questions around identity, intellect, and criticality. They can serve as models for how to think about putting her work into practice.

- **What We Keep (see Chapter 1):** "How will my instruction help students to learn about themselves and/or about others?"
- **Détournement (see Chapter 2):** "How will my instruction build students' knowledge and mental powers?"
- **Surviving the System (see Chapter 5):** "How will my instruction engage students' thinking about power and equity and disruption of oppression?"

For more about Gholdy Muhammad's work in historically responsive literacy, check out the following resources:

- "Author Interview with Dr. Gholdy Muhammad: 'Cultivating Genius'" by Larry Ferlazzo at https://www.edweek.org/teaching-learning/opinion-author-interview-with-dr-gholdy-muhammad-cultivating-genius/2020/01
- "Unearthing Genius and Joy with Gholdy Muhammad" at https://www.youtube.com/watch?v=asItQUf_pl8
- "The Write Time with Gholdy Muhammad & Chris Rogers" at https://www.youtube.com/watch?v=Yp6uwitQVIY

GETTING STARTED WITH THE WORK

When we think about how to engage in this work, we don't have to think about this in giant leaps but rather in small, tangible steps toward change. If the intention of starting this work relates to turning up the volume on our students' voices, we not only have to reflect on the issues that inspire our students to speak up, but we also need to consider what learning experiences can amplify their words. Making these small changes can spark a journey of transformation. As we've worked to implement and strengthen this work over many years, we've had the opportunity to facilitate hard questions from our students, stretch our own thinking with the help of community experts, take risks in trying new technologies, witness wobble and flow from our learners, and, more importantly, grow alongside our students as we all attempt to understand the world around us.

We often get asked by teachers we work with about the entry points to this work. While we acknowledge that change comes with time, we also know that there are a variety of entry points. Looking at big ideas over the years of implementing this work with students, we notice that there are key entry points that continuously emerge.

1. *Prioritize identity work.* Like we see in Gholdy Muhammad's work, identity—or the ability to see yourself in what you're learning—is vital to our students. Learning about our students while they are exploring their own identities not only allows us to understand and build relationships with them, but it also informs us about how to design learning experiences that will matter to our students' lives (for example, see Multigenre About Me Project in Chapter 1).
2. *Implement text selections that invite meaningful questions and interest.* As discussed in the introduction, meaningful and purposeful text selections can unlock a new wave of thinking for all our learners. Strong text selections not only invite our students to develop strong questions, but they also afford insight into perspectives that may never exist within their current context.
3. *Build criticality.* We often think about the role of building criticality as teacher-centered as teachers work to build critical thinking skills within students. But criticality also connects to the learning constructed by our students. Building criticality should not only be present in the learning experiences we design for our learners, but it should also be seen in the learning habits

they are continuously building (for example, see Surviving the System in Chapter 5).
4. *Connect with the community.* Take a moment to dismantle the belief that you're the only expert in the room. This disruption invites you to rethink who, where, and what students can learn from as they engage in not only learning from the community but also as they act in it (for example, see Mentor Moments in Chapter 6).
5. *Reimagine assessment.* Discussed more throughout this chapter, making small changes to how you assess students can be significant to the learning process. Taking steps to provide more specific, constructive feedback, removing punitive measures like zeros in a gradebook, or even incorporating more conferences with students can create a path toward making substantial change.

Most of this book has focused on helping students examine their identities, build criticality, and connect with the community through carefully selected texts. This last chapter is going to explore the last entry point: assessing and grading the work.

Grading the Work

As Stephanie reminded us earlier in this chapter, assessment and grading can be tricky when we try to overlay traditional grading practices on student-centered work, particularly when that work is directed toward taking social action in the community. Most traditional grading practices are very teacher-centered. The teacher decides what skills, standards, or ideas they are looking for in a particular project and grade accordingly. In a student-centered classroom, this can be problematic, particularly when students' curiosities and passions do not take them in a direction we originally imagined a unit might take. And, as Stephanie demonstrated, boiling students' passions down to points can be insulting to students.

Many educators whom we respect would point to rubrics to capture and assess the work students are doing (Feldman, 2018). We're not sold on that approach, either. Crafting a good rubric is difficult. Crafting a rubric that accounts for all students' creativity and ideas is almost impossible. Attempts at this almost always result in a rubric that is so general that it tells the student very little. And when we try to get more specific, we do not allow students to find their own entry points in the work. Rather, students look to the rubric for where to start and are often so focused on what *we* expect them to do that they cannot see any other ways to approach the problem.

Traditional grading and assessment also discourage risk-taking. In addition to trying to hit the appropriate mark on the rubric, students are often limited to one attempt. And the product is more than likely privileged over the process. This leads to students who jump back into the game of school and attempt to please the teacher in order to receive the maximum number of points; students who have already decided they are not good at the game and give up before they start; or students who ignore the parameters put in place by the teacher, follow their passions, and receive a grade that is not reflective of their learning. And all these scenarios defeat the work we are trying to do.

In a perfect world, student work would be untethered from grades. But the reality of the system we work within means that we *do* ultimately have to assess and assign grades to students. So, how do we do this? The following sections provide approaches that center students in the grading and assessment process while also allowing for the risks needed to engage in inquiry for social action.

The 4-Ps of Grading and Assessment

Several years ago, we were introduced to Steve Peha's (n.d.) 3-P grading system on his website "Teaching That Makes Sense." Peha makes the case for breaking students' grades into their participation, progress, and performance, weighting each according to importance, and then mathematically calculating a final grade. Much of Peha's argument makes sense to us, particularly in terms of inquiry work. We're not sold, however, on the way grades are calculated because we abandoned the use of points several years back. How could we keep them after Stephanie's insightful question? So instead, we use his categories to help frame the conversation around grades with our students, giving them the language needed to articulate their performance in our classes and supplying us with language to provide strategic feedback to them. We've also added another P to help frame our conversations: Power. Together, the 4-Ps provide a structure to a feedback-oriented approach to grades that allows students to take risks, ask their own questions, and design solutions to social issues that matter to them. In the next sections, we break apart how we use each of the 4-Ps with our students.

Power. Beginning the year engaging students in a discussion around grades can prompt them to think about who has the power in most grading situations. The answer, as we all know, is the teacher. Yet, if we truly want

to revolve student learning and inquiry around students, we need to adopt approaches that help equalize the power. One approach is working with students to define each of the letter grades in the gradebook. Rather than simply labeling an "A" as excellent or exceeding expectations, ask students to create descriptors that demonstrate what earning an A in our class should look like.

When students make vague statements like "excellent" or "exceeds expectations" (which is ironic, since that is the language most educators use), prompt them to be more concrete in their descriptions. What does work that is excellent look like? What do the students do to exceed expectations? Together, teachers and students can examine examples of student work and identify what sets some work apart from others. From there, we can develop a list of descriptors that capture these differences. Once a list of descriptors has been generated, work together to create a label that can be substituted for the letter grade. One class substituted Risk-Taker for an A, Conservative for a B, Adequate for a C, and Scrub for an F. This class chose to eliminate the D category. This list can be saved as a point of reference for students when they reflect upon their participation, progress, and performance in class. It also provides teachers with language they can use in conversations around grades. And because students created the labels and descriptors, they are more likely to identify exactly where their efforts place them in each of the categories.

In addition to cocreating descriptors around grades with students, we also invite students to be a part of the grading process through the reflection and feedback loop that becomes a regular part of the classroom culture. Rather than giving students grades, engage in dialogue with students to determine the grades that must ultimately be placed in the gradebook. And while teachers are the final decision-makers, more often than not, engaging in dialogue around the descriptors, as well as participation, progress, and power will lead to a grade that both the student and teacher can agree upon. The reflection and feedback loop will be explored more later in the chapter.

Participation. Peha (n.d.) makes the case that participation should account for 50% of a student's grade. If that makes you raise an eyebrow, rest assured it gave us pause at first too. This philosophy flies in the face of many grading conversations that advocate for removing participation from grades all together (Feldman, 2018). Yet, in a classroom that uses inquiry to disrupt and ignite social action, how can students *not* participate? How can we *not* factor in participation when doing this work? Participation provides students with the space to make decisions about the questions they ask and the actions they will take in response to their learning. Practice making decisions will, as Kohn (2013) states, lead to students learning how to make good decisions. This is a skill that we *want* our students to develop if we want them to make positive change in the world, so eliminating participation from grade decisions does not provide a clear reflection of their work in our classes.

The key to considering participation as a large factor in students' grades, however, rests in what we consider to be participation. Participation cannot just mean speaking up in front of the whole class. Rather, it is contributing to the work of the class (Kay, 2018). Participation is a vital aspect of social action. For some students, participation might mean actively contributing to the brainstormed list of potential solutions to a problem, but, for others, it might mean listening to others' ideas and seeking out the resources to help accomplish a task. For some students, participation might mean contacting community members to come speak to the class, but, for others, it might mean listening with intention to those community members' expertise to embed the new information into their work. For some students, participation might mean working bell to bell, building off of other students' ideas, but for others, it might mean coming up with alternate solutions in the quiet of their homes. Just as we need to leave space in our classrooms for students to have a say in what they are learning and how they use their learning, we also need to make space for students to have a say in how they participate. And then we must recognize this participation as we provide feedback to students and determine their grades.

Progress. The key to making social change is progress. Although we'd like to be able to snap our fingers and wipe out injustices in this world, this just isn't possible. Change happens when we take steps toward our goals. The same is true for changes in students' thinking and understanding, whether it's thinking about how to solve the problems of the world or understanding that writing takes practice. Too often, schools don't recognize student progress. The eye is on the summative—the scores on a standardized test, research paper, or project. When we ignore progress, we ignore all the small successes that occur along the way. And it's in these small successes where change happens because they signify movement is being made toward a goal.

Progress can be tricky to account for, especially in an inquiry driven classroom because we may not have the small quizzes and worksheets to point to as evidence of growth. Yet, it's only tricky if teachers rely on themselves to account for progress. While teachers can collect evidence of progress on their own, the most valuable resource for collecting this evidence is our students. Providing and discussing the goals of the learning experiences, whether those are standards, teacher-created objectives, or student-directed ambitions, equips students with the language needed to monitor their own growth. Together, teachers and students can develop indicators to look for as students begin their learning journey. For example, students can identify shifts in their thinking, ways they have taken risks, knowledge they have acquired, or changes in their learning habits. Students can then provide evidence of their growth through portfolios and reflections.

Performance. Admittedly, this approach to assessment and grading flips traditional grading practices because the student's performance is the least considered element contributing to a student's grade. For most of us, this makes us uncomfortable because it goes against everything we've been taught about teaching and learning. Yet, when we deemphasize the final project, we encourage risk-taking. This encouragement of risk-taking can create a chain reaction. The more risks students take, the more likely they are to make true change. The more students see their work making a difference, the more they are willing to participate. The more students participate, the more progress they make. And all of this leads to a much better product than if we start by emphasizing the quality of their performance.

Further, deemphasizing student performance allows for the mistakes and failures students will inevitably experience when taking the risks needed to make meaningful social change. Inquiry is messy. Change is messy. Recording a failing or less than perfect grade doesn't account for its messiness. It just restricts our inclination to try something new. And, more importantly, it perpetuates failing as something negative to be avoided rather than a positive to be celebrated.

Shifting from Grading to Feedback

Once we leave school, very little in our lives revolve around a single grade or score. If we think specifically about professions in related fields, we find that feedback is typically how professionals learn and grow. Editors send manuscripts out for review, and while there may be a rubric here and there, most decisions around publication are made from narrative feedback. Media creators rely on the feedback they receive from creative partners, clicks, listens, and views. Activists gauge success around the numbers who show up to rallies, who sign petitions, who change their minds, who change the systems. And while each of these fields often has a single voice that makes a final decision, they make their decisions based upon the feedback of others. So, why can't teachers frame grades and assessment in the same way?

The Role of the Student in Feedback. Self-reflection is a cornerstone of grading in an inquiry-driven classroom. Just like students take ownership of their learning, they must also take ownership of their grades. When students understand the purpose of a learning experience, they can examine their participation, progress, and performance around the purpose, providing evidence as to why they earn a particular grade.

When working toward a classroom that values social action, self-reflection should be an ongoing process. While Wobble Journals (see Chapter 2) and Well-Remembered Events Reflections (see Chapter 1) allow for students to reflect upon their thinking around topics of study, other reflective structures can aid them in reflecting upon themselves as learners. Weekly emails written by the students to their parents or guardians allow students to reflect regularly on their learning and keep their families updated as well. This adds to the transparency of the learning culture, which is imperative when engaging in inquiry for social action, and it ensures that students are aware of their investment in the learning experiences throughout the year—not just during grade report periods. Further, the emails impact students' long-term learning, allowing them the opportunity to make connections to previous learning experiences as they encounter new ones later in the year.

Providing students with a checklist can help them construct the content of their message. The following example demonstrates how students share what they learned and their evaluation of their participation, progress, and performance:

- Let your guardians know we completed our first blog draft answering the question "What does it mean to be me?": Let your guardian know that you created a new, personalized blog space, brainstormed, and outlined your answer to the driving question, and drafted your blog. This should be posted already.
- Let your guardian know that we collected words that mattered the most to us when it came to **understanding learning**—especially since we do not have a traditionally graded classroom. Let your guardian know whether you raised your hand to share or interacted at your table/with your group (participation) during that discussion.
- **Choose three words** related to our discussions this week and share them with your guardian (performance). Choose words that would be most interesting or new to them. Explain these words in your own way and what you learned (progress).
- Let your guardian know that next week we will be starting a new unit talking about the writing process and talk about some things that you'd be interested in writing about. What interests you when it comes to writing (topics, types of writing, etc.) and/or what would you want to learn more about when it comes to writing?
- Make sure to CC your teacher before sending the email to your guardian!

Students are also provided with a mentor email to use as a model. While these supports are important early in the semester, as students become more comfortable with the weekly emails, they have the freedom to develop them however fits them best.

In addition to their weekly emails, students provide more holistic reflections at each grading period, including when progress reports are due. These can be completed as more narrative reflections or through a Google Form. As students complete their grade reflections, they reflect specifically upon their participation, progress, and performance, as well as upon their learning around specific standards or goals for each of the projects within the grading period. Students provide specific evidence to demonstrate how they've met their goals. Reflection such as this allows them to not only demonstrate their achievement of goals set by the teacher or district, but to also set personal goals, such as Keegan's participation goal:

> I need to start asking more questions regarding my work. Also, I need to work on giving feedback. Also, the quality of my feedback. I need to work on taking notes. And making sure they are detailed.

As this portion of Calvin's grade reflection demonstrates, self-reflections also allow students to recognize important aspects of learning that extend beyond standards and content goals, such as working collaboratively and using feedback from others to continue to develop their ideas.

> In these last 9 weeks, I have gotten much better at working with my peers. I am able to work with my friends and not get distracted, which is a big improvement since the first

quarter. Also, I have been asking for feedback more and getting more out of my feedback too. I always try my hardest on my work. Nobody is ever at the best they can be though, so next quarter I am looking to become even better with feedback, discussions, group work, and leadership.

Creating a culture of self-reflection makes space for honest conversations around grades with students and their families. It also helps to shift the power away from the teacher as the sole dispenser of grades toward a more balanced approach, providing teachers with discussion points as they prepare to submit more formal grades.

The Role of Peers in Feedback. Structuring peer feedback can be challenging, but when students are well coached, peer feedback becomes an integral part of the disruptive inquiry process. Not only does it continue to help balance the power structure in the classroom, but peer feedback also demonstrates to students that different people will bring different perspectives to their work. Working with multiple perspectives is imperative when developing work meant to be shared with the larger community and meant to move toward social change. Effective peer feedback also lightens the teaching load. Taking risks, failing, and tackling a challenge again are important aspects of the learning process, of the inquiry process, of the change process. But if teachers are tasked with giving the sole feedback during the iterative process, it can be overwhelming. Thus, it is important to help students develop their feedback skills early in the school year.

One of the most impactful approaches for developing students' feedback skills was inspired by Disney. Disney animators use a strategy called "Trust Circles," which require those involved in the creative process to circle together and openly share their thoughts on their first drafts. This collaborative conversation showcases an element of professional trust among each other, demonstrates a constant thread of constructive feedback, and provides a launching point for the directors of the film to refine their ongoing work. This approach has been successfully adapted for the classroom, providing students the space and time they need to fully develop their ideas.

To start this process, students can watch a clip from the documentary *Into the Unknown: Making Frozen II* (Harding, 2020), which captures the conversations of the Disney animators. After analyzing how the conversation was structured, as well as the purpose behind the dialogue, students practice their own trust circles, using media and texts they are drafting for their own projects.

Trust circles, like any activity that involves trust, take time to develop. This means that it is important to regularly build in time for students to participate in them. This can be structured in different ways. Designating days where everyone participates in a circle or creating designated spaces in the classroom where students can go whenever the need for a circle arises can both be effective approaches to regularly integrating trust circles into the feedback loop. And each time students participate, the stronger their feedback and collaboration skills become— and the more they look forward to participating in a circle.

While peer feedback does not typically play a role in assigning a summative grade, it can be a substitute in the formative stage. Rather than assigning a grade while a work is in progress, which can hinder the creative process, peer feedback can assist students in their achievement of their ultimate goals. And it does so in a much more powerful way than relying solely on the teacher.

The Role of the Teacher in Feedback. When creating a culture of feedback through self-reflection and peer feedback protocols, the role of the teacher becomes much easier because students recognize that the feedback provided to them is not for a grade but for their continued growth as thinkers and doers. This means, however, teachers must maintain a culture of trust with students and provide feedback that is constructive and helps students meet their goals. It also means that risks are acknowledged— praising students when their risks pay off and allowing them to reattempt the work by redirecting their effort when their risks fail.

So, what does this look like on a daily, weekly, quarterly basis? When examining individual work, provide descriptive feedback that points to the student's successes and shares concrete tips and resources for areas of growth. Mark Barnes's (2015) SE2R (Summarize, Explain, Redirect, and Resubmit) feedback model provides a helpful structure that can assist teachers in more efficiently providing narrative feedback. As most teachers know, patterns emerge across student work, so it's helpful to identify the suggestions and resources most used in feedback and to create a bank of suggestions and resources that can be copied and pasted and then personalized onto student work. This can greatly speed up the feedback process. Consider eliminating a grade from this work to put the emphasis on the student's thinking and processes.

If grades are required by your district, however, it can be helpful to use the descriptors cocreated with students so that they know what those grades mean in the gradebook. If the gradebook only accepts points, don't allow for variation across a letter grade—for example, set everything to 100 points and all As equal 95, all Bs equal 85, and so on. Eliminate the 0 from the gradebook.

Nothing kills a grade or motivation more than a 0. Finally, let students know those grades are all just placeholders. They can be changed at any time because we are always refining our ideas and our products.

Providing feedback to individual work is just one piece of the grading puzzle. Grades recorded on report cards and transcripts should be a holistic picture of a student's time in our class. This means that the self-reflections and student responses to peer feedback need to be figured into the final equation. Using the self-reflections students complete during grade-reporting windows, conference with individual students about their grades while the rest of the class is working on larger projects. Give students the opportunity to make a case for the grade that will be recorded by verbalizing the evidence they have collected. This allows teachers to see the moments of learning and growth that are not always visible, and it provides time for dialogue when the teacher feels they are not in complete agreement with the students' self-assessment. Mutually determining grades using the descriptors developed by the class as a whole helps restore the power balance and provides transparency to grading practices.

CONCLUDING THOUGHTS

It was almost May, and Genius Hour work was wrapping up. Students were busy concluding conversations with mentors, finalizing their give-back, and preparing to present their work to the community. For the most part, it had been going well. Students discovered they *can* make an impact on the world around them—and even learn about the language arts along the way. Despite these successes, however, there was a small buzz among some students and teachers that questioned whether this project was worth the time it takes. After all, students had not taken a single test or written a single research paper or essay the entire school year. How could this be school? Upon hearing this buzz, Sarah realized that it's not enough to be transparent with parents and the community about the questions students are exploring. It is also vital to be transparent and explicit with students about how the experiences described in this book translate to the learning they expect in school. And if we are going to disrupt the system from within, making explicit connections to traditional skill development helps us to find the fissures to make the changes needed to provide space for all students.

For Sarah, this meant stopping planned instruction and brainstorming with students the impact Genius Hour had on their learning. Reflecting upon this experience, we realized that while their emphasis was on Genius Hour, their discussion really reflects disruptive inquiry as a whole. Thus, we wrap up this book by sharing with you the insights we gained from Sarah's conversation with her students.

If There's Noise, Then We Stop, Listen, and Respond

When we question social issues around topics such as race, class, or gender, there is bound to be discomfort among those we work with in schools. Often, discomfort leads to noise as those who are made uncomfortable seek to restore teaching and learning to its previous form. When we hear the noise, we can choose to ignore, to simply listen, or to listen and respond. If we choose to ignore the noise, we risk the success of our efforts. Ignoring signals that we don't care about the noise, and by translation, we don't care about those who are making the noise. This can erode trust within our community, and without trust, we cannot gather the human resources needed to accomplish our goals. If we choose to simply listen, the noise can get overwhelming. It can cause us to question our actions, and sometimes it can prompt us to stop the work to restore quiet to our worlds.

But if we choose to listen and respond, we can identify the motivations behind the noise and address the misgivings. When students are frustrated because we have changed the game of school, we provide the scaffolds that build their confidence, so they are willing to take risks. When they are struggling to discover their passions, we provide multiple exposures to new and different experiences. When they are trapped in the echo chambers of one belief system, we bring in multiple perspectives through community members and diverse sets of texts. When colleagues, administrators, parents, or community members question whether we are teaching our content, we can show them how we are meeting standards and teaching skills. When they fear we are trying to push an agenda, we can demonstrate how we are bringing in multiple perspectives and privileging students' questions rather than our own. When they don't understand how we assign grades, we can invite them into the feedback process and conversation. Listening and responding builds the transparency and trust needed to do the work we describe in this book. It also models for students how to approach differing opinions, which is foundational to making social change.

If There's Standardization, Then We Need to Recognize Humans Cannot Be Standardized

Since the dawn of the industrial age, schools have attempted to standardize education in much the same way as industry has used the assembly line to produce products. But humans are not vacuum cleaners. As much as we try to provide the same curricula and assess students in the same ways, we can never account for the variability in human experiences, thinking, and values that make it impossible for each student to experience school in identical ways. And attempting to map one approach on all students hurts our most vulnerable students.

We recognize that some of you may be bound by rigid pacing guides, strict grading policies, and even unjust legal mandates. If this applies to you, we hope that you can find fissures in your curricula where you can fit in some of the ideas within this book—or that we at least spark some ideas for how you can alter your curricula just slightly enough to account for the nonstandard human voices in your classroom. Small cracks can lead to large change. We just have to start.

But even if you are not in a school that is tightly regimented, all teachers are expected to teach to standards and to develop particular skills. This means that it is vital that we demonstrate how disruptive inquiry *does* meet the standards even if it does so in a nonstandard way. Developing such a case requires that we have research to back us up, which is why we thread respected educational theorists throughout this book. Research is not enough, however. We must also demonstrate how students meet the standards we are expected to teach. As Sarah discovered, one of the most successful ways to do this is to develop a list with students. After brainstorming on the board about the skills students develop during Genius Hour, Sarah captured their thinking in a Google Doc: https://tinyurl.com/5fhv5rmn. As the chart demonstrates, students who engage in Genius Hour are hitting upon multiple skills expected within the language arts—and in ways that respect who students are as humans. This work—and other disruptive inquiry work—also develops other essential skills such as empathizing with others, learning from failure, and engaging as invested citizens that the standards cannot capture because they cannot be measured on a standardized test.

If There's Student Agency, Then We Discover Genius

We began this chapter contemplating the work of Gholdy Muhammad (2020). Muhammad argues, and we concur, that schools overemphasize skills and intellect at the cost of identity and criticality. They also often sacrifice joy. While varied pedagogical approaches can restore balance among the four pursuits, we have found that through disruptive inquiry, students can see themselves in the curriculum, can develop criticality towards texts, and can leverage their skills and intellect to make a difference. Fostering student agency helps our students unearth the genius within themselves.

And we witness this joyful discovery throughout the school year. It was evident in the conversation Sarah had with students around Genius Hour. It is evident in feedback we receive from parents and the community. And it is evident in the work they do. It's a process. Their first attempts are messy. But they get better each time they try. And they often notice their resilience. We want to leave you with the wise words of Emma, which were taken from an assignment that tasked students to write a thank-you note to themselves. We celebrate Emma and all the students like her who have discovered they *can* make a difference in the world.

Thank you Emma,

I have always wanted to show you how much I appreciate you. You are so sentimental, passionate, and resilient. These traits have pushed me to work towards my goals and help others . . . I am so grateful for how passionate you are about the things that bring you joy. This shows through your hard work and determination. You use this passion to help others and make a change in our world. I have seen how once you put your mind to something and build up a passion for something there is nothing that can stop you.

READING YOUR WORLD

This chapter provides you with different ways to consider bringing this work into your own context. As you consider your own ways forward, we prompt you to think about your own students like Stephanie. The amount of space provided to Stephanie to shape her own learning during the year gave her the confidence to advocate for a grading process that made the most sense to her as a learner. We want students to have this kind of confidence. How can you listen to your own students and develop routines and structures that respond to the needs they identify for themselves?

As you begin the work described in this book in your own teaching context, consider the fissures in your curriculum that provide a place to start. For some, the starting point might be examining grading and assessment practices. Shifts in how we grade students also lead to shifts in how we design our instruction. But, as Stephanie demonstrated, the opposite is also true. Changing how we design instruction may ultimately lead to shifts in grading and assessment, but if starting there makes you uncomfortable, look for another place to begin. We don't have to do it all at once. We just have to begin.

REFLECT, MOTIVATE, AND ACT

Reflect on Our Current Practices

- *What are small changes you can make to your teaching practices at this moment?*
- *What barriers might you face when making these changes?*
- *What do you hope to communicate to your learners and stakeholders when making this change?*

Motivate Teachers to Discover Their Genius

- *How can listening to students inform your practices and create sustaining change to your classroom culture?*

- *How might making changes to your assessment practices meet/support/encourage the individual learner?*

Take Action Toward Student-Centered Inquiry

- *What steps can you take to infuse disruptive inquiry into your practice?*
- *How can your students partner with the community to take action?*
- *What might be a simple, actionable step you could take to shift your assessment practices to a student-centered approach?*

References

Anderson, R. C., & Pearson, P. D. (1984). A schema-theoretic view of basic processes in reading comprehension. In P. D. Pearson (Ed.), *Handbook of Reading Research* (255–291).

Azzam, A. M. (2013). Handle with care: A conversation with Maya Angelou. *Educational Leadership, 71*(1), 10–13.

Bakhtin, M. M. (2010). *The Dialogic Imagination: Four Essays* (Vol. 1). University of Texas Press.

Bakhtin, M. (2013). *Problems of Dostoevsky's Poetics* (Vol. 8). U of Minnesota Press.

Barnes, M. (2015). *Assessment 3.0: Throw Out Your Grade Book and Inspire Learning.* Corwin Press.

Bautista, M. A., Bertrand, M., Morrell, E., Scorza, D. A., & Matthews, C. (2013). Participatory action research and city youth: Methodological insights from the Council of Youth Research. *Teachers College Record, 115*(10), 1–23.

Beach, R., Boyd, A. S., Webb, A., & Thein, A. H. (2022). *Teaching to Exceed in the English Language Arts: A Justice, Inquiry, and Action Approach for 6–12 Classrooms* (3rd ed.). Routledge.

Bishop, R. S. (1990). Mirrors, windows, and sliding glass doors. *Perspectives, 6*(3), ix–xi.

Carter, K. (1994). Preservice teachers' well-remembered events and the acquisition of event-structured knowledge. *Journal of Curriculum Studies, 26*(3), 235–252.

Csikszentmihalyi, M., & Csikzentmihaly, M. (1990). *Flow: The Psychology of Optimal Experience* (Vol. 1990). Harper & Row.

Debord, G., & Wolman, G. J. (1956). A User's Guide to Détournement, trans. *Ken Knabb (2007), Situationist International Anthology. Berkeley: Bureau of Public Secrets*, 8–13.

Deci, E. L., Koestner, R., & Ryan, R. M. (2001). Extrinsic rewards and intrinsic motivation in education: Reconsidered once again. *Review of educational research, 71*(1), 1–27.

Dewey, J. (1903). Democracy in education. *The elementary school teacher, 4*(4), 193–204.

Dewey, J. (1923). *Democracy and Education: An Introduction to the Philosophy of Education.* Macmillan.

Eisner, E. W. (2002). The kind of schools we need. *Phi delta kappan, 83*(8), 576–583.

Eisner, E. W. (2013). What does it mean to say a school is doing well? *Curriculum Studies Reader E5* (pp. 313–321).

Ellison, T. L., & Solomon, M. (2019). Counter-storytelling vs. deficit thinking around African American children and families, digital literacies, race, and the digital divide. *Research in the Teaching of English, 53*(3), 223–244.

The Enneagram Institute. (2021). *The Traditional Enneagram.* https://www.enneagraminstitute.com/the-traditional-enneagram

Fecho, B., Graham, P., & Hudson-Ross, S. (2005). Appreciating the wobble: Teacher research, professional development, and figured worlds. *English Education, 37*(3), 174–199.

Feldman, J. (2018). *Grading for Equity: What It Is, Why It Matters, and How It Can Transform Schools and Classrooms.* Corwin.

Freire, P. (1972). *Pedagogy of the Oppressed.* Herder and Herder.

Garcia, A. (2019, May 8). Fence-testing in the hyphenated present. *The American Crawl.* https://www.theamericancrawl.com/?p=1734

Garcia, A., & O'Donnell-Allen, C. (2015). *Pose, Wobble, Flow: A Culturally Proactive Approach to Literacy Instruction.* Teachers College Press.

Giroux, H. A. (1988). *Teachers as Intellectuals: Toward a Critical Pedagogy of Learning.* Greenwood Publishing Group.

Groenke, S. L., Haddix, M., Glenn, W. J., Kirkland, D. E., Price-Dennis, D., & Coleman-King, C. (2015). Disrupting and dismantling the dominant vision of youth of color. *English Journal*, 35–40.

Gutiérrez, K. D., Larson, J., Enciso, P., & Ryan, C. L. (2007). Discussing expanded spaces for learning. *Language Arts, 85*(1), 69–77.

Gutiérrez, K. D. (2008). Developing a sociocritical literacy in the third space. *Reading research quarterly, 43*(2), 148–164.

Hobbs, R. (2020). *Mind Over Media: Propaganda Education for a Digital Age.* W. W. Norton & Co.

Howe, C., & Abedin, M. (2013). Classroom dialogue: A systematic review across four decades of research. *Cambridge Journal of Education, 43*(3), 325–356.

Johannsen, C. C. (2011, April 22). *Higher education under attack: An interview with Henry A. Giroux.* Truthout. https://truthout.org/articles/higher-education-under-attack-an-interview-with-henry-a-giroux/

Juliani, A. J. (2014). *Inquiry and Innovation in the Classroom: Using 20% Time, Genius Hour, and PBL to Drive Student Success.* Routledge.

Kay, M. R. (2018). *Not Light but Fire: How to Lead Meaningful Race Conversations in the Classroom.* Stenhouse.

Keene, E., & Zimmermann, S. (1997). *Mosaic of Thought: Teaching Comprehension in a Reader's Workshop.* Heinemann.

Kellner, D., & Share, J. (2007). Critical media literacy is not an option. *Learning Inquiry 1*, 59–69.

Kirkland, D. (2019). More than words: Teaching literacy to vulnerable learners. *Literacy Today, 37*(2), 10–12.

Koenig, S. (2014). *Serial* [Audio podcast]. Serial Productions. https://serialpodcast.org/season-one

Kohn, A. (2013, October 29). A dozen essential guidelines for educators. *Alfie Kohn.* https://www.alfiekohn.org/blogs /dozen-essential-guidelines-educators/

Krishnaswami, U. (2019, January 17). *Why stop at windows and mirrors?: Children's book prisms.* The Horn Book Inc. https://www.hbook.com/story/why-stop-at-windows -and-mirrors-childrens-book-prisms

Luke, A., & Dooley, K. (2011). Critical literacy and second language learning. *Handbook of research in second language teaching and learning,* 856–868.

Luke, A., Garcia, A., & Seglem, R. (2018). Looking at the next twenty years of multiliteracies: An exchange. *Critical Literacy, Schooling, and Social Justice* (pp. 297–304).

McNair, A. (2017). *Genius Hour: Passion Projects That Ignite Innovation and Student Inquiry.* Routledge.

Mirra, N., Garcia, A., & Morrell, E. (2015). *Doing Youth Participatory Action Research: Transforming Inquiry with Researchers, Educators, and Students.* Routledge.

Mirra, N. (2018). *Educating for Empathy: Literacy Learning and Civic Engagement.* Teachers College Press.

Morrell, E. (2015a). *The 2014 NCTE Presidential Address: Powerful English at NCTE Yesterday, Today, and Tomorrow: Toward the Next Movement. Research in the Teaching of English.* 49. 307–327.

Morrell, E. (2015b). Teaching English POWERFULLY: Four challenges. *English in Texas, 45*(1), 5–7.

Muhammad, G. (2020). *Cultivating genius: An equity framework for culturally and historically responsive literacy.* Scholastic.

Muhammad, G. E., & Haddix, M. (2016). Centering black girls' literacies: A review of literature on the multiple ways of knowing of black girls. *English Education, 48*(4), 299–336.

National Center for Education Statistics. (2020, September). *Race and ethnicity of public school teachers and their students.* U. S. Department of Education NCES 2020-103. https://nces.ed.gov/pubs2020/2020103/index.asp

Paris, D., & Alim, H. S. (Eds.). (2017). *Culturally Sustaining Pedagogies: Teaching and Learning for Justice in a Changing World.* Teachers College Press.

Peha, S. (n.d.). *The 3P grading system: An easier, faster, better way to evaluate students and their work.* Teaching That Makes Sense. https://www.ttms.org/

Pink, D. H. (2011). *Drive: The Surprising Truth About What Motivates Us.* Penguin.

Purcell, J. H., Burns, D. E., & Purcell, W. (2020). *The Interest-Based Learning Coach: A Step-by-Step Playbook for Genius Hour, Passion Projects, and Makerspaces in School.* Routledge.

Reynolds, J. (2018, May 28). *Ten Things I've Been Meaning to Say to You.* PowellsBooks.Blog. https://www.powells.com /post/lists/ten-things-ive-been-meaning-to-say-to-you

Rief, L. (1992). *Seeking Diversity: Language Arts with Adolescents.* Heinemann.

Romano, T. (2000). *Blending Genre, Altering Style: Writing Multigenre Papers.* Heinemann.

Romano, T. (2013). *Fearless Writing: Multigenre to Motivate and Inspire.* Heinemann.

Silverman, K. (2014). *About.* Big Talk. https://www.youtube .com/c/Makebigtalk/about

Stanford d.school. (2018). *Design thinking bootleg.* https:// dschool.stanford.edu/resources/design-thinking-bootleg

Vasquez, V. M., Janks, H., & Comber, B. (2019). Critical literacy as a way of being and doing. *Language Arts, 96*(5), 300–311.

Vygotsky, L. S. (1978). *Mind in society: The Development of Higher Psychology Processes.* Harvard University Press.

Wesch, M. (2018). *The art of being human.* CreateSpace Independent Publishing Platform.

Whalen, S. P. (1999). Finding flow at school and at home: A conversation with Mihaly Csikszentmihalyi. *Journal of Secondary Gifted Education, 10*(4), 161–165.

Teaching Resources

Acevedo, E. (2018). *The poet X.* Quill Tree Books.

Ad Fontes Media. (n.d.) *The media bias chart.* Ad Fontes Media. https://adfontesmedia.com/

Adichie, C. N. (2009, July). *The dangers of a single story* [Video]. TED Global 2009. https://www.ted.com/talks/chim amanda_ngozi_adichie_the_danger_of_a_single_story ?language=en

Ahmed, S. (2019). *Internment.* Little, Brown and Company.

Anderson, L. H. (2011). *Speak.* Square Fish.

Anderson, L. H. (2015). *The impossible knife of memory.* Penguin.

Green, J. (2008). *An abundance of Katherines.* Penguin.

Harding M. (Director). (2020). In A. Astley & J. Condon (Esecutive Producers), *Into the Unknown: Making Frozen II.* The Walt Disney Company. https://www.disneyplus.com/series /into-the-unknown-making-frozen-2/6PWutGrMQzCI

Jacobson, J. R. (2015). *Paper things.* Candlewick Press.

Jones, K. L., & Segal, G. (2019). *I'm not dying with you tonight.* Sourcebooks Fire.

Kendi, I. X. (Host). (2021, June 16). *Be Antiracist: The Juneteenth mixtape* [Audio podcast]. Pushkin. https://www .pushkin.fm/episode/the-juneteenth-mixtape/

Khorram, A. (2018). *Darius the great is not okay.* Penguin.

Kubrick, S. (Director). (1980). *The shining.* The Producer Circle Company.

Lee, H. (2010). *To kill a mockingbird.* Random House.

London, J. (1903). *The call of the wild.* The Macmillan Company.

Lowry, L. (1993). *The giver.* Houghton Mifflin.

Myers, W. D., & Myers, C. (1999). *Monster.* HarperCollins Publishers.

Nelson, J. (2015). *I'll give you the sun.* Speak.

Reynolds, J. (2015). *The boy in the black suit.* Simon and Schuster.

Reynolds, J., & Kendi, I. X. (2020). *Stamped: Racism, antiracism, and you: A remix of the National Book Award-winning Stamped from the beginning.* Little, Brown Books for Young Readers.

Ribay, R. (2020). *Patron saints of nothing.* Penguin Books.

Shapiro, B., & Wax, N. (2018). *What we keep.* Running Press.

Sinek, S. (2009, September). *How great leaders inspire action* [Video]. TEDxPuget Sound. https://www.ted.com/talks/simon_sinek_how_great_leaders_inspire_action?language=en

Slater, D. (2017). *The 57 bus: A true story of two teenagers and the crime that changed their lives.* Farrar, Straus & Giroux (BYR).

Spielberg, S. (Director). (1993). *Jurassic Park* [Film]. Universal Pictures.

Stark, K. (2016, September 23). *Why you should talk to strangers* [Video]. TED. https://www.youtube.com/watch?v=rFpDK2KhAgw

Stone, N. (2017). *Dear Martin.* Ember.

Stone, N. (2022). *Dear Justyce.* Ember.

TED. (2009, September 30). *Tim Brown urges designers to think big* [Video]. YouTube. https://youtu.be/UAinLaT42xY

TED (2012, November). *Colin Stokes: How movies teach manhood* [Video]. TEDxBeaconStreet. https://www.ted.com/talks/colin_stokes_how_movies_teach_manhood

Thomas, A. (2017). *The hate u give.* Gyldendal A/S.

Vice News Tonight. (2020). *Is America getting better? We asked Americans* [Video]. Vice Video. https://video.vice.com/en_us/video/is-america-getting-better-we-asked-americans/5d729ddfbe4077371c0b1e36

Wood, Z. A. (2018, April). *Why it's worth listening to people you disagree with* [Video]. TED2018. https://www.ted.com/talks/zachary_r_wood_why_it_s_worth_listening_to_people_you_disagree_with

Yoon, N. (2015). *Everything, everything.* Delacorte Press

Zentner, J. (2017). *Goodbye days.* Crown Books for Young Readers.

Zentner, J. (2021). *In the wild light.* Crown Books for Young Readers.

Index

About the Authors

Robyn Seglem is a professor of middle grades English language arts and literacy at Illinois State University. Prior to completing her PhD at Kansas State University, Robyn taught middle and high school ELA in various Kansas City suburbs. She maintains her National Boards certification and has served on the committees to revise the ELA National Boards for Professional Teaching Standards and the Five Core Propositions. Her research focuses on literacy, technology, inquiry, and innovation in teaching. Robyn currently serves as a coeditor for the National Council of Teacher Education's middle-level journal, *Voices from the Middle*.

Sarah Bonner is an experienced teacher currently teaching 8th-grade language arts at Heyworth Junior High School in Heyworth, Illinois. She is also a certified reading specialist, current doctoral candidate, and an adjunct professor for Illinois State University for the School of Teaching and Learning. Her research interests include inquiry, literacy, design-based research, and innovation in teaching.